ORGANIZING EMPIRE

D0088537

PURNIMA BOSE

ORGANIZING EMPIRE

Individualism, Collective Agency, and India

DUKE UNIVERSITY PRESS | DURHAM & LONDON 2003

© 2003 Duke University Press   All rights reserved

Printed in the United States of America on acid-free paper ∞

Designed by Rebecca M. Giménez   Typeset in Quadraat by

Keystone Typesetting, Inc.   Library of Congress Cataloging-

in-Publication Data appear on the last printed page of this book.

FOR BASANA AND BIBHUTI BASU,

in loving memory

CONTENTS

ACKNOWLEDGMENTS

This project started as a dissertation under the guidance of Barbara
Harlow, with the able assistance of Elizabeth Butler Cullingford, Bernth
Lindfors, Ann Cvetkovich, and Richard Lariviere. I consider myself particularly fortunate to have studied with Barbara Harlow, whose geopolitical and institutional analyses, intellectual fearlessness, and generosity of
spirit continue to serve as a model. Without her persistent reminders of
the necessity of examining the writing of Dutt and Cousins, combined
with her ubiquitous deadlines, this project could not have been conceptualized or completed. Its central concern with organizing was very
much influenced by the activist climate at the University of Texas at Austin
during the late 1980s and early 1990s. A number of activists and academics, in some cases both, commented on the manuscript at an early stage;
for such input, I am grateful to Hossam Aboul-Ela, Danica Finley, Rachel
Jennings, Laura E. Lyons, Luis Marentes, Louise Meintjes, Louis Men-
doza, Supriya Nair, and S. Shankar. Other activists—in Austin and in
Bloomington, Indiana—helped formulate the organizational questions
which inform this study through their example, including Pedro Bustos-
Aguilar, Steve Carr, Milton Fisk, Amber Gallup, Carrie Hattic, Suzanne
Henry, Charley MacMartin, Kathy Mitchell, Hatem Natsheh, Ana Sisnett,
Sandy Soto, and John Zuern.

I am indebted to Bipasa Bose Nadon for aiding me with the legal
research for chapter 1, Joginder and Harbans Bhola for generously providing source material on the Jallianwala Bagh massacre, Jane Manaster
for introducing me to tombs and tomes, Sangeeta Ray for her extremely
helpful suggestions on chapter 3, and Fred Kameny for his excellent
editorial advice.

A number of my colleagues at Indiana University read and meticulously commented on drafts of this manuscript: Patrick Brantlinger has been an exemplary senior colleague, a wonderful mentor, and supportive at every stage of this project; Tom Foster and Janet Sorensen have offered much intellectual and emotional support over the years; Robyn Wiegman's constructive suggestions helped reconceptualize an earlier incarnation of this manuscript, and I am extremely thankful. Eva Cherniavsky generously read and provided invaluable commentary on countless drafts of this manuscript. As numerous graduate students, junior faculty, and members of the Bloomington community know, Eva exemplifies the best ideals of feminist practice. And Jeffrey C. Isaac, unlikely ally and valued interlocutor, who, in spite of the long hours he devotes to antiracist and anti-sweatshop organizations, would not identify himself as an "activist," has left his intellectual imprint on this project in ways which, I hope, make him uneasy.

Friends and family who have been supportive in other ways include Basana and Bibhuti Basu—whose stories about the nationalist movement and partition first sparked my interest in this period—Amitabha K. Bose, Cathy Bowman, Ellen Brantlinger, Bharati and Kamal Datta, Saugato Datta, Roopali Mukherjee, Flynn Picardal, Katrin Sieg, and John Zuern.

My favorite ideologue, Zhaleh Breen, has provided much in the way of encouragement and humor through the writing process. Saleem Bose gave careful consideration to this manuscript, tearing through its pages. Sudesh and Samir K. Bose took a keen interest in this project and were supportive in countless ways that are better left unenumerated. And finally, I am most grateful to Laura E. Lyons—comrade, confidante, and collaborator—who over the last fifteen years has shared the aggravations and provisional triumphs of many of the political and intellectual campaigns that inform my thinking. Besides being extremely constant in her friendship, Laura through her warmth and wit has transformed the petty tragedies of the last few years into farce, helping to give a feminist and comical perspective to experiences that thankfully do not have much significance on a world historical scale. I look forward to many more years of friendship and collaboration with Laura.

|||||

An earlier version of chapter 3 appeared in *Genders* 23 (1996) as "Engendering the Armed Struggle: Women, Writing, and the Bengali 'Terrorist'

Movement." Portions of chapter 1 were published in *boundary 2* 26 (1999) in an article written with Laura E. Lyons, "Dyer Consequences: the Trope of Amritsar, Ireland, and the Lessons of the 'Minimum' Force Debate." I thank the editors at New York University Press and Duke University Press for permission to reprint this material.

INTRODUCTION

[Resistance to Imperialism] cannot occur without the willingness of men and women to resist the pressures of colonial rule, to take up arms, to project ideas of liberation, and to imagine (as Benedict Anderson has it) a new national community . . . Nor can they occur unless either economic or political exhaustion with empire and the cost of colonial rule are challenged publicly, unless the representations of imperialism begin to lose their justification and legitimacy, and, finally, unless the rebellious 'natives' impress upon the metropolitan culture the independence and integrity of their own culture, free from colonial encroachment.—*Edward Said*

Organizing Empire: Individualism, Collective Agency, and India seeks to demonstrate the complexity and (in)commensurability of the multiple narratives which constitute our access to British colonial history. It insists that dominant and widely circulated Raj histories and memoirs can be read against the more obscured practices and narratives of nationalist and popular anticolonial activists and organizations.[1] Such an investigation raises questions regarding the nature of dominance, hegemony, and resistance, particularly concerning the subjects who make history—in every sense of the phrase—and the ways in which the agents of struggle can or cannot be recognized within elite-imperial narratives. I explore these questions historically through archival materials including parliamentary debates, popular colonial histories, newsletters of organizations, biographies, and novels. The chapters of this book share a thematic and theoretical treatment of individualism and collective agency. I argue that the figure of the individual provides both the means by which repressive colonial and neocolonial power works to displace its own recognition of its constitutive violence and also ways to theorize feminist and nationalist resistance.

Each chapter offers a case study of individualism by focusing on a representative individual, or group of individuals, and analyzing her, his, or their self-fashionings in relation to the colonial state and organized, collective resistance to British rule. Chapter 1 investigates "rogue-colonial individualism" by examining how the repressive authority of the state is projected onto its most visible agent, in this case the putative author of the infamous Amritsar massacre, General Dyer, who is then repudiated as the pathological instigator of an aberrant "incident." Chapter 2 treats "feminist-nationalist individualism," as well as the tension between individuated leadership and the will to a horizontal representation of women's collective social agency. In tracing the split self-fashioning of the Irish suffragette Margaret Cousins in Ireland and India, this chapter suggests how the authority of a nationalist movement's individual representatives might be displaced in the process of feminism's international circulation. Chapter 3 examines the discursive operations of "heroic-nationalist individualism" in the memoir of a Bengali insurgent, Kalpana Dutt, focusing specifically on the generative contradictions between the form of the memoir, so central to nationalist hagiography, and the project of cathecting an emancipated social collective through this very narrative medium. And finally chapter 4, on "heroic-colonial individualism," addresses the phenomenon of "raj nostalgia" in the 1970s and 1980s, to explore how the retrospective construction of colonial administrators as the empire's heroic servants ambivalently registers the emergence of displaced ex-colonial populations as a dissident political force in the metropolis.

The four case studies, then, represent a range of subject-positions within the context of British imperialism in twentieth-century India. The range is by no means exhaustive, but the differences among the subject-positions illuminate the constraints that the colonial situation of domination and subordination placed upon conceptions of individual agency and activism. Two of the case studies (chapters 1 and 4) deal with individuals and organizations that supported the British Raj. The other two (chapters 2 and 3) treat individuals and organizations that resisted and sought to overthrow the colonial regime. Chapters 1 and 2 also offer a comparative analysis of agency in relation to imperial domination in two colonial contexts, India and Ireland. And chapters 2 and 3 concern feminist as well as anti-imperialist forms of activism and agency.

Before engaging questions about subaltern identity and collective agency, however, it is necessary to trace the emergence of the ideology of individualism in seventeenth-century political theory in relation to its transmutations under colonial and nationalist ideology. The persistence of individualism in both ideologies has serious implications for how we theorize dominance, hegemony, and resistance in the colonial context.

INDIVIDUALISM AND COLONIALISM

Organizing Empire maps the shifting uses of the term "individualism," once used to denote part of a larger social collective but now denoting something distinct from it. Tracing the shift makes it possible to illuminate the suppressed collective aspect of the ideology of individualism within a colonial context. Broadly conceived, individualism is a set of ideas that emphasizes the importance of the individual, the individual's interest, and a conception of the subject as a free and autonomous agent who exercises choice in the absence of a controlling state authority (Marshall 304). The word "individualism" is derived from "individual," which in turn has its origins in the sixth-century Latin *individuus*, a negative adjectival form of *dividere*, "to divide" (Williams, *Keywords* 161). The meaning of "individual," as Raymond Williams explains, encapsulates a paradox that posits the individual both as being distinct from others and as embodying a "necessary connection" to others through membership in a group (161). This contradiction is a result of the long evolution of the term in a range of discourses, inflecting the word with theological, scientific, political, and economic valences (161). The modern sense of the term "individual" and its early-nineteenth-century derivative, "individualism," is marked by its prior applications: to the essential unity of the Trinity in medieval theology, to the physical and biological coherence of insentient and sentient entities in the seventeenth and eighteenth centuries, to the relation between the self, natural law, and the sociopolitical order during the Enlightenment.

In *The Political Theory of Possessive Individualism*, Crawford Brough MacPherson argues that in the writings of John Locke in particular, political philosophy in the late seventeenth century signaled a movement away from previous understandings of the individual, who was no longer regarded as a "moral whole" nor as part of a larger social collectivity, but rather as a proprietor of "his" self, in which the concept of private property became even constitutive of subjectivity. (Since women were barred from property ownership, the gendering of pronouns is appropriate here.) MacPherson maintains that "the difficulties of modern liberal-democratic theory" inhere in the "possessive quality" of seventeenth-century individualism, which conceived of the individual as "essentially the proprietor of his own person or capacities, owing nothing to society for them" (3).[2] "The relation of ownership," he explains, "having become for more and more men the critically important relation determining their actual freedom and actual prospect of realizing their full potentialities, was read back into the nature of the individual" (3). To the extent that the individual "[wa]s proprietor of his person and capacities," he was considered free. Freedom thus became "a function of possession" as well as "freedom from dependence on the wills of others" (3). As the basic unit of the social formation, the individual interacted with other "free equal individuals" who were "proprietors of their own capacities and of what they ha[d] acquired by their exercise" (3). Society was based on "relations of exchange between proprietors," with the political apparatus conceived of as "a contractual device for the protection of proprietors and the orderly regulation of their relations" (269).

The notion of proprietorship underwriting possessive individualism—in its seventeenth-century and later articulations as described by MacPherson—becomes radically exaggerated in the context of early-twentieth-century British colonialism, giving rise to rogue-colonial individualism and heroic-colonial individualism. If, as Frantz Fanon persuasively argues, the colonial world is a Manichean one, in which the settler and the native constitute and are constituted by their differences from one another, it is also true that the discursive category of the "colonizer" is itself governed by the logic of an internal binary opposition which divides colonial officials into rogues on the one hand and heroes on the other—even while the colonizer in actuality consists of multiple, generally self-contained, competitive social-class factions, namely the governmental apparatus, the economic sector, missionaries, and the military. While colonial discourse generally casts its official agents in the heroic mold, it rhetorically displaces colonial violence by singling out those officials who exceed the limits placed on the use of force as determined by the colonial state. Such officials are seen as rogues by some, heroes by others. Both articulations of colonial individualism, however, are underwritten by a distinctly colonial notion of proprietorship in which the metropolitan-colonial subject exercises proprietorship over the person of the native and the territory and resources of the colony. Proprietorship thus acquires an element of political domination as well as of territoriality. In other words, the possessive quality of colonial individualism derives from the center's territorial possession of the periphery and a concomitant ideological justification which postulates that metropolitan-colonial society possesses a higher moral authority than its native counterpart, legitimizing its domination of natives in those same territories.

Within the logic of colonial individualism, society is not conceived of as a system of exchange between free, equal individuals whose existence is autonomous from the colonial state. Rather, colonial individualism, like the caste system whose prejudices it also absorbed, is founded on a notion of radical inequality; in the eyes of the colonial state, the metropolitan-colonial classes occupy a higher status than the native classes on the basis of an incontrovertible material advantage, which derives from a preferential legal system founded on racialist assumptions (Balandier 45). Unlike the possessive individualism elaborated by MacPherson, which seems to disengage and isolate the individual from a larger social formation (though it too is based in extreme material inequality and hierarchy), colonial and nationalist forms of individualism openly articulate the self in relation to the colonial state, positing the self either as the agent of the colonial state or as its dissident.

INDIVIDUALISM AND NATIONALISM

Frantz Fanon, in his teleology of nationalist consciousness *The Wretched of the Earth*, charts the development of the native intellectual from her or his interpellation through the colonial ideological and repressive state apparatuses to her or his affiliation with the struggle for national liberation. Contending that such a process entails the "eradication of the superstructure" provided by the colonial bourgeoisie, which values "the triumph of the individual," "clarity," and "beauty," he notes that "individualism is the first to disappear. The native intellectual had learnt from his masters that the individual ought to express himself fully. The colonialist bourgeoisie had hammered into the native's mind the idea of a society of individuals where each person shuts himself up in his own subjectivity, and whose only wealth is individual thought" (46). As the native intellectual becomes immersed within the various formal structures of the national liberation struggle—interacting with other natives within specific organizational contexts—she or he learns a new vocabulary, replacing the old one of bourgeois individualism with one which includes words such as "brother, sister, friend" that values horizontal, more egalitarian, social relations over vertical, hierarchical ones (47). Fanon predicts that "such a colonized intellectual, dusted over by colonial culture will . . . discover the substance of village assemblies, the cohesion of people's committees, and the extraordinary fruitfulness of local meetings and groupments" (47). Sustained contact and work within an organized national liberation movement empower the native intellectual to reconceptualize the basic unit of society in collective terms.

Fanon's narrative of the formation of political consciousness in relation to the native intellectual's subjectivity predicates a rupture between a colonial ideology grounded in individualism and a nationalist ideology rooted in collectivity. According to him, it is the experience of organizing within indigenous structures such as those based in local territoriality and kinship ("village assemblies" and "local meetings") along with emergent class-based groups ("people's committees") that signal the transition into nationalist consciousness for the native intellectual. His analysis of decolonization is remarkably prescient—particularly his warning that a neocolonial global configuration can render "independence" a nominal affair, leading to insignificant improvements in the quality of lives of majority populations in former colonies. Yet Fanon's account of the process of political conscientization, whereby the native intellectual passes through colonial individualism and matures into a nationalism informed by a commitment to collectives, constructs a too-rigid opposition between the two ideologies. Rather, I argue that the ideology of individualism haunts the very structures of nationalist and activist accounts of political agency and collective struggle.

Indeed, individualism and nationalism converge in that both ideologies draw on what Richard Handler terms "an epistemology of entivity," the presupposition that nations, like individuals, have an attributable, objective existence. Nations are analogous to individuals to the extent that both entities "possess" and are "bound" by unique attributes or characteristics (R. Foster 253). This shared epistemology suggests that the nation is apprehended by its members as being both "a collective individual" and "a collection of individuals" (Handler 39). Insofar as its members perceive the nation through bounded biological metaphors that imbue it with consciousness—constructing the nation as an "existent entity" which is a "living individual"—the nation is granted agency. Handler notes: "The nation can be shown to build, struggle, and create; it can be said to have a soul, spirit, and personality; it can be treated as a friend or parent. Most important, the metaphorical individual can be discussed in terms of its freedom to choose and its ability to control its own destiny" (41). Understood as a collective individual, the nation can exercise an autonomous will and choice which can prove critical for the project of self-determination (41). Alternatively, figured as a collection of individuals, the nation becomes, in Aristotelian fashion, more than the sum of its individual members who, in turn, represent a specific type or character (43). In this other formulation of the nation as species being, Handler explains, the nation becomes "bounded physically by the attributes that distinguish it from all others, and temporally by its endowment with an evolutionary 'beginning'" (44). Nationalist ideology combines both senses of the nation, as a collective individual and as a collection of individuals, by positing the nation as "an individuated being" that is a unique constituent of some encompassing order—itself composed of other individuated beings, who, in turn, are constituted internally as a collection of individuals related to each other by their likeness (R. Foster 253). In other words, each individual (such as an Indian) becomes a synecdoche of the collective individual (such as India), which is differentiated from other collective individuals (such as Britain) (253).

DOMINANCE, HEGEMONY, AND RESISTANCE

In noting the convergence of the category of individualism in imperial, feminist, and Indian nationalist discourses, I do not intend to collapse important distinctions between formations of dominance and resistance. As Jeffrey C. Isaac asserts, domination "refers to a structurally asymmetrical relationship, whereby one element of the relationship," in this case the colonial state, "has power over another," in this case the native, by "virtue of its structural power to direct the practices of the other" (84). Emphasizing the structural dimensions of domination, Isaac cautions against understanding the term solely as an "event," urging that it be alternatively conceptualized as a "situation or condition" (85). An investigation into the legal and parliamentarian discourse of one event, nonetheless, *can* disclose the ways in which domination informs the entire structural operation of colonialism, including its ideological justifications. The peaceful protest of Indians at Amritsar in 1919, for instance, provided the pretext for the colonial state to exert overt power over its native subjects. General Dyer, in his capacity as a representative of the colonial state, massacred several hundred of the protesters to curtail nationalist activities in the region and avert what he believed was a second mutiny.

The brutality of that event, I argue, is symptomatic of the colonial situation more generally and reveals the inherent contradictions that structure the rhetoric of the colonial rule of law: between the colonial state's espousal of universal rights on the one hand, and the effective lack of realization of those rights for individual native subjects on the other. Colonial modernity offers a new and distinctive mode of political rationality, in which the colonial state directs its efforts at the "destruction and reconstruction of colonial space so as to produce not so much extractive-effects on colonial bodies as governing-effects on colonial conduct" (Scott 203). This new rationality requires the creation of a "legally instituted space where legally defined subjects could exercise rights, however limited those might have been" in practice (208). In spite of the actual inequality that inheres within the structure of colonial relations, the colonial rhetoric of the law differentiates in *effective* rights and rationality between colonial and native subjects even as it draws on a postulate of equal natural rights and rationality. Such a dynamic is evident in the parliamentary debates surrounding General Dyer's massacre of Indians at Amritsar.

The discourse of rights in colonial contexts suggests that the dynamic between dominance, hegemony, and state power is radically dissimilar under colonialism to that of bourgeois-democratic state formations in which consent plays such an important role. Antonio Gramsci has noted that hegemony has both ethico-political and economic dimensions, given that it "must necessarily be based on the decisive function exercised by the leading group in the decisive nucleus of economic activity" (*Gramsci Reader* 211–12). Hegemony can thus be understood as the projection by the ruling class of its own interests as national ones, translating its economic interests into political facts; it exists in "active forms of experience and consciousness" by virtue of its saturation of political and economic institutions and relationships (Williams, *Keywords* 145). Insofar as hegemony results in "the formation of a 'new' ideological terrain," manifest in political, cultural, and moral terms, it can only be actualized by securing the consent of subordinated social classes (*Gramsci Reader* 423). "Undoubtedly the fact of hegemony presupposes that account be taken of the interests and the tendencies of the groups over which hegemony is to be exercised," Gramsci writes, "and that a certain compromise equilibrium should be formed" (211). Hegemony becomes a link in a chain of associations that includes civil society, consent, and direction in contrast to a chain of associations tied to political society, coercion, and domination (423).

However, the relationship between hegemony and dominance in bourgeois-democratic state formations does not accurately account for the anomalies and contradictions of colonial rule. Ranajit Guha maintains that liberal historiography's failure to distinguish between "the universalizing tendency of capital as an ideal and the frustration of that tendency in reality" has led to a distorted analysis of power relations under colonialism, whose primary thrust has been that "dominance under colonial conditions has quite erroneously been endowed with hegemony" ("On Some Aspects of the Historiography of Colonial India" 224). Rather, power in colonial India is constituted by the interaction between dominance and subordination, each of which is in turn determined by the contingent relationship between coercion and persuasion on the one hand and collaboration and resistance on the other. Hegemony refers to a condition of dominance in which persuasion greatly exceeds coercion (231). Guha explains:

> Liberal historiography has been led to *presume* that capital, in its Indian career, triumphed over the obstacles to its self-expansion and subjugated all precapitalist relations in material and spiritual life sufficiently enough to enable the bourgeoisie to speak for all of that society as it had done in its historic incarnations in England in 1648 and France in 1789. Resistance to the rule of capital has thus been made to dissolve ideally into a hegemonic dominance. There is not recognition therefore in either of the dominant historical discourses that in reality the universalist project . . . hurtled itself against an insuperable barrier in colonialism. (228)

Many of the experiences of the vast majority of the Indian population were never integrated into the hegemony of the colonial and native bourgeoisies (41). The British metropolitan-bourgeoisie's failure to universalize its class interests on the terrain of ideology in India led to "a compromise with precapitalist particularism under colonial conditions of its own creation," whose political ramifications include a configuration of power in which dominance was actualized without hegemony, resulting in what Guha calls a "spurious hegemony" ("Dominance without Hegemony" 274). Yet it is worth remembering that no system of domination is entirely capable of determining or even predicting "the range of subject positions" that arise within it and the multiple responses to the colonial state's authority (Parry 85).

If dominance without hegemony signifies the general condition of colonialism in these pages, my use of the term "resistance" is delimited to describe opposition to the colonial state resulting from the decision of individual subjects to affiliate with one another and to organize into collectives to attain specific political ends. The coping mechanisms for people living under colonial rule span the ideological spectrum from collaboration with the colonial state to acquiescence to its dictates to active opposition against its governance. Military occupation extracts a certain level of heroism from even the most detached of natives, as it disrupts and informs all aspects of quotidian existence for those living within its purview. This kind of courage, a bravery of the mundane, which attaches to individual subjects under military occupation and colonialism can be more readily assimilated within conventional narratives of heroism, long familiar from British novelistic narrative practices, that usually figure heroism as a revaluation of the prosaic in the construction of individual subjectivity. Without diminishing the daily acts of courage required of those who live under colonial regimes, the category of resistance is restricted here to organized collective challenges to colonial-state power. My primary focus, in other words, is the relationship between resistance and collective agency in less conventional heroic narratives of the individual subject which issue from activist efforts.

I have found it necessary to examine colonial, neocolonial, and Indian nationalist accounts of the last thirty years of the Raj, instead of merely focusing on one of these discourses, because neither colonial nor nationalist discourse exists in a sociohistoric vacuum, isolated from the influences of the other, as a unitary, self-contained ideology. As Aijaz Ahmad remarks, "cultural contradictions within the imperialized formations tend to be so very numerous—sometimes along class lines but also in cross-class configurations, as in the case of patriarchal cultural forms or the religious modes of social authorization—that the totality of indigenous culture can hardly be posited as a unified, transparent site of anti-imperialist resistance" (7–8). Imperial and nationalist ideologies exert some reciprocal compulsion on one another, littering Indian nationalist discourse with the ideological residues of imperial discourse and, hence, making it what Partha Chatterjee calls a "derivative discourse." Commenting on the typological presuppositions that underwrite nationalism, Chatterjee argues that there is an "inherent contradictoriness in nationalist thinking, because it reasons within a framework of knowledge whose representational structure corresponds to the very structure of power nationalist thought seeks to repudiate" (38). Being attentive to the processes by which the colonized assumed oppositional stances towards the colonial state requires questioning how dominance is constituted in ideology (Hall 135).

Chapters 1 and 4, which respectively analyze the discursive operations of rogue-colonial individualism in the parliamentary debates on General Dyer's culpability in the Amritsar Massacre and heroic-colonial individualism in the memoirs of British colonial officials and their wives, provide two case studies of how dominance is constituted in ideology to produce a spurious hegemony. Ascertaining the discursive operations of individualism in colonial and neocolonial discourse enables a more nuanced evaluation of nationalism that avoids treating it as inherently progressive or categorically retrograde. By tracing the residues of colonial and neo-colonial articulations of individualism in feminist and nationalist discourses, we can better determine the historical limitations of specific feminist and nationalist positions. Chapters 2 and 3, which respectively focus on autobiographical accounts of Margaret Cousins's feminist organizing in Ireland and India and Kalpana Dutt's involvement with the Bengali terrorist movement, investigate the limitations of feminist-nationalist individualism and heroic-nationalist individualism. Part of these limitations, which are primarily based in their religious, class, and caste orientation, issues from the elite-subaltern identity of their authors. After delineating a brief taxonomy of colonial, neocolonial, and nationalist individualism, I will turn to the category of the elite-subaltern, explicating it in relation to questions of political agency and organizing.

A TAXONOMY OF INDIVIDUALISM

Rogue-Colonial Individualism In chapter 1, I investigate what I am calling "rogue-colonial individualism." Unlike feminist-nationalist individualism, heroic-nationalist individualism, and heroic-colonial individualism, rogue-colonial individualism is not a self-representation of individual agency; it is rather an articulation of how the colonial state manages to mollify critics of overt colonial brutality by scapegoating colonial officials, such as General Dyer, as anomalous rogue players in need of legal or parliamentary discipline for exceeding the acceptable limits placed by the colonial state on the use of force. Rogue-colonial individualism arises in those instances, such as the Jallianwala Bagh massacre in Amritsar, in which native civilians are slaughtered by colonial officials, even though the civilians are engaged in peaceful protest against the colonial state. It is expressed by the colonial political apparatus in the dominant idiom of moral outrage that invokes the piety of the colonial rule of law, promulgating the misleading notion that natives have equal natural rights before the colonial state which ultimately acts in their interest by punishing such wanton transgressions. In the case of the Amritsar massacre, the contradiction between the rhetoric of the colonial rule of law and the colonial state's effective discrimination between its metropolitan-colonial and native subjects is rendered all the more acute given that the victims of the carnage were protesting against legislation which sanctioned the detention of nationalists without even a modicum of legal due process.

Rogue-colonial individualism relies on the discursive strategy of ascribing intentionality to the key participants in colonial massacres in two ways: first, it constructs the motives of the colonial officials accused of using excessive force as being misguided and overzealous; and second, it simultaneously refuses to assign hostile intentions to the native protesters, thus implicitly affirming their license to demonstrate against the colonial state and perpetuating the illusion that natives have constitutional rights and are encouraged to exercise them. Rogue-colonial individualism, then, nowhere challenges the colonial state's authority to exercise domination over its native subjects and, hence, leaves intact the structurally asymmetrical relationships that bind the colonial center to its peripheral territories.

Feminist-Nationalist Individualism In chapter 2, I analyze an articulation of feminist-nationalist individualism through the writings of Margaret Cousins, a suffragette who emigrated from Ireland to India and helped launch the Indian women's movement for political representation and social equality.[3] Individualism in Cousins's writings is crucially linked to her understanding of the nationalist projects in Ireland and India and their conjuncture with feminism. For her, individualism becomes irreducibly connected to questions of feminist agency, national identity, and the authority to write the history of social movements. Her articulation of feminist-nationalist individualism, grounded as it was in a commitment to solidarity, challenges the assumptions of what Gayatri Chakravorty Spivak calls "feminist individualism in the age of imperialism," a concept modeled on MacPherson's possessive individualism ("Three Women's Texts" 263). Spivak claims that feminist subjects, in the period of high imperialism, are constituted and interpellated as individualist through the dominant "registers of childbearing and soul making," respectively comprehended as "domestic-society-through-sexual-reproduction cathected as 'companionate love'" and "the imperialist project cathected as civil-society-through-social-mission" (263). "As the female individualist, not-quite/not-male, articulates herself in shifting relationship to what is at stake," Spivak explains, "the 'native female' as such (*within* discourse, as a signifier) is excluded from any share in this emerging norm" (263–64; emphasis in original). In contrast to the feminist-individualist subject, theorized by Spivak, whose identity seems to be predicated on the discursive erasure of the gendered-native subject, Cousins's feminist-nationalist individualism sought to facilitate the native female's emergence into the realm of feminist politics and historiography by respecting her authority to document and narrate the Indian women's movement. Clearing a discursive space for the enunciation of Indian women's demands for electoral representation and social equality necessitated that Cousins deemphasize her own important contributions to the Indian women's movement.

Feminist-nationalist individualism is constituted by three major features: first, it positions the individual qua activist-subject in relation to an organized collective based on the individual's national identity, determining appropriate modes of activism for different colonial locations; second, it is grounded in the discourse of political rights, specifically the right to electoral representation; and third, the possessive quality—and limitations, ultimately—of this type of individualism reside in the ways in which feminist-nationalist individualism narrowly circumscribes these rights, restricting them to members of the bourgeoisie. While Cousins developed a theory of solidarity, based on her anomalous position as an Irish woman active in Indian women's organizations, a position which granted her less visibility in that movement, her account of the Irish suffrage movement is overdetermined by an individualism that magnifies her contributions to feminist activism by assigning to herself a foundational role in the establishment of a modern Irish political tradition. Her failure to acknowledge the work of other Irish women in the Irish Women's Franchise League, whose activist efforts were crucial to the success of the Irish suffrage campaign, is in direct contrast to her treatment of the activism of Indian women.

Heroic-Nationalist Individualism In chapter 3, I examine an articulation of heroic-nationalist individualism in the writings of Kalpana Dutt, a Bengali woman who participated in the armed struggle against colonialism in what is called, nonpejoratively in the Indian nationalist context, the "terrorist movement." Heroic-nationalist individualism has several distinguishing features, including a belief in the efficacy of armed struggle waged by an elite segment of the native population, which identifies "success" with "blood sacrifice" (in this case, on the model of the Irish Easter Rising of 1916), and according to which individual acts of bravery encourage others to become nationalists. In other words, through the use of political violence, this type of individualism strives to create native heroes who will both challenge the colonial state's monopoly on the use of force and inspire others to engage in armed struggle.

Heroic-nationalist individualism offers a special, gendered concatenation of individualism, nationalism, and Hinduism. India becomes gendered as a female, figured sometimes as mother and other times as the Goddess Kali, who requires the heroic sacrifice of her sons and daughters to restore her honor, which has been violated by colonial rule. The individual qua nationalist subject is idealized here as an upper-caste, male *ksatriya* (warrior), who functions to intervene in the degrading British discourse of the martial races by specifically challenging the stereotype of the Bengali *babu* as weak, effeminate, and nonmartial. Heroic-nationalist individualism, then, seeks to substitute, in literal terms, a Hindu, masculine subject imbued with courage and physical strength for the effeminate, bookish, and comic caricature of the Bengali male used by colonial authorities to discredit nationalist aspirations and activities. Because this articulation of individualism occurs through a woman combatant in an explicitly nonfeminist manner, heroic-nationalist individualism distances the issue of gender, except in the most conventional patriarchal Hindu terms, from questions of nationalism and political agency.

Heroic-Colonial Individualism In chapter 4, I investigate an articulation of heroic-colonial individualism as it appears in the memoirs and newsletters of former colonial officials and their wives. Heroic-colonial individualism shares with nationalism the tendency to posit the community of colonial officials and their wives as a collective individual. Indeed, the colonial diaspora—military and civilian representatives of the colonial regime—evolved a distinct version of national identity (explained in chapter 4 as "Anglo-Indian" nationalism), which was nonetheless colonial in that it was grounded in territorial and political conquest. "Anglo-Indian" nationalism constructs colonials who were serving on the subcontinent as an entity separate from and morally superior to that of their metropolitan compatriots residing in Britain. In addition to projecting the colonial diaspora as a collective individual, heroic-colonial individualism has two other primary features: first, it constitutes colonial officials and their wives as heroic subjects through recourse to a rhetoric of law and order; and second, it fetishizes, both at the literal and discursive levels, deceased British colonials, attempting to memorialize them for posterity. The white man's burden, here, has been transformed into a historiographical mission.

Colonial officials and their wives represent themselves as heroic individuals who rescue and protect hapless natives from being slaughtered by other natives. This type of individualism disavows, in part, the violence of colonialism by transferring it on to natives and creating a native pathology that essentializes South Asians as inherently prone to irrational violence. In "On Some Aspects of the Historiography of Colonial India," Guha sketches the ideological and generic attributes of colonial and neocolonialist historiography, noting that it has particular difficulty conceptualizing Indian nationalism in class terms and is only capable of assessing the mass articulation of nationalism, "of the people *on their own" "independently of the elite,"* in very limited terms ("On Some Aspects of the Historiography of Colonial India" 39; emphasis in original). Mass support for Indian nationalism, he observes, can only be understood in these accounts "negatively, as a law and order problem, and positively, if at all, either as a response to the charisma of certain elite leaders or in the currently fashionable term of vertical mobilization by the manipulation of factions" (39). Subaltern mobilization tends to occur horizontally, "through the traditional organization of kinship and territoriality or in class associations depending on the level of the consciousness of the people involved," and to be "relatively more violent" than elite mobilization (40). Like colonial and neocolonialist historiography, heroic-colonial individualism thematizes the mass articulation of Indian nationalism as spontaneous eruptions of what in the South Asian context is called "communal" violence (that is, sectarian violence).

Heroic-colonial individualism also fetishizes the dead in ways that are peculiar to the national phase of commemoration which generally elects the dead over the living (Gillis 11). The First World War provided a modality of memorialization qualitatively and quantitatively different from that of earlier epochs insofar as nations began to feel the necessity of leaving material evidence of all their dead in the form of graves and inscriptions (11). This kind of valorization of the dead is apparent in the discourse of heroic-colonial individualism and ventriloquized through organizations such as the British Association for Cemeteries in South Asia (BACSA). With a membership drawn from ex-colonial officials and their wives, BACSA attempts to maintain and restore the graves of their compatriots who expired in the colonies and to amass an archive of colonial memorabilia. The access to mementos, images, and graveyards in South Asia that BACSA provides to its members aids in congealing their nostalgic, heroic memories of colonialism and facilitates the publication of family histories. The family history thus becomes the paradigmatic genre through which the British national memory of colonization is personalized, in the process making available a sanitized representation of colonial relations which masks the brutality of the colonial project. Heroic-colonial individualism revives and preserves a monologic memory of colonialism which, ironically, affects a disengagement with the trauma of colonial rule inasmuch as it discourages a critical assessment of that past, instead inducing amnesia of civil and human rights violations of native subjects by the colonial regime.

SUBALTERN AND ELITE-SUBALTERN IDENTITIES

Almost all the nationalist figures I treat are in some sense elite-subaltern subjects. *Organizing Empire* locates elite-subaltern subjectivity in the social space that emerges between discourses of agency, individualism, and political organizing as they are primarily expressed in narratives of the self, namely in the genres of biography and autobiography. The trope of the individual animates colonialist and nationalist elitist historiography, by primarily crediting the development of Indian nationalist consciousness and state formation to elite personalities and the institutions they inhabited. Colonialist and neocolonialist historiography narrates Indian nationalism through a paradigm of "stimulus and response," describing the process whereby the native elite acquired political consciousness as learning "the maze of institutions and the corresponding cultural complex introduced" by the British for the purposes of colonial governance (Guha, "On Some Aspects of the Historiography of Colonial India" 37–38). Colonialist and neocolonialist elitist historiography understands the motivations of the native elite for participating in the nationalist movement as arising from expectations of power, economic gain, and social privilege rather than out of any "lofty idealism" or commitment to social justice. "[I]t was the drive for such rewards," Guha notes, "with all its concomitant play of collaboration and competition between the ruling power and the native elite as well as between various elements among the latter themselves, which, we are told, was what constituted Indian nationalism" (38). Nationalist and neonationalist elitist historiography, in contrast, narrates Indian nationalism as an expression of idealism, as the story of how the native elite "led the people from subjugation to freedom" (38). The history of Indian nationalism becomes a "spiritual biography" of individual elite natives, whose chief modality is

> to uphold Indian nationalism as a phenomenal expression of the goodness of the native elite with the antagonistic aspect of their relation to the colonial regime made, against all evidence, to look larger than its collaborationist aspect, their role as promoters of the cause of the people than that as exploiters and oppressors, their altruism and self-abnegation than their scramble for the modicum of power and privilege granted by the rulers in order to make sure of their support for the Raj. (38)

Where colonialist and neocolonialist elite historiography employ the idiom of collaboration and self-interest, nationalist and neonationalist elitist accounts draw on an idiom of altruism and political obligation to a larger national collective. Both kinds of historiography, however, explain nationalist consciousness and political agency through the figure of the individual, who is inevitably represented as a unique and charismatic person, capable of mobilizing others through the sheer force of her or his personality.

Against such individualist modes of historiography, Guha, and the Subaltern Studies Group more generally, advocate investigating how the nationalist movement was informed by relations of domination and exploitation. They do so by excavating and recovering the political domain of what Gramsci calls the "subaltern." The signifier "subaltern," in the work of the Subaltern Studies Group, designates those "of inferior rank," naming a "general attribute of subordination in South Asian society whether this is expressed in terms of class, caste, age, gender and office or in any other way" (Guha, "On Some Aspects of the Historiography of Colonial India" 35). The term "subaltern" emphasizes the deviation from an ideal: in Guha's words, "*the demographic difference between the total Indian population and all those whom we have described as the 'elite'*" (44; emphasis in original). Because of the "uneven character of regional economic and social developments," the category of the "elite" is itself heterogeneous in its composition and consists of both foreign and indigenous groups. The foreign elite included "British officials of the colonial state and foreign industrialists, merchants, financiers, planters, landlords and missionaries," while the indigenous elite was further divided into an all-India level, comprising "the biggest feudal magnates, the most important representatives of the industrial and mercantile bourgeoisie and native recruits to the uppermost levels of the bureaucracy," and regional and local levels (44). In addition to the classes which constituted the indigenous elite at the all-India level, regional and local elites also included those individuals and groups who "*acted in the interests of the [elite] and not in conformity to interests corresponding truly to their own social being*" (44; emphasis in original).

As Eva Cherniavsky explains, "the 'subaltern classes' represent an 'ideal category,' comprised in the abstract of all those who do *not* belong to 'dominant foreign groups' or 'dominant indigenous groups,' at either the 'all-India' or 'regional and local' levels" (97; emphasis in original).

As an "ideal category," however, the subaltern is paradoxically not a fixed, stable, transhistorical identity. Rather, subaltern identity is constructed through a difference that is predicated on power relations which are themselves enacted within multiple social registers. For example, an individual can belong to an elite group on the basis of class privilege and be subaltern on the basis of her gender. The category of the subaltern is a relational one, determined by the structure of social hierarchy within a given locale or region. The emplotment of a subaltern history, which refuses to write the history of episodic insurgency through the conventions of a law-and-order narrative, acknowledges the subaltern's status as what Cherniavsky terms a "differential subject" (97).

Mapping the social relations between the elite and subaltern classes within the Subaltern Studies project, Spivak notes the existence of at least four social-class formations: "dominant foreign groups," "dominant indigenous groups on the all-India level," "dominant indigenous groups at the regional and local levels," and the subaltern classes ("Can the Subaltern Speak?" 284). The first two groups, according to Spivak, compose the elite whereas the last two groups have varying degrees of subaltern status. Indeed the third group, consisting of "the dominant indigenous groups at the regional and local levels," acts as the "floating buffer zone of the regional elite-subaltern" (285). As an "intermediate" grouping, the regional elite-subaltern group functions as a "*deviation* from an *ideal*—the people or subaltern—which is itself defined as a difference from the elite" (285). Cherniavsky explains, "That is, the 'subaltern classes' are defined as the non-elite, while the 'regional elite-subaltern' are defined in their *difference* from this *differential* ideal, as the not non-elite" (97). Ultimately, however, the "constitution of the elite-subaltern subject in and as a double negation . . . does not reduce to an affirmation" given that she or he is not "the subject in and of a dominant discourse" (97).

Paraphrasing Cherniavsky, we might observe that the contradictions of elite-subaltern status (of existence as a "not non-elite") become legible specifically with reference to the discursive constructions of individualism (102). While strategically drawing on the ideology of individualism in the service of feminism and anti-imperialism, both feminist-nationalist individualism and heroic-nationalist individualism are marked by the limits of the elite-subaltern identities of their authors. Margaret Cousins and Kalpana Dutt could lay claim to subalternity by virtue of their gender and their status as colonized subjects. But each woman also occupied an elite status within several social registers such as those of class and religion. Though she was an ardent Irish nationalist, Cousins's background was middle-class and Anglo-Irish. Moreover, once she emigrated to India, Cousins was clearly a partisan of Hinduism, as evidenced by her having attributed the contemporary status of Indian women to a "fall" wrought by the spread of Islam on the subcontinent. For her part, Dutt came from a bourgeois, Hindu family. The elite backgrounds of both women circumscribed the extent to which they were able to conceptualize the nationalist project in progressive terms, under which national liberation and the formation of the nation-state were understood to be coterminous with the granting of a universal franchise and the development of decentralized institutional sites which would foster participatory democracy. Instead of articulating a crudely negative version of Indian nationalism as being incompatible with some identities such as membership in the lower class or a religious minority, their versions of nationalism instead affirmed indirectly certain identities by positing the nationalist subject as middle-class and Hindu. While the nationalist subject, in other words, was not constructed as a negation, as not being not-Muslim or as not being not-lower class, Cousins's and Dutt's elite-subaltern status is nevertheless visible in the bourgeois, Hindu construction of the nationalist subject that was so integral to both feminist-nationalist individualism and heroic-nationalist individualism.

CAN THE ELITE-SUBALTERN ORGANIZE?

At the end of her seminal essay on the conditions of subalternity and their relationship to representation, "Can the Subaltern Speak?," Gayatri Spivak reflects on possible readings of a little-known incident from the nationalist period, the suicide of an elite-subaltern subject, Bhuvaneswari Bhaduri. Spivak writes:

> A young woman of sixteen or seventeen, Bhuvaneswari Bhaduri, hanged herself in her father's modest apartment in North Calcutta in 1926. The suicide was a puzzle since, as Bhuvaneswari was menstruating at the time, it was clearly not a case of illicit pregnancy. Nearly a decade later, it was discovered that she was a member of one of the many groups involved in the armed struggle. She had finally

been entrusted with a political assassination. Unable to confront
the task and yet aware of the practical need for trust, she killed herself. (307)

"Bhuvaneswari had known that her death would be diagnosed as the
outcome of illegitimate passion," Spivak speculates, and "had therefore
waited for the onset of menstruation" (307). According to Spivak, Bhaduri's suicide constitutes an "interventionist" and "subaltern" rewriting
of the "social text of sati-suicide," in that the young woman appropriated
"the sanctioned motive for female suicide"—the death of the husband—
even as she violated caste prescriptions for "purity" by postponing her
suicide till she was ritually "impure" (307–8). Bhaduri's menstrual
blood, considered impure and polluting in the idiom of Hindu social
practices, becomes evidence of and testifies to her sexual purity.

The willful misreading of the suicide as "a case of illicit love" and
its erasure from the annals of elite nationalist narratives confirms, for
Spivak, that "the subaltern as female cannot be heard or read" (308). In
this formulation of the female subaltern, a constitutive aspect of subaltern identity is its "exclusion from the symbolic" and its corresponding
lack of access to discursive modalities of self-representation (Cherniavsky 97). As Asha Varadharajan comments, the " 'native' represents the
ineffable, ontological residue of the failure of representation; the impos-
sibility of theory; the sign of the inadequacy of self-reflection" (xxiv).[4]
And if this formulation of subaltern identity has bleak consequences for
representation in the discursive-mimetic sense, its implications for collective action are equally troubling. Indeed, Spivak maintains that the
interpretive manipulation of female agency persistently forecloses on
"the possibility of collectivity itself" ("Can the Subaltern Speak?" 283).

Yet we might inquire how questions of agency, gender, and collective
action can be reread into this scene of elite-subaltern nonarticulation. As
Barbara Harlow notes in her insightful reading of this incident in Barred:
Women, Writing, and Political Detention, Spivak's anecdote implicitly raises
a number of concomitant questions regarding gender and the role of
women in organized resistance groups which suggest that the dominant, patriarchal structure of political opposition has remained intact
in spite of the suicide's apparent "challenge to traditional authority"
(34). The practical effects of the suicide, Harlow points out, are that the
"politician targeted for assassination remains alive" while "the woman

charged with carrying out his death has herself been sacrificed" (34). Interrogating the suicide and its possible readings, she asks:

> What remains unexplained still is what may have impeded Bhaduri in her mission: her own "weakness," material circumstances, a break-down in the organization's political coordination? Who failed whom? And what, further, is the character of the trust so needed that the woman must die at her own hands in order to preserve it? How has the construction of trust been gendered? How, that is, must Bhaduri, in her particular function as a female member of the resistance, be obliged to prove herself and maintain the confidence of her male comrades? (34)

Harlow's reading of Bhaduri's suicide argues for the necessity of shifting the analysis of nationalist narratives from a register that posits a generalized, gendered subject of resistance to a register that would examine the material practices of specific resistance groups in relation to their ideologies of gender and to the tasks that they assign women within the movement. Such a shift entails a progression away from theorizing how individual subjects are interpellated through a general set of social codes to an analysis of how individual combatants function within particular organizational contexts. Harlow's comments invite us to ask after the structure of command, gender hierarchies, and constructions of trust, duty, and honor that animate specific resistance organizations. The questions that she poses speak to the necessity of interrogating the relationship between the material practices of nationalist organizations and their gender ideologies, particularly as that relationship has an impact on and determines the decision, by individual insurgents, to engage in a variety of actions in the service of the anticolonial struggle.

Such work requires conceptualizing subalterns and elite-subalterns as being subjects of history in both senses of the phrase, as constituting a legitimate subject of historiographical study and as being actors who subject history to the processes of transformation through multiple and diverse forms of situated action. While this kind of work and its focus on agency have been dismissed by poststructuralist and postmodern theories of the subject as being a form of information retrieval and of reinstating an overly romanticized understanding of subaltern consciousness and agency, feminism as both a scholarly enterprise and a political practice requires the reconstitution of an archive underwritten by the categories of "women" and, I would add, collective action (Weed xvii).[5] The project of feminist historiography begins by identifying the individuals, events, and organizations which made and continue to make up a given epoch, considering how these entities are embodied in official documentation, informal sources, and unwritten symbolic practices like rumor and street theater. The compilation of such materials and the reconstruction of the participation of individuals within social movements—while always leading to historical inferences which are conjectural, tentative, and open to refutation—is crucial for assembling an archive of feminist activism and for establishing and tracing feminist genealogies of struggle.

Indeed, given that the native subject "is the effect of many determinants, numerous interpellations and various social practices," resulting in the "formation of differentiated and incommensurable subjectivities," a historiographical project that remains committed to a notion of agency and the possibilities of mobilization can also be simultaneously skeptical of attempts to resurrect a singular and monolithic version of subaltern and elite-subaltern consciousness (Parry 85). As Benita Parry remarks,

> A postcolonial rewriting of past contestation, dependent as it is on a notion of a multiply (dis)located native whose positions are provisional, and therefore capable of annulment and transgression, does not restore the foundational, fixed and autonomous individual; what it does resort to is the discourse of the subject inscribed in histories of insubordination produced by anti-colonial movements, deciphered from cryptic cultural forms and redevised from vestiges perpetuated through constant transmutation in popular memory and oral traditions. (85)

Arguing a similar point, David Lloyd urges that the "subaltern" be read as a product and effect of multiple discourses insofar as "the social space of the 'subaltern' designates not some sociological datum of an objective and generalizable kind, but is an effect emerging in and between historiographical discourses" ("Discussion outside History" 263).

Organizing Empire reconstitutes elite-subaltern subjectivity, or in Lloyd's terminology, the elite-"subaltern subject effect," by probing the interstices between discourses of agency, individualism, and political organizing. Agency is understood here in relation to feminist and nationalist subjects and their capacity for willed, voluntary political action, under the auspices of larger, organized collectives, directed toward dismantling the colonial state and establishing a gender-neutral form of citizenship within the emergent post-independent state. A crucial aspect of my treatment of agency, in other words, is the *collective* nature of elite-subaltern resistance to the colonial state as it is manifest in feminist and anticolonial movements.

Movements can be distinguished from more sporadic forms of political protest such as riots, rebellions, and episodic insurgency on the basis of their duration. According to Sidney Tarrow, movements are "*collective challenges by people with common purposes and solidarity in sustained interaction with elite, opponents and authorities*" (3–4; emphasis in original).[6] A contentious episode can only become transformed into an anticolonial movement when nationalist subjects sustain collective action against the colonial state (Tarrow 5). This transformation cannot occur unless natives are economically and politically exhausted with empire and willing publicly to confront colonial rule (Said, *Culture and Imperialism* 200). Concurrently, as Edward Said notes, the representations of imperialism must "begin to lose their justification and legitimacy" and the "rebellious 'natives' [must] impress upon the metropolitan culture the independence of their own culture, free from colonial encroachment" (200). Anticolonial movements emerge when the price of living under colonial occupation, calculated economically, socially, and psychologically, becomes too high to be sustained and when shifts in the political opportunity structure create openings and incentives for collective actions (Tarrow 6). "The magnitude and duration of these collective actions," Tarrow asserts, "depend on mobilizing people through social networks and around identifiable symbols that are drawn from cultural frames of meaning" (6).

For the elite-subaltern subjects of this study, Cousins and Dutt, the social networks that were activated were primarily caste based and territorially centered in their neighborhoods and schools. As the dominant cultural frame of meaning, Hinduism provided both women with identifiable symbols of domesticity and militancy for mobilizing other women and nationalists in their organizing campaigns on the subcontinent.

Agency and elite-subaltern identity, understood within the context of feminist and anticolonial movements, are embodied in concrete political organizations. Political organizations are generally conceived of as collections of individuals who cohere for purposive action. But for mobilization to occur, individuals must already be socially organized in various ways. "Although it is individuals who decide whether or not to take up collective action," Tarrow explains, "it is in their face-to-face groups, their social networks and their institutions that collective action is most often activated and sustained" (21). Indeed, the word "organization" evokes the individual as an organic entity: one of its meanings is "the connexion and co-ordination of parts for vital functions or processes" within a living or sentient being (Burchfield 923). Yet the word also names "the action of putting into systematic form," of "arranging and coordinating . . . parts into a systematic whole" for a definite purpose (923). This definition of "organization" has four important elements: disaggregated parts, coordination, structure, and purposiveness. Political organizations are group structures in which the disaggregated parts of the group are coordinated by agents for a purpose, namely to effect some kind of social change at a range of levels spanning the grassroots to the global.

My approach to agency and political organizations follows what sociologists term the "goal model" or "rational model" of analysis, in which organizations are conceptualized as having five major characteristics. First, political organizations are considered collectives; second, their activities are "oriented toward the attainment of a specific purpose"; third, their ends are given, knowable, or recoverable; fourth, their "central internal processes involve 'decision-making'"; and fifth, their degree of success or failure can be judged by standards of efficiency and effectiveness (Wilson 10–11). Subscribing to such a model of political organizations does not contradict the "natural-system model" of organizational analysis and its contention that political organizations are "miniature social systems" in which the attainment of specific goals may be ancillary to other unstated objectives such as the imperative for the organization to engage in self-perpetuation (Wilson 11). It does, however, shift the analytic emphasis from the ways in which the attitudes, values, and expectations of individual participants have an impact on the organization to questions of structure, hierarchy, decision-making processes, and the accountability of the leadership to those whom they claim to represent and serve. The primary concerns of this book are individuals and how they narrate their agency within and through political organizations to challenge the power and authority of the colonial state, but also how that state deploys discourses of individualism in the face of such provocations to its authority.

THE STATUS OF INDIA-IRELAND LINKS

Mapping the four major types of individualism in colonial, neocolonial, and nationalist discourses also suggests alternative means of analyzing imperialism and nationalism that challenge the disciplinary proclivities of postcolonial studies which are bound to the single-site-and-discrete-period model.[7] In "Ethnography in/of the World System," George Marcus provides a useful model for pursuing the comparative dimensions of research that posits connections between seemingly discontinuous contexts. Among his different methodological suggestions for this kind of research, two in particular have influenced me, namely his injunction to "follow the thing" and to "follow the life or biography" (108–9).[8] Following the thing "involves tracing the circulation through different contexts of a manifestly material object of study (at least as initially conceived), such as commodities, gifts, money, works of art, and intellectual property" (106–7). For instance, the circulation of biographies of Irish nationalists among Indian nationalists, and telegrams exchanged in solidarity between the two groups, which I discuss in Chapter 3, attest to the existence of resistance networks among nationalists in both sites. Following the life or biography can be valuable because, according to Marcus,

> Life histories reveal juxtapositions of social contexts through a succession of narrated individual experiences that may be obscured in the structural study of processes as such. They are potential guides to the delineation of ethnographic spaces within systems shaped by categorical distinction that may make these spaces otherwise invisible. These spaces are not necessarily subaltern spaces (although they may be most clearly revealed in subaltern life histories), but they are shaped by unexpected or novel associations among sites and social contexts suggested by life history accounts. (110)

General Dyer's and Margaret Cousins's life histories, traced in chapters 1 and 2, disclose the structural links in the imperial grid, demonstrating how certain colonial sites, such as Ireland, functioned as schools in repression and training for colonial administrators and military officials eventually posted in other sites, such as India; these life histories also expose the systematic linkages between seemingly disparate feminist and nationalist struggles.

Tracing the contours of anticolonial movements through geographical associations and modalities of resistance militates against imperialist attempts to view and isolate these struggles as local phenomena occurring in discrete national sites. Such a multisited analysis challenges the hierarchical and intranational categorizations of struggle in terms of imperial, nationalist, subaltern, and elite-subaltern formations, offering instead a lateral view of an alternative organization of global networks whose possibilities are enabled by colonialism but whose significance lies in the ways these groupings turn the colonial system against itself. Exclusively nationalist frameworks are inadequate for a complete understanding of either colonial power or anticolonial resistance.

Yet while I explore the links between India and Ireland in various degrees of detail throughout *Organizing Empire*, this book is not meant to be an exhaustive account of the structure of the British colonial state or of the circuits of intellectual exchange among nationalists around the globe. Rather, the recurring references to links between India and Ireland are offered as a preliminary foray into multisited research, to indicate new scholarly directions for postcolonial studies.[9]

ROGUE-COLONIAL INDIVIDUALISM: GENERAL
DYER, COLONIAL MASCULINITY, INTENTIONALITY,
AND THE AMRITSAR MASSACRE

On April 13, 1919, in the Indian city of Amritsar, General Reginald Edward Harry Dyer ordered his Gurkha and Baluchi soldiers to fire upon an
unarmed crowd, estimated at between ten and twenty thousand, assembled in an enclosed compound, the Jallianwala Bagh, to protest the
Rowlatt Act, which allowed for detention without trial. The crowd had
gathered in defiance of his proclamation earlier that morning:

> No person residing in the city is permitted or allowed to leave the city
> in his own private or hired conveyance or on foot without a pass. No
> person residing in Amritsar city is permitted to leave his house after
> 8. Any persons found in the streets after 8 are liable to be shot. No
> procession of any kind is permitted to parade the streets in the city, or
> any part of the city, or outside of it, at any time. Any such processions
> or any gathering of four men would be looked upon and treated as
> an unlawful assembly and dispersed by force of arms if necessary.
> (United Kingdom, Parliament, *Report of the Committee* 28)

Dyer's troops opened fire, without warning, on the peaceful gathering in
the Jallianwala Bagh, discharging some 1,650 rounds, killing 379 people
and wounding 1,137 (29). After his troops had fired for ten minutes, Dyer
ordered them to retreat without making any medical provisions for the
injured. Because of the 8 P.M. curfew in the region, it was extremely difficult for the friends and families of the victims to retrieve their corpses
and to tend to the wounded.[1] As a well-documented use of lethal force
against a colonized population, the Jallianwala Bagh massacre made
clear that British colonialism, in spite of its claims to be a project in
liberal humanism, articulated in the political idiom of the "improve-

ment" or "civilizing" of the natives, relied on force in order to secure and maintain its rule (Guha, *Dominance* 275). General Dyer's massacre provoked a crisis among the metropolitan bourgeoisie, because it rendered visible the contradictions that structured every aspect of British Indian colonial relations.

British "*bourgeois culture hits its historical limit in colonialism*," Ranajit Guha argues. "None of its noble achievements—Liberalism, Democracy, Liberty, Rule of Law, etc.—can survive the inexorable urge of capital to expand and reproduce itself by means of the politics of extra-territorial, colonial dominance" (*Dominance* 277; emphasis in original). Indeed, a precondition of maintaining colonial rule was the failure of the metropolitan bourgeoisie to actualize its own universalist project, thus leading to a number of contradictions which informed the specificity of the British colonial formation on the subcontinent (274). These contradictions included, for example, parliamentary rule over a state formation which lacked the concept of citizenship for the vast majority of its subjects, the development of capitalism predicated on a neofeudal organization of property, and a liberal education purposefully promulgated to perpetuate the natives' loyalty to an autocratic regime (271–72). Analyzing the relations between dominance and subordination within colonial India in light of such contradictions, Guha notes that each of these terms is constituted by a "pair of interacting elements" which "imply each other *contingently*": dominance is made up of the interaction of coercion and persuasion, while subordination is determined by the interaction of collaboration and resistance (229–30; emphasis in original). In the British Indian context, according to Guha, coercion always obtained over persuasion given that there could be "no subjugation of an entire people in its own homeland by foreigners without the explicit use of force" (233). Because dominance was secured by coercion, emphasizing the use of force rather than consent, British dominance on the subcontinent was actualized *without* hegemony, requiring, in the process, the "fabrication of [a] spurious hegemony" (283).

Guha's insistence on repositioning hegemony within the "trajectory of real historical power relations" is instructive for an analysis of the crisis in the British House of Commons occasioned by Dyer's carnage in Amritsar. The parliamentary debates reveal the discursive operations of rogue-colonial individualism through which a "spurious hegemony" was established. While General Dyer was investigated for violations of military procedure, the parliamentary debates illustrate how military-civilian relations are constructed by rhetorical strategies that contain violations against the colonial regime's own ideological articulation. Colonial discourse creates an opposition between those officials whom it deems "good," agents whose behavior conforms to the colonial norm, which is the regulated use of force, and those whom it deems "bad," agents whose actions fall beyond the norm by using force blatantly. Confronted with pressure from angry natives and their metropolitan sympathizers, who are outraged by incidents of excessive force, the colonial regime creates a safety valve to dissipate some of this tension and avert nationalist challenges to the colonial state and scrutiny of the colonial project as a whole. Through the process of individuation, a specific person is scapegoated in a discursive manifestation of rogue-colonial individualism.[2] As demonstrated by the public reaction to the Amritsar massacre, the ideology of rogue-colonial individualism often emphasizes the importance of ascertaining the "intentionality" of the principle personalities involved. Through methods of individualizing the participants into rogue-colonial officials, the systemic workings of colonial power are renegotiated and the function of violence such as surveillance and discipline is itself displaced by other, less threatening narratives.

The law becomes the primary vehicle through which the colonial regime affects the disarticulation between its governance and its reliance on force that is so central to rogue-colonial individualism. By providing a mechanism through which the use of force can be regulated and potentially criminalized, through the censure of the most egregious offenders of colonial brutality such as General Dyer, the authoritarian nature of colonial rule is obscured by the trappings of bourgeois democracy. Yet the ambiguities of the law constantly threaten to unravel this spurious hegemony and rend the fabric of colonial ideology. In its generic sense, the law signifies a body of rules of action or conduct that is prescribed by a controlling authority—generally the state—which has binding force on its citizens (Black's 612). The boundaries of jurisprudential discourse, however, are themselves fluid given that the law is derived from three major sources: judicial precedents, legislation, and custom. Diffuse in origins, the law is manifest in multiple forms, textual and extratextual, including civil law, criminal law, martial law, common law, and international law. The extratextual sources for the law additionally perplex the imperative to adjudicate, since these sources are not stable categories but are subject to historical processes and interpretive fluidity. As the oral texts of "custom" change over time so too do the meanings attached to them through the process of interpretation. It is perhaps the multiple manifestations of the law, in the context of colonialism, that have contributed to the vexed status of massacres in jurisprudential discourse.[3] Paraphrasing Guha, we might note that the law reaches its historical limit in colonialism. For while we might conceptualize the law ideally as a system of norms that exists to safeguard the bodily integrity and liberty of individual subjects, what the parliamentary debates of the Amritsar massacre expose is the law as the solemn expression of the will of the supreme power of the colonial state (Black's 612).

This chapter examines the debates on General Dyer and the Jallianwala Bagh massacre in the House of Commons to show the centrality of the law to the ideology of rogue-colonial individualism. As illustrated by the parliamentary debates on the Amritsar massacre, the law serves to obfuscate the brutal foundations of colonial rule while constructing a spurious hegemony as part of colonialism's apparatus of self-justification. Though the various official representatives of the British state were by and large united in their commitment to the idea of Empire, their conceptions of the proper aims and responsibilities of the colonial project were by no means unified or monolithic. As David Scott explains in "Colonial Governmentality," " 'the colonial state' cannot offer itself up as the iteration and reiteration of a single political rationality"; rather, different political rationalities and configurations of power, which were often discontinuous with earlier ones, emerged at given moments within the structures of the colonial state (197; emphasis in original). The Jallianwala Bagh massacre and the attendant discussion of General Dyer were underpinned by the competing political ideologies, geopolitical interests, and party agendas of those political and military officials who participated in them. My method in this chapter is to read the various interpretations of Dyer's intentionality against the conflicting motivations, both domestic and international, that underwrite their pronouncement.

An investigation of the discursive operations of intentionality and the law within the parliamentary debates additionally demonstrates how colonial subjects are interpellated through the military apparatus and suggests how different colonial locations, such as India and Ireland, are linked in the imperial grid. General Dyer's career exposes the isomorphic parallels between these two colonial sites by showing how Ireland functioned as a training ground for counterinsurgency in other parts of the Empire. This interpellation is of course structured by gender and race, and its articulation in the discourse of rogue-colonial individualism illustrates the peculiar conjuncture between patriarchy and colonial domination operative in the British Indian context. As General Dyer's explanation of his intentions reveals, massacre becomes a way of asserting colonial masculinity over the natives. While General Dyer emerges as a Janus-faced figure in these accounts—either the valiant military man discharging his duties under mutinous circumstances or a monstrous aberration of a colonial system predicated on the rule of law—the natives are gendered as male, embodying the potential of a radical nationalism that threatens to solidify into an armed struggle, modeled on that of Sinn Fein and the IRA, against the colonial state. Absent in these narratives are the South Asian women and children who were present in the Jallianwala Bagh and massacred by Dyer's troops. The parliamentary debates concerning General Dyer's conduct at Amritsar illustrate how the multiple expressions of Dyer's culpability or, depending upon one's perspective, heroism occurred within a narrowly circumscribed field, focused on ascertaining the "intent" of the principal participants, that never impugned colonialism and its relationship to deadly force. The ideology of rogue-colonial individualism seeks to distance the colonial enterprise from its constitutive violence by criminalizing those colonial officials who engage in explicit and excessive brutality against natives.

DYER INTENTIONS: MASSACRES AND COLONIAL MASCULINITY

While factual clarity is rarely an aspect of international disputes such as colonial massacres, with the Amritsar massacre the factual details of the event were not disputed; yet these details caused less of a reaction from the British public than did Dyer's explanation of his intentions in ordering the attack on civilians. Both Dyer's critics and his supporters drew on the concept of intentionality, nuancing it in different ways, either to condemn his actions or to validate them. The invocations of intentionality functioned on two different registers, namely the individual and the collective. Dyer and his partisans justified the massacre by arguing that he had acted out of anticipatory self-defense, maintaining that the collective intent of the crowd was to initiate a second Mutiny. His critics, in contrast, insisted on limiting the discussion to questions of Dyer's individual intent and responsibility, to distance him from the military establishment and the colonial rule of law. That intentionality could be used to rationalize fundamentally contradictory stances on Dyer's conduct is symptomatic of its lack of clarity as a legal category. In jurisprudential discourse, "intention" has been associated most often with criminal law and is generally linked to malice aforethought. Determining the relationship between intention and malice aforethought in criminal cases, furthermore, has been crucially dependent on questions of objectivity and probability (Dine 72).

According to Black's Law Dictionary, "intent" signifies the "design, resolve, or determination with which [a] person acts." Because "intent" is a "mental attitude which can seldom be proved by direct evidence," it "must ordinarily be proved by circumstances from which it can be inferred" (Black's 559). "Intent" thus describes a "state of mind existing at the time a person commits an offense and may be shown by act, circumstances and inferences deducible therefrom" (559). One of the earliest statements of intent, Foster's Crown Law of 1762, assumes that those charged with murder acted out of malice aforethought and places the burden of proof on the defendant, stating: "In every charge of murder, the fact of the killing being first proved, all the circumstances of accident, necessity, or infirmity are to be satisfactorily proved by the prisoner, unless they arise out of the evidence produced against him: for the law presumeth the fact to have been founded in malice unless the contrary appeareth" (quoted in Dine 72). Before the Criminal Evidence Act of 1898, however, defendants were barred from giving evidence in their behalf in murder cases and, consequently, the court was denied direct evidence of the defendant's mental state at the time of the offense (Dine 73). The two unsettled questions revolving around ascertaining intent and malice aforethought, according to Janet Dine, are:

> 1) do the jury need to examine the mind of the defendant or may they take an objective stand and assume that his mind worked in the way an ordinary reasonable juror's mind would work?; 2) as nothing in human affairs is certain, no person can say that they can, with absolute certainty, achieve a particular result. The result of a particular human action can therefore only be described as falling on a particu-

lar point on a scale of certainty ranging from highly unlikely to virtually certain. At which point along this scale is a particular result intended? Is it intended when it was foreseen as likely, highly likely, virtually certain? (72)

These unresolved questions of objectivity and probability have facilitated what Andrei Marmor calls the "expertise thesis" which maintains that when authority is invested in an individual on the assumption that she or he is "more likely to have a better access to the right reasons bearing on the pertinent issue, it would typically be most sensible to take the authority's intentions into account" when her or his "directives require interpretation" (178).

In testifying to the Hunter Committee, the committee officially appointed by the British government to investigate the massacre and what were quaintly known as other "disturbances" in north India, Dyer foregrounds his identity as a military officer, legitimizing his authority on the basis of military expertise and access to conditions on the ground. He narrates his "intentions" by stressing that his objectives were calculated from a military perspective. Believing that there was evidence of a widespread rebellion which was not confined to Amritsar alone, he felt that his duty at the Jallianwala Bagh was not limited to dispersing the crowd but was "to produce a moral effect in the Punjab" (United Kingdom, Parliament, *Report of the Committee* 30). Dyer had ascertained, in his words, that the "situation was very very serious" and "had made up" his "mind . . . to do all men to death if they were going to continue the meeting" (112). He explains:

> I fired and continued to fire until the crowd dispersed, and I consider this is the least amount of firing which would produce the necessary moral and widespread effect it was my duty to produce if I was to justify my action. If more troops had been at hand the casualties would have been greater in proportion. *It was no longer a question of merely dispersing the crowd*, but one of producing a sufficient moral effect from a military point of view not only on those who were present, but more especially throughout the Punjab. There could be no question of undue severity. (30; emphasis in original)

Dyer's statement regarding the massacre is an admission of what is known in jurisprudential discourse as "constructive intent": a reasonable expectation that casualties, or the "willful and wanton" infliction of injuries to others, would result from his actions (*Black's* 217). Constructive intent is here legitimized by a rhetorical move that both delocalizes a political protest—decontextualizing it from events in Amritsar and projecting it on a regional scale to the entire Punjab—and simultaneously, though implicitly, alters the nature of that protest, transforming it from a civilian event to a potential military insurrection. In surmising that the crowd consisted of "rebels" because it had gathered in defiance of his proclamation, Dyer drew on circumstantial evidence and decided that he had "to give them a lesson" (*Report of the Committee* 113).

Dyer's testimony indicates that a crucial aspect of maintaining the peace in Amritsar and in the Punjab included upholding British military prestige, thereby asserting colonial masculinity and dominance over the natives through the exercise of force.[4] For example, after admitting that he could have dispersed the crowd without firing on it, Dyer explains that he rejected this option out of the anxiety that the crowd would make a laughingstock out of him. "I could disperse them for some time," he reveals, "then they would all come back and laugh at me, and I considered I would be making myself a fool" (114). This possibility would have been all the more personally abhorrent to Dyer considering that he subscribed to the adult-child paradigm of colonial relations. In response to the suggestion that he had done "a great disservice to the British Raj" by firing on the crowd, Dyer asserts, "I thought it would be doing a jolly lot of good and they would realise that they were not to be wicked" (116). Characterizing the crowd as a naughty group of children capable of becoming dangerous hooligans, he casts himself in the role of the adult who was their reluctant disciplinarian. Dyer's testimony illustrates Jenny Sharpe's observation that "the crisis produced by anticolonial rebellion is managed through a recoding of European self-interest as self-sacrifice and native insurgency as ingratitude" (*Allegories* 8). Indeed, the rhetoric of self-sacrifice and native ingratitude permeates Dyer's explanation for his actions: "it only struck me at the time it was my duty to do this and that it was a horrible duty. I did not like the idea of doing it, but I also realised that it was the only means of saving life and that any reasonable man with justice in his mind would realise that I had done the right thing; and it was a merciful act, though a horrible act, and they ought to be thankful to me for doing it" (116). By applying the "reasonable man"

measure to justify his actions—thus universalizing his pathological in-
fantilization of the natives onto other hypothetically fair-minded persons—Dyer genders and racializes the colonial rule of law as only in-
terpretable by male Britons. His display of force at Amritsar, as his
statements demonstrate, was meant to showcase the power of the colonial military apparatus and to shore up the subject-position of its male
agents. One member of the Commons would later characterize Dyer's
elaboration of these intentions in his statement to the Army Council as
"manly and splendidly frank and open" (United Kingdom, *Parliamentary
Debates* 1779).[5]

Colonial male subjectivity relied in part on the ideological promulgation of British males as the guardians of British women and children
who, as a result of their inferior status in the hierarchy of colonial power,
were vulnerable to becoming objects of native violence. Underwriting
much of Dyer's desire to teach a "lesson" to the natives was the fear that
a second Mutiny was imminent and that this would have dire consequences for British women and children. Of all the violent acts committed by Indians during the Amritsar disturbances before the massacre,
which included the brutal killing of five European men, Dyer viewed the
attack on a female missionary, Marcella Sherwood, as the most serious.
While bicycling in Amritsar, she had been bludgeoned by a group of men
and left for dead on a city lane. "The attempted murder of Miss Sherwood," he writes in his rebuttal to the Hunter Committee report, "was
probably the most dastardly outrage in the whole rebellion" (United
Kingdom, *Statements of Brig.-Gen. Reginald E. Dyer* 17). According to his
biographer, Dyer, "who had a very tender reverence for women saw Miss
Sherwood lying on a pallet . . . swathed in bandages, between life and
death" sometime after she had been attacked (Colvin 196–97). Shortly
afterward, he determined a suitable punishment to mete out to those
unfortunate Indians who happened to find themselves on the street in
which she had been assaulted. His notorious "crawling order" decreed
that any Indian who wanted to travel on that lane was required to get on
all fours and crawl through it. Such punishment was appropriate in
Dyer's estimation because, as he states, "we look upon women as sacred,
or ought to," and the site of the assault had to be sanctified by Indians
who were accustomed to prostrating themselves in places of worship
(quoted in Colvin 197). Here, the colonial rule of law, in this case martial

law, is used to instantiate the British as a divine presence whose worship is constituted by the appropriation of native religious rituals. Punitive colonial measures against Indians take on the legitimacy of Hindu authority in the process, even as they uphold British male power.

Dyer's construction of colonial male subjectivity as fulfilling the guardian function for British women and children threatened by the potential of native violence is reaffirmed by numerous Englishwomen who viewed him as "the Savior of the Punjab" and who leapt to his public defense. As an anonymous Englishwoman declared in Blackwood's Magazine in April 1920, "No European who was in Amritsar or Lahore doubts that for some days there was a very real danger of the entire European population being massacred, and that General Dyer's actions alone saved them" ("Amritsar" 446). Dyer's defenders in the Commons turned to the testimonials of memsahibs in particular to support the claim that the Amritsar disturbances signaled the beginnings of another Mutiny. Many of these testimonials contain references to the Mutiny, which served as a trope for acts of violence against Englishwomen. Miss Sherwood herself wrote to one member of parliament on Dyer's behalf and asked that he enter her letter into the record. Her letter reads, "I should like to say, that loving the [Indian] people as I do, having worked amongst them for years, and still hoping to go back to India, I am convinced that there was a real rebellion in the Punjab, and that General Dyer saved India and us from a repetition of the miseries and cruelties of 1857" (quoted in United Kingdom, Parliamentary Debates 1757). Another Englishwoman outlines the deplorable conditions in the fort, to which the women and children had been evacuated out of fear for their safety in the civil lines: "The children had no milk, but only bully beef, and there were no sanitary conveniences in the Fort. We had a terrible time, recalling the days of the Mutiny, which was a very, very bad time for the English women and children" (1757). "I wish to do my part in strongly protesting against the injustices being done to General Dyer," another Englishwoman writes, "who, I believe, did his duty and saved us from unspeakable horrors" (1757). The insistent repetition of the mutiny theme in references to the "miseries and cruelties of 1857," the "unspeakable horrors," and as "a very, very bad time for the English women and children" reveals a collective colonial memory of trauma which refuses to be more precisely narrated. As Jenny Sharpe explains in Allegories of Empire: The Figure of Woman in the Colonial Text:

During the 1857 revolt, the idea of rebellion was so closely imbricated with the violation of English womanhood that the Mutiny was remembered as a barbaric attack on innocent white women. Yet Magistrates commissioned to investigate the so-called eyewitness reports could find no evidence to substantiate the rumors of rebels raping, torturing, and mutilating English women. During the course of the nineteenth century, Anglo-Indian fiction gave coherence to the Mutiny narratives by lending a literary imagination to what was "unspeakable" in the first-hand reports. (2)

Rape, as a discursive category which arose during the Mutiny, functions as a "highly charged trope that is implicated in the management of rebellion" because it provided the necessary pretext for ruthless counterinsurgency measures against natives (Sharpe, *Allegories* 2).

Such testimonials as those of the memsahibs aided Dyer's defenders in gendering and nationalizing the victims of native violence as British women and children. In order to support their case, the Dyerites had to gender and nationalize the crowd gathered in the Jallianwala Bagh as male and as Indian. Since the status of victimhood was reserved for women and children of their own race and nationality, speaker after speaker in the House of Commons contended, as the Hunter Committee report did, that there were no native women and children present during the firing.[6] Since Indian women did not begin to take an active role in the nonviolent movement till the emergence of Gandhi as a national leader sometime after the massacre, it is unlikely that many were present in the Jallianwala Bagh. The Indian National Congress Report does not contain any allegations that women were present at the site of the massacre (V. N. Datta 105).[7] However, at least one survivor of the massacre, Sardar Atma Singh Siddhu, reported the presence of women at the peaceful demonstration, and his assertion is supported by Secretary S. K. Mukerji whose records reveal that two women were killed in the massacre.[8] A number of Indian sources also maintain that a large number of children were in attendance at the rally. Mohammed Ismail, for instance, estimates there were four to five hundred children in the crowd (Furneaux 29). Another survivor of the massacre, Lala Guranditta, recounts seeing a young boy, about twelve years old, lying dead with the corpse of a toddler cradled in his arms (Furneaux 22). On hearing of the attack, Mian Sikander Ali rushed to the Jallianwala Bagh to search for his younger son. He remembers:

I reached the Bagh at about 7.15 p.m. entering in through the main entrance on the north. I managed to extricate his dead body from a large heap of corpses near the outlet to the east of the well. The deceased had a bullet mark on his calf, and a big opening a little over his forehead. Close to my son, lay my cousin named Ismail. He also had received a bullet on his calf, and his right jaw had been lacerated. A near relation of Ismail, named Hasan, had also come to the Bagh in search of the latter. We both removed the corpses with the greatest difficulty, as there was no one to help us. There were a number of children among the dead. I saw an aged man lying prostrate on the ground with a two years old baby in his arms. Both appeared to be lifeless. The number of dead and wounded, then lying in the garden, was about two thousand. (quoted in Furneaux 26–27)

These accounts do not specify the gender of the children. Yet given that purdah restrictions among Hindus, Muslims, and Sikhs do not typically begin before the onset of puberty, it is probable that the children included both girls and boys.

The gendering of the victims of colonial violence as male and the insistent repetition that children were not in evidence in the Jallianwala Bagh that afternoon aided Dyer's supporters in justifying the massacre as a form of anticipatory self-defense. To advance such a claim, they had to impute a collective intent to the crowd and characterize it as a potential military threat. Dyer's defenders resorted to several arguments to establish the hostile intentions of the crowd. Chiefly, these were that the very presence of the crowd, which was engaged in protest against the colonial government, was proof of its "dangerous mood," that its size signaled a threat to Dyer's forces, and that the crowd was armed with "dangerous weapons" (Parliamentary Debates 1749). Lieutenant General Sir Alymer Hunter-Weston, who tried to moderate between the pro- and anti-Dyer factions, for example, asked members of parliament to transport themselves imaginatively to the scene of the massacre and provided them with a narrative of the probable circumstances facing Dyer:

On arriving at the entrance to the park, he finds himself in face of a huge assembly of many thousand people. They *appear* to him to be in a dangerous mood, and he knows that it is *possible* that they are armed with lathis—long bamboo clubs, often ringed with iron, dangerous weapons in hand to hand fighting. The nearest men are within a few yards of him, and a determined rush *may* easily overwhelm his little force of fifty native soldiers armed with rifles, and forty armed only with kukris, the Gurkha knives. . . . It *might* well be that any hesitation on his part, any failure to use, and to use at once, the necessary force, *might* be the spark which would set alight the conflagration of another mutiny. (1749–50; emphasis mine)

As the italicized words indicate, the claims regarding the dangers posed by the crowd were delivered in the conditional mode rather than the indicative and thus were speculative rather than based in fact. Dyer's defenders often substituted speculation for actual evidence to make their case, a strategy which removed all concrete criteria for rendering judgments of intentionality. Perhaps the most blatant expression of this kind of speculation occurs in Ian Colvin's description of the crowd in his 1925 biography of Dyer. "The character of the mob," he writes, "may also be presumed from the events which had gone before" (176):

They had met in defiance of the proclamation to listen to their favorite orators. There is no reason to doubt that those who sat at the feet of Durga Das were substantially the same crowd as those who had murdered the Bank managers and looted the Bank go-downs. Lord Meston, no friend of General Dyer, afterwards admitted in the House of Lords that the mob was being harangued "presumably not in the interests of peace and order but with incitations to violence." "The point," he continued, "had been much debated, whether they were armed. It is perfectly true that they had no lethal weapons, that they had no firearms, and it is also alleged that they were not ostensibly armed with bludgeons. But I have never known an Indian crowd of that type and of that character that had not a very large supply of bludgeons somewhere or other near. And those who know the Indian *lathi*, heavily shod with iron, five feet long, capable of battering out a man's brains in a few seconds, will realise how dangerous a weapon that bludgeon might be, and would be, in the hands of infuriated men at close quarters. Any mob so armed is dangerous, and the mob that faced General Dyer was undoubtedly dangerous. If there had been any faltering or hesitation, it is quite certain that General Dyer's men might have been rushed and overwhelmed and cudgelled to death. (176–77)

Colvin presents no evidence that the crowd consisted of the same people who had committed earlier acts of violence against Europeans. The rhetorical phrase "there is no reason to doubt" conveniently glosses over this omission of facts. Colvin also enlists Lord Meston and his testimony to the House of Lords to buttress the assertion that the crowd was extremely dangerous. In his speech, Meston admits that the crowd was not armed with either guns or lathis. Yet based on his previous experience of Indian crowds, he concludes that it *must have* stashed a large supply of lathis within the vicinity. In order to make such a claim, Meston had to ignore the topography of the Jallianwala Bagh. While the entrance to the compound was sandwiched between two strips of raised ground, most of the Jallianwala Bagh consisted of a flat, open field with several widely spaced trees dotting its perimeter and harbored few hiding places that could conceal a large number of lathis. Furthermore, Meston's argument relies on a model of hand-to-hand combat which is at odds with the military and spatial configuration of the scene. A more accurate assessment of the scene would have likened it to a firing squad: on one side were arrayed the military forces, spread across the elevated earth in a double line, and on the other a group of unarmed, crouching Indians listening to a speech.

The Hunter Committee inquiry could find no evidence that the crowd was "provided with firearms," although it too relies on the conditional mode in surmising that "some of them *may* have been carrying sticks" (29; emphasis mine). Several eyewitnesses dispute the allegations that some in the crowd were armed with lathis. Pratap Singh, a survivor of the massacre, describes the aftermath of the shooting to the Congress subcommittee and comments on this point: "I got up and saw bodies on all sides, and went towards the back of the garden. The bodies were so thick about the passage, that I could not find my way out. I had my son with me and men were rushing over the dead bodies. . . . I never saw any lathis (sticks) the whole time I was there, neither among those sitting nor on the ground afterwards" (quoted in Furneaux 25–26). Still another eyewitness, Lala Karan Chand, relates searching for his brother among the dead: "The Bagh was like a battlefield. There were corpses scattered everywhere in heaps, and the wounded were crying out for water. I saw many bodies of children. . . . I never saw any lathis at all in the Bagh when I was searching for my brother" (quoted in Furneaux 27–28).

The construction of the native victims of colonial violence as armed, adult males, primed for rebellion because they were brimming with hostile intentions toward the Empire, aided colonial officials in casting the Amritsar carnage as a kind of preventive military measure which successfully thwarted a second Mutiny. However, the concept of anticipatory self-defense touted by Dyer's supporters fails to meet the accepted requisites for lawful self-defense as elaborated in the *Digest of International Law* (1906). Secretary of State Daniel Webster, reacting to the British destruction of the steamship *Caroline* at Niagara Falls, offers the classic formulation of the customary right of self-defense in limiting it to cases in which the "necessity of that self-defense is instant, overwhelming and leaving no choice of means, and no moment for deliberation" (quoted in Malone 412). Furthermore, as Linda Malone explains, lawful self-defense requires that "the response be strictly limited to the object of stopping or preventing the danger and must be reasonably proportionate to what is required for achieving this object" (412). With the Amritsar massacre, General Dyer's response to the civilian protest fails to pass the twin tests of necessity and proportionality. Self-defense, according to international law, cannot be exercised in *anticipation* of some perceived threat to the state but only in *response* to an actual armed attack. Given that the protesters were not armed, nor directly engaged with Dyer's troops, they did not pose a physical threat to the crown forces. Had Dyer wished to limit his objective to dispersing the crowd, he could have done so by issuing orders to that effect. Dyer's commands to his soldiers to fire without warning on civilians, killing a significant number in the process, so that he could administer a "lesson" to potential insurgents in the region, was a disproportionate response to a peaceful political protest. The Jallianwala Bagh massacre represents the solemn expression of the will of the supreme power of the colonial male military subject. Masculinity combined with militarism, in the context of Amritsar, resulted in a massacre.

SHIFTING INTENTIONS

The debates on General Dyer and the Jallianwala Bagh massacre in the House of Commons illustrate how the ideology of rogue-colonial individualism never assailed colonialism and its reliance on deadly force. Both Dyer's supporters and his critics draw on the rhetorical strategy of individuation, constructing him as either a heroic military officer courageously performing his duties under extremely dangerous circumstances or as an abominable aberration of the colonial rule of law, who has seriously mistaken his military obligations. The singular focus on individual responsibility and culpability, articulated through narratives of intentionality, obscures the systemic workings of colonial power and dominance. That the debate on Dyer was so narrowly circumscribed is evident from the responses of such ideologically diverse politicians as the Liberal Samuel Edwin Montagu and the Conservative Sir Winston Churchill, who agreed that the massacre violated the British rule of law. Party affiliations were no predictor of what position a given member of parliament would take on the question of Dyer's culpability. To cite another instance, Sir Edward Carson, a member of the Conservative Party who ordinarily agreed with Churchill on colonial policy, sharply differed with him on his opinion of the general, who Carson felt should not be punished for an "error of judgement" (*Parliamentary Debates* 1714). While Montagu, Churchill, and Carson all used similar discursive strategies focused on ascertaining the intent of the principal participants in marshaling their arguments against or for Dyer, they were motivated by a range of geopolitical considerations in India, Ireland, and the rest of the Empire: Montagu sought to advance a limited form of parliamentarianism in India; Churchill to preserve the Empire through an affirmation of the colonial rule of law; and Carson, to defeat Irish Home Rule through repressive counterinsurgency measures. The pronouncements of the three on Dyer are underwritten by different administrative colonial agendas which supported the legitimacy of colonial rule. An examination of the intentionality that structures these pronouncements reveals the constitutive relations of power which animate the colonial regime in its various discursive guises.

A brief chronology of the parliamentary measures to discipline Dyer might be in order. Montagu, who was then secretary of state for India, concurred with the Hunter Committee's censure of General Dyer and published its report on May 27, 1920, without first forwarding its conclusions to Dyer or allowing Sir Michael O'Dwyer, the lieutenant governor of Punjab during the massacre and one of Dyer's staunchest supporters, an opportunity to rebut the committee's findings. For his part, Churchill pressured the Army Council to relieve Dyer of all his military responsibilities and to retire him at half-pay. Along with O'Dwyer, Sir Edward Carson, another Irishman who was an ardent loyalist and the first signatory to the "Ulster Solemn League and Covenant," championed Dyer's cause. Churchill announced in the House of Commons on July 7, 1920, the decision by the Army Council to retire Dyer. In response, Carson introduced a motion to reduce Montagu's salary by £100 to express dissatisfaction with the government's treatment of Dyer. This resolution was followed by one similar in substance but different in intent, introduced by the floor whip for the Labour Party, Ben Spoor, which sought "to condemn all responsible for the Government of India's policy" (Fein 132–33). These resolutions resulted in a furious debate between the pro- and anti-Dyer factions regarding the nature of his intentions, the collective intent of the crowd, anticipatory self-defense, minimum force, and concepts of justice.[9] The Dyerites worried that the general had been denied due process and that he was being punished unfairly while the anti-Dyer faction maintained that the primary issue was that he had violated the implicit rules governing the proper administration of force and had thus transgressed the colonial rule of law. Both groups marshaled the concept of "intentionality" to bolster their arguments. Dyer's detractors focused on his intention of "teaching" Indians a "lesson" by inflicting as many casualties as possible and his failure to ascertain the peaceful collective intent of the crowd assembled at the Jallianwala Bagh. Dyer's partisans justified his actions by claiming that he had intended to avert a second Mutiny and that he was motivated by the desire to guard British life and property. In their view, Dyer had correctly gauged the hostile intent of the protestors and acted accordingly.

The state, Antonio Gramsci explains, "operates according to a plan" by urging, inciting, soliciting, and punishing those under its purview to regulate their behavior in accordance with proscribed norms. Deviations from these norms, either through "criminal action or omission," cannot "merely be judged generically as 'dangerous'" but require a "punitive sanction, with moral implications," to sustain the way of life created by the state (*Selections from the Prison Notebooks* 247). Gramsci notes that "[t]he Law is the repressive and negative aspect of the entire positive, civilizing activity undertaken by the State" and incorporates both a "prize-giving" function and a disciplinarian function insofar as "praiseworthy and meritorious activity is rewarded, just as criminal actions are punished," often "in original ways, bringing in 'public opinion' as a form of sanction" (247). In the polarized discussion of General Dyer's conduct at Amritsar, we can see both the prize-giving and the disciplinarian functions of the law in operation. Those who sought to censure Dyer tried to brand him a "terrorist," a rogue-colonial military official acting outside the democratic norms which constituted, in their opinion, the ideological foundation of the British Empire. Summoning a rhetoric which was remarkably similar to that of his critics in its emphasis on the law and justice, Dyer's supporters, in contrast, cast him as a heroic victim who had been betrayed by the system of colonial rule which he had served so well. Both the disciplinarian and prize-giving aspects of the debates on the Jallianwala Bagh massacre were conducted in a political idiom which invoked morality and the colonial rule of law.

Montagu initiated the debate by creating an opposition between two modes of colonial rule, one based on "terrorism" and "subordination" and the other on "partnership" (*Parliamentary Debates* 1710). Linking the former to General Dyer, Montagu asserted that Dyer's statement of intent regarding his response to the Amritsar protest illustrated that he was operating under a "doctrine of terrorism" (1707). He declared:

> If an officer justifies his conduct, no matter how gallant his record is—and everybody knows how gallant General Dyer's record is—by saying that there was no question of undue severity, that if his means had been greater the casualties would have been greater, and that the *motive* was to teach a moral lesson to the whole of the Punjab, I say without hesitation . . . that it is the doctrine of terrorism. . . . Once you are entitled to have regard neither to the *intentions* nor to the conduct of a particular gathering, and to shoot and to go on shooting, with all the horrors that were here involved, in order to teach somebody else a lesson, you are embarking upon terrorism, to which there is no end. (1707; emphasis mine)

Dyer's error, according to Montagu, was that he attached regional significance to what was essentially a local protest by failing to determine accurately the collective intent of the crowd. In Montagu's estimation, collective intent could have been partially gauged by observing the "conduct of [the] particular gathering." Rejecting the notion that Dyer had acted out of anticipatory self-defense, Montagu believed that "terrorism" is constituted by a symbolic element that instills fear in the populace by subjecting a portion of it to violence as an example for others. Such symbolic violence is rooted in "racial" arrogance toward Indians and violates the "canons of modern love of liberty" which are a part of British democracy (1708). "However good" Dyer's "motive" to guard British life may have been, Montagu concluded, he had "infringed the principle which has always animated the British Army and infringed the principles upon which our Indian Empire has been built," namely those "principles of liberty" and "democracy" (1708–9). As someone acting outside the moral norms of the Empire, Dyer becomes, in Montagu's assessment, an anathema, an anomalous figure who must be disavowed as a rogue-colonial individual.

While Montagu's condemnation of Dyer draws on a rhetoric of the law which is abstracted in its invocation of such categories as "liberty" and "democracy," Dyer's supporters sought to discredit his criticism of the general by resorting to a rhetoric of the law grounded in the particularity of procedure. Sir Michael O'Dwyer reconstructed the chronology by which Montagu learned of the massacre, implicitly suggesting that Montagu's moral outrage at Dyer was belated and motivated by political expediency. According to O'Dwyer, he had briefed Montagu about the events at Amritsar at least twice before their disclosure in the British media in December 1919 (Parliamentary Debates 1024–25). O'Dwyer had reported the details of the massacre, excluding Dyer's explanation that he intended to produce a "sufficient moral effect" to forestall further agitation in the Punjab, in two separate interviews with Montagu on June 30, 1919, and July 24, 1919 (1025). However, Montagu maintained that he did not know the specifics of the Jallianwala Bagh carnage until he read about them in the press. As the correspondence between O'Dwyer and Montagu makes clear, the discrepancy between the two men's accounts hinges on their different understanding of the term "details." As his letter to Montagu of December 30–31, 1919, indicates, O'Dwyer believed that the crucial details of the "Amritsar occurrences" consisted of verifiable facts:

> I have a distinct recollection . . . that at our conversation of 30th June I brought out the fact that Dyer, on 13th April, having already formally warned people that he would disperse any gathering by force, did not think it necessary to give any further warning to the gathering which assembled an hour or two later in defiance of his proclamation. I certainly explained then that two British police officers were with him when he fired, and that the District Magistrate, thinking a gathering in defiance of the proclamation impossible, had gone off to look after the 80 panic-stricken women and children who had collected in the

Fort for safety after the murder of Europeans on the 10th. I also said that Dyer's rough estimate of the death casualties was 200; but my memory was not clear as to whether he had fired 1,400 or 1,600 rounds. (1025)

In Montagu's estimation, the crucial details of the massacre necessarily include Dyer's explanation of his intentions and actions. In his "private and personal" telegram to O'Dwyer of February 2, 1920, Montagu writes: "In any case the details I was referring to were these: That Dyer is reported to have stated in his evidence that the crowd might have dispersed without his firing on them, that he fired without warning, and that he stopped firing because his ammunition was exhausted. I do not remember that you ever dealt with these things" (1026). O'Dwyer found this explanation of Montagu's position unsatisfactory, as demonstrated by his public revelations of their correspondence in the *Morning Post* on June 8, 1920.

Dyer's defenders seized on what they perceived as Montagu's duplicity for concealing his early knowledge of the massacre. His charges against Dyer, they argued, amounted to hypocrisy and a desire to appease Indian nationalists to pursue his own political agenda. From the beginning of his appointment as secretary of state for India in 1917, Montagu had declared his intentions of working towards the Indianization of the administrative apparatus "with a view to the progressive realisation of responsible government in India as an integral part of the British Empire" (quoted in Wolpert, *New History of India* 294). To formulate an appropriate structure for moving toward this goal, he visited India with the express purpose of conducting discussions with British officials and representative Indians.[10] Montagu's conclusion from these talks was that parliamentary government was viable in India (Edwardes 198). His proposals for change were embodied in the principle of "dyarchy," which divided responsibilities for governance between British officials in India and elected members of native legislative councils. Under Montagu's proposal, the former group would retain control over the most powerful branches of government, as they were in charge of revenue legislation and the armed forces, while the latter group would be entrusted with such responsibilities as administering education and regulating public health (Edwardes 200). "Any legislative authority which these bodies might have, however," as Michael Edwardes points out, "was rendered nugatory by the fact that such legislation as they might refuse to pass could still become law by being 'certified' by the viceroy" (199). Though these reforms were enacted by royal proclamation in December 1919, the success of their implementation depended on the cooperation of the bourgeois leaders of the Indian nationalist movement.[11] Montagu's reforms had the potential to curb nationalist demands for complete independence by co-opting an influential segment of this leadership into the structure of colonial governance. Montagu's condemnation of Dyer and his denial of prior knowledge of the details of the massacre must be read alongside his desire to win over Indian nationalists to his electoral scheme.

If Montagu's responses to Dyer were conditioned by his wish to advance his political reforms, the attacks on him by Dyer's champions were motivated, in part, by antisemitism.[12] As Helen Fein argues in *Imperial Crime and Punishment*, Montagu had been marginalized in the imperial bureaucracy for his Liberal leanings, his reformist impulses, and his Jewish identity (134). Indeed, he used his Jewish background to build alliances with Indians by referring to himself on numerous occasions as "an Oriental" (Wolpert, *New History of India* 295). The Dyerites deflected criticism from the general onto Montagu by blaming him for encouraging Indian nationalist unrest (Fein 135). In a letter to the *Times*, Thomas Jewell Bennett, a member of Commons, characterized the debate in the House as being "charged with personal antipathy towards Montagu—not free, as I am well warranted in saying, from the racial prejudice which worked mischief in France during the anti-Dreyfus controversy" (quoted in Fein 135).[13] The publication of an edition in February 1920 of the *Protocols of the Elders of Zion*, which attributed communism, revolution, and war to an international Jewish conspiracy, fed into antisemitic attacks against Montagu. The *Morning Post* printed extracts from the *Protocols* over the course of August 1920. One of its editorials opines: "in Palestine, ruled like India by a Jew, both Christian and Mohamedan are accusing the British Government of broken faith. . . . The course of events, in fact, is following the Bolshevik indications of the Bolshevik purpose with very remarkable accuracy" (quoted in Fein 135).[14] The racialization of Montagu as a Jew, combined with references to Bolshevism, characterized him as a dangerous outsider of the Empire, bent on overturning the colonial rule of law.

Like his liberal colleague Montagu, Sir Winston Churchill, a member of the Conservative Party, then secretary of state for war and a strong advocate of British imperialism, drew on the concept of intentionality and the rhetoric of the colonial rule of law in his condemnation of Dyer. Churchill, as Montagu had done before him, faulted Dyer for inadequately judging the collective intent of the crowd. He noted that these intentions could be properly divined by asking two fundamental questions:

> Is the crowd attacking anything or anybody? . . . Are they trying to force their way forward to the attack of some building, or some cordon of troops or police, or are they attempting to attack some band of persons or some individual who has excited their hostility? . . . That is the first question which would naturally arise. The second question is this: Is the crowd armed? That is surely another great simple fundamental question. By armed I mean armed with lethal weapons. . . . At Amritsar the crowd was neither armed nor attacking. (Parliamentary Debates 1726)

By framing the issue in this way, Churchill was able to infuse concrete criteria into the category of "intentionality" where Dyer's supporters had previously defined it only in speculative terms. His understanding of the concept of minimum force was similarly matter of fact. The military officer "should confine himself to a limited and definite objective," Churchill declared, "that is to say to preventing a crowd doing something which they ought not to do, or to compelling them to do something which they ought to do" (1727).[15] In establishing these criteria for determining collective intent, Churchill echoed the guidelines for the lawful exercise of self-defense in customary international law, which maintain that there must be an actual armed attack to justify the state's use of force.

Churchill observed that he had "a difference of opinion" on the Dyer case with many of those with whom he generally felt himself "in the strongest sympathy" "on the general drift of the world's affairs" (1730). His commitment to imperialism rested on the moral conviction that it was a form of governance deriving its authority from the law, and he understood that the Jallianwala Bagh massacre had grave implications for the stability of the British Empire and the retention of India. Such a formulation of colonial rule had to disavow the use of force as a legitimate means of securing compliance with state objectives. "Governments who have seized upon power by violence and by usurpation have often resorted to terrorism in their desperate efforts to keep what they have stolen," he announced, "but the august and venerable structure of the British Empire, where lawful authority descends from hand to hand and generation after generation, does not need such aid" (1729). Churchill's image of interlocked hands across generations serves to naturalize British colonial rule in presenting it as an English birthright. While the family metaphor underwriting this image represents the British, India and its inhabitants are represented as property to be bequeathed as an imperial inheritance from one British generation to the next.

Echoing Montagu's distinction between colonial rule based on "co-operation" and sheer "terrorism," Churchill condemned Dyer's actions by distinguishing the "British way of doing things," based on the rule of law, from "foreign" methods. British colonialism, for him, "has always meant and implied close and effectual co-operation" with Indians. In contrast, he charged foreign countries with relying on force to buttress their powers and rhetorically situated Dyer within this group for his use of excessive force at Amritsar. Like many of Dyer's critics, Churchill described the Jallianwala Bagh carnage as an incidence of "frightfulness." "There is surely one general prohibition which we can make," he stated, "I mean a prohibition against what is called 'frightfulness' . . . the inflicting of a great slaughter or massacre upon a particular crowd of people, with the intention of terrorising not merely the rest of the crowd, but the whole district or the whole country" (1728). At the time of the parliamentary debates on Dyer, the term "frightfulness" was often employed to describe German brutality in France and Belgium during the First World War, signifying "a deliberate policy of terrorizing the enemy (especially noncombatants) as a military resource" (Burchfield 1163). By invoking the term "frightfulness" in relation to Dyer, Churchill aligns him with what was then referred to as "Prussianism," constructing him as being "unBritish" and distancing him from the whole machinery of the British Empire. The discursive operations of rogue-colonial individualism, as Churchill's pronouncements on Dyer indicate, require making a foreign outsider of the problematic colonial official, who is in the final analysis a representative of the colonial state.

Churchill doggedly asserted that Dyer's conduct at Amritsar represented an anomalous instance in British colonial rule:

> However we may dwell upon the difficulties of General Dyer during the Amritsar riots . . . one tremendous fact stands out—I mean the slaughter of nearly 400 persons and the wounding of probably three or four times as many, at the Jallian Wallah Bagh on 13th April. That is an episode which appears to me to be without precedent or parallel in the modern history of the British Empire. It is an event of an entirely different order from any of those tragical occurrences which take place when troops are brought into collision with the civil population. It is an extraordinary event, a monstrous event, an event which stands in singular and sinister isolation. (*Parliamentary Debates* 1725)

Yet even as he attempted to isolate Dyer's actions and to disassociate British colonialism from the use of deadly force, Churchill was forced to admit that "tragical occurrences" generally result when the military is called upon to assist civilian authorities. That he had to acknowledge such clashes suggests that they were frequent enough to warrant some mention. Indeed, Churchill continued by noting that "collisions between troops and native populations have been painfully frequent in the melancholy aftermath of the Great War" (1725). Nor were confrontations between the military forces and civilians localized in India; Churchill cited "numerous cases" of this nature in Egypt and also in Ireland (1725, 1732). The failure of the colonial regime to actualize its own universalist project—in terms of extending democracy, liberty, and the rule of law to subjects in its conquered territories—is denied through rhetorical strategies which contain violations against the colonial state's ideological articulation by casting them as anomalous incidents. By Churchill's own admission, however, these incidents were widespread and occurred frequently, suggesting that they were symptomatic, albeit in the most crude form, of the brutality of the colonialism. As Ian Colvin, Dyer's biography, baldly remarks on the Jallianwala Bagh massacre, "The death of some hundreds of such people—rebels or their associates—does not seem, when we consider the million men recently lost in its defence, an extortionate price to pay for the safety of an empire" (329).

Like Montagu and Churchill, Sir Edward Carson invoked the category of intentionality and the rhetoric of the law in his response to the massacre to arrive at opposite conclusions regarding General Dyer's conduct at the Jallianwala Bagh. As Churchill had attempted to do before him, Carson posed the question of intent in epistemological terms. Yet whereas Churchill had elaborated concrete criteria for ascertaining collective intent, Carson offered a hermeneutics for determining intentionality by challenging his colleagues to "try and put themselves in the position of the man whom they asked to go and deal with these difficult circumstances. . . . He had to decide as to whether this was a riot, an insurrection, a rebellion, a revolution" (*Parliamentary Debates* 1714). Figured in the language of concentric circles, he perceived a local event as posing the threat of a far-reaching revolution. For Carson, the situation was indeed serious and evocative of an earlier crisis on the subcontinent. He reminded his audience:

> In reference to the very action which you are going to break [Dyer] for, or have broken him for, after his thirty-four years of honourable service, you have to admit it may have been that which saved the most bloody outrage in that country, which might have deluged the place with the loss of thousands of lives, and may have saved the country from a mutiny to which the old mutiny in India would have appeared small. (1714)

Imputing a hostile collective intent to the crowd, Carson, like those memsahibs who supported Dyer, legitimized the massacre by narrating it as a form of anticipatory self-defense against a second Mutiny.

The rhetoric of the rule of law is manifest in Carson's concern that Dyer has been denied due process. Pleading for fairness toward Dyer, he denounced the abstract rhetoric of the rule of law employed by Montagu and Churchill, declaring, "You talk of the great principles of liberty which you have laid down. General Dyer has a right to be brought within those principles of liberty. He has no right to be broken on the *ipse dixit* of any Commission or Committee, however great, unless he has been fairly tried—and he has not been tried" (1712). Yet this invocation of the rule of law and the attendant principle of liberty was somewhat disingenuous given that the issue under debate was not whether parliament thought the general should be punished by depriving him of his liberty, but whether it concurred with the Army Council's recommendation to retire him. In framing the rule of law in terms of the lack of due process for General Dyer, Carson cast him as the hapless victim of the arbitrary decisions of the colonial state.

Carson's support of Dyer, as Helen Fein reveals, was not motivated by any vigorous belief in due process and the rule of law, but by his status as a representative of Ulster and his general distrust of the government's willingness to arrange for a favorable settlement for his unionist constituency in Ireland (133). Concerned that Irish Home Rule would result in Catholic hegemony over the Protestant majority in the northern counties, Carson and his faction rallied to Dyer's defense for several reasons. First, the Dyer debate provided Carson with the opportunity "to embarrass the government" by showing that there was dissension within its ranks regarding its treatment of one of its own servants (Fein 133). As contemporary observers noted, however, the more important reason for Carson's spirited defense of Dyer was that he wanted the government to pursue a similar policy in Ireland, modeled on the imposition of martial law in the Punjab (Fein 133). In the August 10, 1920, issue of the *Statesman*, one journalist analyzes Carson's response to the Dyer affair by commenting,

> so far as Sir Edward Carson is responsible for those disciplinary movements [against Montagu] the cause is doubtless to be found in the position in Ireland. . . . Instead of with a sword in one hand and an olive branch in the other the Government, in [the Carsonites'] opinion, ought to confront the recalcitrant population with swords in both hands. . . . They have shown it on such questions as the Dyer affair and again in divisions of a more general character, none of them of any special interest to Ulster. (quoted in Fein 133–34)

That Carson did not have a consistent position regarding rebellions in the colonies leant credence to such interpretations. While he upheld Dyer's use of force to quell a native protest at Amritsar, he had encouraged fellow unionists to organize paramilitary units, such as the Ulster Volunteer Force (which numbered eighty thousand by 1913), to oppose home rule in Ireland (Evans and Pollock 82). The motivations which underwrote Carson's defense of Dyer emanated from his loyalist politics and his desire to preserve colonial rule in Ireland.

A system of force in an unstable equilibrium, such as a colonial state formation, will find on the parliamentary terrain the legal rhetoric to help maintain an illusory stability. Parliamentary debates provide the opportunity for the law to exert both its prize-giving and its disciplinarian functions. Yet as the discussions of the Jallianwala Bagh massacre reveal, these debates seldom unravel the contradictions which structure colonial rule. Political parties and parliamentary speeches instead reaffirm the ideological rationales of the colonial state. "If the State represents the coercive and punitive force of juridical regulation of a country," Gramsci notes, "the parties—representing the spontaneous adhesion of an élite to such a regulation, considered as a type of collective society to which the entire mass must be educated—must show in their specific internal life that they have assimilated as principles of moral conduct those rules which in the State are legal obligations" (*Selections from the Prison Notebooks* 267). The parliamentary debates on General Dyer and the Jallianwala Bagh massacre present the spectacle of politicians pontificating on the virtues of British democracy, liberty, and the rule of law without any recognition that such values might be incompatible with extraterritorial conquest and the maintenance of these territories through the use of repressive state apparatuses such as the police and the army. Alliances between Conservatives and Liberals were forged in the interests of assigning blame for the massacre, through recourse to the ideology of rogue-colonial individualism, and in the urgency of preserving the British myth that the Empire embodied a humanitarian version of colonialism based on the rule of law.

COMMON LAW, MARTIAL LAW, AND THE MINIMUM FORCE DEBATE

The colonial rule of law invoked so vociferously during the parliamentary debates on General Dyer's conduct in Amritsar, as a perusal of the events leading up to the massacre illustrates, was itself laden with ambiguities inhering in the confusion over the properly constituted authority and jurisprudence operating in Punjab.[16] Two major factors account for the strained relation between the military and civilian populations: namely, uncertainty over which branch of the law, martial or civil, had primary jurisdiction in the region and, more generally, the militarized nature of the police forces operative in British colonies. Several days before the massacre, the civilian authority, Miles Irving, who was then deputy commissioner of Amritsar, abdicated power and relinquished civil control of the city to General Dyer, in response to native unrest that was the result of a confrontation between the military and a crowd that had assembled to protest the detaining of the local nationalist leaders Saif-ud-Din Kitchlew and Satya Pal. During that earlier confrontation, twenty Indians had been killed (V. N. Datta 92). The crowd's subsequent murder of five

Europeans caused the civil authorities to panic and to cede their authority to the military. Yet even though Dyer began to exert de facto control over the city on April 11, 1919, the Punjab authorities did not officially declare martial law till two days after the massacre, on April 15, 1919. Even though Deputy Commissioner Irving, according to the dictates of colonial law, was legally responsible for the area, General Dyer did not bother to consult him or seek his approval before opening fire in the Jallianwala Bagh.

The status of the law during periods of civil unrest, as in Amritsar, is further complicated by the dual application of common law and martial law to the behavior of the army in such contexts. British common law derives its authority from judicial decisions rather than from legislative enactments. According to *Black's Law Dictionary*, common law "consists of those principles, usage and rules of action applicable to government and security of persons and property which do not rest for their authority upon any express and positive declaration of the will of the legislature" (189). Rather, they are conferred their legitimacy "solely from usages and customs of immemorial antiquity, or from the judgements and decrees of the courts recognizing, affirming, and enforcing such usages and customs . . . particularly the ancient unwritten law of England" (*Black's* 189). Acting as the palimpsest under which other modalities of the law are layered, common law subsumes those emergency actions undertaken by military and civilian officials in periods of civil unrest.

As Andrei Marmor observes, "all efficacious legal systems have *de facto* authority" insofar as "the law either *claims* that it has legitimate authority over its subjects" or "is held to possess it, or both" (114; emphasis in original). In a colonial state, however, the state's claim to authority—given its differential treatment of subjects based on their ethnic and national identities—is not universally recognized and may come under attack from insurgent quarters. It is often the very absence or suspension of civil liberties in colonial contexts which leads to native protest in the first instance and precipitates the periodic crises which inevitably punctuate colonial rule. At Amritsar, for example, civil unrest was the native response to the detention of nationalist leaders. In such cases, the colonial regime abandons any pretense of operating under the restraints of a rule of law, resorts to the imposition of martial law, and necessarily suspends habeas corpus. Martial law, A. W. B. Simpson explains, implies the replacement, in part or the whole of the country, of the civil power in every aspect of government, administrative as well as judicial, by the military, acting not under any specific legal provision but on the fundamental principle giving to military commanders the power and the duty to take charge when all the means provided for government under existing law have broken down. (3–4)

Expressing the supreme will of the military commander in the field, martial law applies to the soldier and within "the reasonable necessities of the occasion" to the citizen (McKinney 437). The clause "the reasonable necessities of the occasion" in this formulation of martial law provides a gap in defining the jurisprudential limits of martial law, which is subject to variable interpretations. Martial law confers on the military commander the power of arrest, summary trial, and prompt execution. Once proclaimed, it transforms the land into a military camp, mutating the law of the land into the rules of the camp (McKinney 437). Martial law, once imposed, supersedes all civil authority during the period in which it is in operation and applies to all persons within the territory.

As the parliamentary debates of the Amritsar massacre and the declaration of martial law in Punjab demonstrate, the ambiguity between martial law and common law is often articulated circuitously through the principle of "minimum force." In rehearsing their arguments over individual culpability and collective intent, both Dyer's critics and his supporters turned to the principle of minimum force, projecting it along two separate axes that could be differentiated temporally. While his supporters maintained that his actions were preventive, intended to forestall an unruly population from rebellion in some future time, his critics insisted that minimum force had to be evaluated according to the needs of the present and advocated using force only in reaction to an actual confrontation between troops and civilians. The invocation of the principle of minimum force by both groups attests to its vexed status in the law and its inherent ambiguity. During periods of civil unrest, the conduct of the army is subject to the authority of English common law. In such periods, as Charles Townsend notes, "the executive has the right and the duty to 'repel force with force', but the degree of force used must be no more and no less than is absolutely necessary to restore the peace" (19). Common law permits the executive to "set aside the ordinary legal system" as long as the necessity for forcible acts to restore order can afterward be established in the ordinary courts (Townsend 19). The 1914 edition of the *Manual of Military Law*, issued by the British War Office, offers the following vague guidelines on the use of force: "The law which commands the suppression of unlawful assemblies, riots, and insurrections necessarily justifies the civil power in using the necessary degree of force for their suppression. The difficulty is to ascertain what is this necessary degree of force, and the danger of making a mistake in the matter is serious, as any excess in the use of force constitutes a crime" (223). Such stipulations place state personnel in an extremely tenuous position, since they can be disciplined for using either too much force or too little. Given the difficulties of recreating the urgency of crisis retrospectively, military officials have had to rely on acts of indemnity to safeguard them against judicial inquiries (Townsend 19–20).

Under British common law, civilians and soldiers are not differentiated on the basis of their function in relation to the state. Soldiers, who are armed with lethal weapons and who are under the jurisdiction of military law, have the same status as ordinary citizens. Common law specifies that each person, whether citizen or soldier, must come to the aid of the civil authorities when called upon for assistance (Mockaitis 18). Decisions regarding the necessary level of force to be deployed are left to individual discretion, case by case (Townsend 43). The question of civil emergency, in other words, is ambiguously defined. Townsend explains: "If troops were called out to preserve or restore order, their officers went into action guided only by a forcible but indistinct sense of social constraint" (43).

The blurring of the boundaries between martial and common law in the British system, evident in the confusion over the principle of minimum force, inheres in the structure of the ideological state apparatus of the law, and there are similarly blurred boundaries between the repressive state apparatuses of the military and civilian police forces in the colonial state formation. While the British state distinguished between its military and civilian police forces within its contiguous borders, both in terms of the institutional organization of these forces and their weaponry, these differences were less evident in the colonies. Within Britain, the police force consisted of a decentralized and unarmed constabulary which was epitomized in the reassuring figure of the "bobby on the beat" (Townsend 23). Yet this model of policing civilian populations was rarely exported to the colonies, where instead the preferred model was the highly militarized and armed Royal Irish Constabulary (RIC) (Townsend 24).[17] According to Townsend, the RIC "was military in organization, training, appearance, and, for a long time, attitude" (47). The military nature of the RIC became even more apparent in 1920, when the British government shored up the RIC's power by altering its recruitment base from Irishmen to demobilized soldiers from Britain, expanding these forces, and equipping them with such military weapons as rifles and Lewis guns (Townsend 57). A shortage of uniforms for the expanded forces resulted in the issue of mixed uniforms, consisting of the regular RIC black-green trousers and military khaki shirts, and earned for the forces the name "Black and Tans." The uniforms thus became a literal signifier of the RIC's liminal position between the civilian and military branches of the colonial state. A Special Auxiliary Division of the RIC, consisting of former army officers, was established by Major General Sir Hugh Tudor, who was the chief of the RIC. Although this force was technically part of the police, it tended to act autonomously and was associated with many of the atrocities directed at the populace (Mockaitis 70). Both the regular RIC constables and the Auxiliaries had very little police training "and lacked traditional police discipline" (Mockaitis 19). Given these factors, it is not surprising that their members had difficulty adhering to the principle of minimum force and often were charged with terrorizing the general public with arson, torture, and murder. The continuities between the civil police force and the army, in the colonial context, result from their having been drawn from the same pool and issued the same weaponry.

In Amritsar in 1919, when the law and the regular police force were unable to curtail civil disturbances or peaceful protest, the civil authority called upon the military for assistance. However, when the military performed the very function for which it was trained—killing—Parliament demanded an investigation of the massacre and clamored for disciplinary action against the military command. When the law broke down, the colonial authorities called in the military, and when the military broke down, the colonial authorities called in the law. In such cases, the law provides the continuity between the repressive and ideological state apparatuses by furnishing the cover under which military engagement becomes increasingly naturalized as part of the ordinary colonial landscape. By rationalizing the military presence through an elaborate set of provisions regulating the behavior of British troops, the colonial authorities codify military occupation within the ideological trappings of civility. Thus, attention is deflected from the summoning of the military by the colonial state in the first instance to cope with the native reaction to colonial rule.

INTERPELLATING THE COLONIAL MILITARY SUBJECT

For what George Marcus calls "multi-sited ethnography," tracing the life histories of individuals can "reveal juxtapositions of social contexts through a succession of narrated individual experiences" that may be otherwise obscured (110). In other words, life histories can help to delineate spaces within systems, such as colonialism, shaped by categorical and geographical distinctions that may render these spaces, under different conditions, invisible. The trajectory of General Dyer's life history discloses the ways in which military officials are interpellated under colonialism through an educational state apparatus that stresses both the acquisition of practical experience in counterinsurgency and the study of the law. Dyer's career also reveals some of the structural links between Ireland and India that are ordinarily concealed.

As Dyer knew from his own experience and those of his fellow officers, lessons in the "proper" use of force were often learned in one colonial location to be employed at a different one. The British state regularly transferred colonial personnel, administrators, and military officials from one colonial arena to another for the express purpose of counterinsurgency.[18] Within the imperial grid, Ireland often functioned as the first stop in many colonial careers, a site where military and administrative personnel gained practical training in colonial repression before their posting in South Asia. Examples of military men who served in both locations include Fredrick Sleigh Roberts and Sir Hugh Henry Rose. Sir John Anderson was also active in both colonial territories, applying the expertise he had gained in Ireland, implementing widespread administrative detention against republicans, to Bengali nationalists. Before serving in India, General Dyer had been posted in Belfast, in 1886, as a subaltern with the First Battalion of the Queen's Royal West Surrey Regiment.[19] The First Battalion included among its ranks Charles Monro, who later became General Sir Charles Monro and Dyer's superior as the commander-in-chief of India from 1916 to 1920 (Colvin 11). Following the thread of Dyer's career trajectory "is thus especially potent for suturing locations" in the social landscape of colonialism that do not seem obviously connected, like India and Ireland, but that function to interpellate military subjects through practical training (Marcus 108–9).

As suggested by Dyer's life history, and his having had his first military posting in aid of the civil authorities, tense military-civilian relations have long been a periodic and integral part of colonialism. Ian Colvin's casual narrative of Dyer's first assignment, in his biography of Dyer, does not convey the seriousness of the events surrounding it:

> Home Rule for Ireland was the question in debate, and the factions of Belfast were carrying on the discussion with rivets, brickbats, and guns. In the summer and autumn of 1886 the Queen's were "employed for several months in the difficult and unpleasant duty of picketing the streets to prevent disturbances between Orangemen and Nationalists." The Battalion was popular with both sides, and lost only one man murdered—and then only because he was thought to belong to another regiment not so well liked. (11–12)

Notwithstanding Colvin's description of the Queen's Royal West Surrey Regiment as a kind of peacekeeping force, the civil "disturbances" in Belfast that Dyer helped to suppress were some of the most violent in nineteenth-century Ireland, resulting in more deaths than in the Emmet rebellion in 1803, the Young Ireland rising in 1848, the Fenian rebellion of 1867, or the Land War of the 1870s and 1880s. The consequences of clashes between nationalists, loyalists, and the colonial forces include the deaths of approximately fifty people, physical injuries to 371 police officers, the expulsion of 190 Catholics from the shipyards, the looting of thirty-one public houses, and extensive property damage (Bardon 149–50).

The six-hundred-page report of the government inquiry into the Belfast disturbances laid much of the blame on the "fighting talk of politicians" who had incited loyalists to resist the attempts of Prime Minister W. E. Gladstone, a Liberal, to introduce a home rule bill for Ireland. Chief among these politicians was Lord Randolph Churchill, a prominent Conservative and the father of Sir Winston Churchill. The elder Churchill undertook a speaking tour in Belfast to oppose home rule efforts, and he concluded one address to a group of Unionists with the following exhortation:

The combat deepens, on ye brave
Who rush to glory or the grave;
Wave Ulster, all thy banners wave,
And charge with all thy chivalry. (quoted in Bardon 147)

In an open letter published shortly after this speech, Churchill announced: "Ulster will fight and Ulster will be right" (quoted in Bardon 147). Responding to Churchill's call, some loyalists began to gather arms in preparation for the struggle they foresaw. Many other Ulster Liberals deserted Gladstone and helped to defeat the home rule bill by a slender margin of thirty votes in Parliament in 1886 (147). In the final tally, ninety-three Liberals voted against the measure (147).

In addition to the practical training that General Dyer received in counterinsurgency in Ireland, he was interpellated through the ideological state apparatus of the military-educational system, which emphasized, as part of its curriculum, military law. Immediately before joining the Queen's Royal West Surrey Regiment in Ireland, he had graduated from the Royal Military Academy at Sandhurst, in July 1885, with "proficiency in Military Law and Tactics" (Colvin 11). Dyer's background provides ample evidence that he was well versed in the contemporary regulations applicable to martial law which governed the interactions between the military and civilian populations. For instance, in 1894 he took a furlough from the army to study military law and military history, with an emphasis on the Napoleonic Wars, for the Staff College entrance examination (Colvin 32–33). It was this training, as well as his subsequent schooling at Staff College, that equipped him with the expertise necessary to serve a five-year term as an instructor in military law.

> "I had had special occasion and opportunity to study principles in this connection," he writes in his statement to the Army Council, "as for five years I held the staff appointment of Deputy-Assistant Adjutant-General for instruction in military law, and the administration of martial law during civil disturbances was necessarily a subject of study by me in that capacity. I had this principle very clearly before me during the whole time I was in Amritsar, and I never at any time failed to act up to it to the best of my judgment and capacity." (*Statements of Brig.-Gen. Reginald E. Dyer* 5)

Indeed, Dyer justifies his decision to fire on civilians by citing the guidelines offered in the *Manual of Military Law*, with which he must have become conversant during his years as a martial law instructor. He argues that he was faced with an "insurrection" and that he was thus authorized to use force to contain and defuse it:

> The rules regulating the action of the military during civil disorders, as stated in Chapter XIII of the Manual of Military Law distinguish clearly three things (1) Unlawful Assembly; (2) Riot; (3) Insurrection. It is conceded that I was faced not with unlawful assembly or riot, but with insurrection . . . of insurrection it is said (page 224)—"The existence of an armed insurrection would justify the use of any degree of force necessary effectually to meet and cope with the insurrection." (*Statements of Brig.-Gen. Reginald E. Dyer* 12)

The *Manual of Military Law* goes on to clarify this directive: "These cases are practically confined to riots in which violent crimes, such as murder, house-breaking, or arson, are being committed, or are likely to be committed and to insurrections in which an intention is clearly shown to attempt by force of arms the overthrow of the government, or the execution of some general political purpose" (224). Though Dyer does not quote these lines from the manual directly, they are echoed in his justification of the firing. In responding to the Army Council, Dyer stresses that the crowd confronting him in the Jallianwala Bagh "was in substance the same mob that had been in course of organization for some days and had committed the hideous crimes of the 10th April [i.e., murder] and was the power and authority which for two days had ruled the city in defiance of the Government" (12). His rebuttal of the Hunter Committee report, then, legitimized his actions by making them meet the criteria for open insurrection established in the *Manual of Military Law* for regulating troops who were called to aid the civil power.[20]

That General Dyer could rationalize his massacre of nearly four hundred persons by calling upon his knowledge of military law, particularly the provisions pertaining to martial law, illustrates the contradictions inherent in the rhetoric of the colonial rule of law. According to Ranajit Guha, the " '[r]ule of law' is the name given by the common sense of politics" to British colonialism (Guha, "Dominance without Hegemony" 276). "As an amalgam of the institutional and conceptual aspects of [the

British legal system]," Guha notes, "it has come to acquire the status of a code mediating all perceptions of civil conflict" and in colonial India every configuration of power is articulated through this code (276). The rule of law, however, presupposes that "all who owe allegiance to the state are equal" before it (256). The colonial state gives the lie to such a code, because the state's "legitimacy is based ultimately on the right of conquest" over subjects who are not its citizens and who consequently have no rights (256). Within such a formation, the declaration of martial law is a signal that the state is declaring war on those who do not accept its authority. Lacking the characteristics of international conflicts, these government wars are instead "waged against persons regarded as rebels or insurgents who, if not killed in military operations or summarily punished under martial law, may be tried as traitors or criminals" (Simpson 4). Martial law renders bare the systemic violence of colonialism and the hypocrisy of the colonial rhetoric of the rule of law. Under its imposition, natives identified as subversive by the colonial state are treated worse than combatants in regular wars or criminals under ordinary circumstances (Simpson 4). Indeed, in metropolitan Britain in the first two decades of the twentieth century, nowhere is there an example of the summary execution of hundreds of supposed criminals comparable to the massacre in Amritsar.

A FAMILY AFFAIR: PATRIARCHY, PATHOLOGIES, AND COLONIAL PROCLIVITIES

General Dyer's conduct at Amritsar has made a lasting impression on the imagination of writers and filmmakers, for it continues to circulate in diverse narrative forms such as scholarly accounts (V. N. Datta's *Jallianwala Bagh*, 1969, and Helen Fein's *Imperial Crime and Punishment*, 1977), novels (Salman Rushdie's *Midnight's Children*, 1980, and Paul Scott's *The Jewel in the Crown*, 1966), and films (Richard Attenborough's *Gandhi*, 1982, and the BBC's production of *The Jewel in the Crown*, 1984). I turn now to a novel, Stanley Wolpert's *Massacre at Jallianwala Bagh*, that relies on much of the documentation of the massacre discussed in the preceding pages. This fictional account illustrates the power and resilience of those earlier interpretations of Dyer's actions by replicating the discursive strategies of rogue-colonial individualism which inform much of the official docu-

mentation. While the novel offers a critique of the massacre, it pathologizes the origins of the violence by explaining Dyer's actions on the basis
of a groin injury which he sustained in Akora. This physiological condition functions, in the text, to explain Dyer's mental state and his decision
to use lethal force against civilians.[21] That such a thoughtful historian as
Stanley Wolpert would attempt to understand the Amritsar carnage by
probing Dyer's psychology in relation to his physiology, rather than by
investigating the colonial system that he was a product of, speaks to the
endurance of the ideology of rogue-colonial individualism. This ideology
has enormous power, in part because it occludes the collective workings
of the colonial system by rendering them as merely the experiences of the
individual agents of that system. But Wolpert takes this individualizing
one step further by literalizing the threat to the masculinity of the rulers
in the injury sustained by Dyer at Akora.

Wolpert, who has made significant contributions to South Asian historiography, published his novel based on the Amritsar massacre, *An
Error of Judgment*, in 1970. This fictional representation was then re-
published under the title *Massacre at Jallianwala Bagh* in 1988. The change
in title between the first and second editions suggests that Wolpert
wanted to convey a stronger sense of outrage at Dyer's actions. The novel
has a dual narrative structure that strives to convey the complexity of the
actual events surrounding the massacre: the external frame narrative
treats the Hunter Committee inquiry into the Punjab disturbances and
the embedded narrative describes Dyer's actions in Amritsar. While
the embedded narrative unfolds in a linear fashion, the point of view
is third person limited and rotates among the major historical personalities associated with the massacre and its subsequent investigation.
In shifting the spatial and temporal setting of the narrative from Lahore
in November 1919 to Amritsar in April 1919, Wolpert moves between
many narrative perspectives, adopting those of Sir William Hunter, General Dyer, Dr. Kitchlew, Dr. Satya Pal, Miss Sherwood, Hansraj, Sir Michael O'Dwyer, and several other characters. The multiple historical
voices populating the novel express differentiated socio-ideological reactions to the massacre and constitute what M. M. Bakhtin terms the
"heteroglossia" of an "epoch" (300). Insofar as the frame narrative is
told through Sir William Hunter's point of view, it is identified with
the authority of the state and the colonial rule of law; thus, it exer-

cises a "centripetal" function by simultaneously "homogenizing" and "hierarchicizing" the "centrifugal" forces of the embedded narrative which threaten to "disperse" and "decrown" its discursive authority (Bakhtin 425).

Massacre at Jallianwala Bagh quite literally situates its critique of colonial violence in the body of the white, colonial, military male subject. This colonial subject, General Dyer, is disclosed as the site of dysfunctional sexuality and perverse desire. The novel characterizes him as a sexually contradictory figure who is simultaneously chivalrous and sexually obsessed with his countrywomen. Colonial militarism, Wolpert implies, is a thoroughly gendered affair which draws its partial justification by casting colonial women as the potential victims of an excessive and violent native libido. In its highly sexualized representation of Dyer, who periodically fantasizes about his niece Alice and who remembers his violent sexual encounters with his wife Mary, the novel insinuates that colonial masculinity, rather than native male desire, constitutes the real threat to colonial women. While Wolpert successfully demonstrates the conjunctural relationship between colonialism and the British metropolitan patriarchy, he is less adept at extending this analysis to native women, who, as in the official documentation of the massacre, are all but absent from the narrative.

In Wolpert's novel, General Dyer's early fury at the disturbances in Amritsar is sparked by the news that Englishwomen have been assaulted by native men, thus necessitating, in his mind, that he don the mantle of protector of his countrywomen. On being informed that an Englishwoman, Mrs. Easdon, had escaped from a crowd of Indians who were incensed at her callousness to their wounded comrades—to whom she had refused medical treatment—Wolpert attributes the following reflections to Dyer: "The wire he'd received this morning had mentioned two Englishmen dead, but the shock of this report about natives attacking Englishwomen left him numb with rage at the monstrous gall of those savage beasts" (8). Invoking the dichotomies of colonial discourse, so eloquently elucidated by Abdul Jan Mohamed, Dyer's characterization of native men figures them in the most formulaic and animalistic terms. The general's overly sexualized and racialized representations of native men have their origins in the tales of horror of demonic, native men imprinted into Dyer's memory by his family:

There was a stench of blood and carrion in the smoke-laden air of that grimy station. A black cloud hovered over the city. He had seen it driving in, the awful genie of death and terror whose home is India, rubbed from his lamp over Amritsar, grinning darkly at the damage done to White life and property. . . . He knew it well, that special brand of Terror, the anguish and fear burned indelibly into every bloodshot eye turned toward him, beseeching, begging his help. He'd known it all his life . . . where ghosts of The Mutiny lurked behind every shadow, and his father, uncles, and brothers relived all the scenes of murder, arson, and rape from Meerut to Cawnpore, from Delhi to Lucknow. Those were lessons none of them could afford to forget. (5)

Dyer has been nurtured on stories of native violence toward the British: as he informs the civil authorities, he has suckled on "the withered tit" of the "sordid soil" and knows the "bitch whore" of India as well as he knew his "sainted mother" (10). Significantly, these tales have been transmitted by his male relatives, his father, uncles, and brothers, illustrating how colonialism and patriarchy are reproduced at the ideological level, through oral discourse, over multiple generations. Populated with the "genie of death and terror" and British "ghosts" of "The Mutiny," the subcontinent becomes transmogrified, in Dyer's horrific vision, into an eerie and threatening landscape. Yet even in this scenario, where the native challenge to colonial rule is acknowledged in such explicit and frightening terms, Dyer confidently asserts the British claim to ownership of the land which is figured as "White property."

The assaults against Mrs. Easdon and Miss Sherwood provide the necessary impetus for the general to render violence against the natives, even those who are collaborators employed by the colonial state in its police forces. It is the British women's names that he invokes as he brutalizes Inspector Ashraf Khan for failing to come to the aid of the hapless European men who were murdered earlier in the National Bank of India, just several hundred yards from the police station. As Dyer smashes his fist into Khan's face, he intones the names of Mrs. Easdon and Miss Sherwood and those other "martyrs, those innocents slaughtered here yesterday, who would, with the victims of Calcutta's Black Hole, and Cawnpore's bloody Well, be inscribed for Eternity in the hagiology of Empire" (15). The British victims of native violence are automatically canonized and become a part of the ideological apparatus of the colonial state to be summoned, as needed, in the service of colonial vengeance and military savagery against insurgents and collaborators alike. If Mrs. Easdon and Miss Sherwood represent, in Dyer's mind, the sacred purity of British civilization, Ashraf Khan signifies their manichean other, the salacious native man with "unnatural" appetites:

> Inspector Ashraf Khan was a heavy-set swarthy man, a man of many lusts, Rex suspected, fine foods and voluptuous women, hashish, and perhaps young boys. He was a singularly greedy serpent, the foulest form of native low life, sleek and corpulent, lazy, lecherous, bred here as all of India's police were, on the yeast of crime, prostitution, dope addiction. (13)

Figured in the phallic metaphor of the "serpent" that evokes the Christian imagery of the Fall, the Inspector embodies, in Dyer's opinion, the native proclivity toward excessive sensual desires of all sorts, including the bodily, the culinary, and the hallucinatory.

In *Massacre at Jallianwala Bagh*, the patriarchal, racialist aspects of colonialism cohere in Dyer's relationship to his niece Alice and his obsessive apprehension regarding her safety and the temptation she offers to native men. As he leads a column of troops through Amritsar, several hours before the massacre, Dyer remembers an earlier affront to his niece by a native male. Like Ashraf Khan, the unnamed native man is represented here in explicit zoological imagery that characterizes him as a lubricious creature and the binary opposite of the "innocent" Alice:

> [Dyer] . . . had been thinking of Alice. He tried to imagine how all of this vile scene might look to her innocent eyes, and it sent a shiver of despair through his rugged frame. Poor babe that she was, how terrifying these savage faces, these ugly black bodies, would have appeared to her. He had taken his niece to see Delhi and the Taj with Mary [his wife] just a fortnight ago, and driving through the old city of the capital, they had been accosted by a mob of young men, one of whom jumped onto the rear bumper of his motor and peered grinning apelike through the window. Luckily, Alice hadn't turned to see that lecherous face with saliva drooling from its red wretched lips, and the bugger dropped out of sight before either lady realized some-

one had attempted to attack them. The mere memory of it made Rex's brain feel cold. (188)

Rendered as a simian, the native man exudes a bestial lust for the virginal Alice, thereby constituting a threat and challenge to colonial rule. For General Dyer, the danger of native male sexuality and violence is actualized several hours later, in the Jallianwala Bagh, when several thousand people gather in defiance of his proclamation. Images of native male sexual potency consume Dyer, transfixing his gaze on the genitalia of the South Asian men around him. Clearly viewing these parts as a kind of armament that can be wielded against colonial women, he orders his troops to "aim for their balls" (211).

> [Dyer] watched as one of the tallest beasts, a particularly vicious brute, whose tool was half an arm long and kept swinging as he raced naked across the field, and almost escaped to use that vile rod in subduing helpless women, virginal girls—watched him suddenly throw up both arms and come arching over backwards, caught by a bullet in his spine, to lay writhing, kicking out in all directions, to no avail, going limp at last, half arm and all, dead as the humping donkey deserved to be. (212)

Dyer's fixation with the phallic proportions of the native male, and the description of his death as a quasi-orgasm which leaves the native man's body "limp," suggest the operation of transference: Dyer has projected onto native men his own desire to dominate colonial women.

Indeed, *Massacre at Jallianwala Bagh* exposes General Dyer as embodying the actual threat of male violence to colonial women. As he watches "the buggers go down," he feels "every fiber of his flesh tingl[e] with excitement" and he grows increasingly aroused as the violence around him begins to saturate his consciousness (211). The continuous shower of bullets evokes the memory of his first sexual encounter with his wife Mary:

> He remembered the morning he and Mary spent before they were married, in the central hill country, the badlands of India. She'd come down from Cawnpore with the regiment, the Colonel's daughter, ripe as a mango in May, her hair flaming crimson. He'd been picked as her "escort" by the Old Man, and was so new to the game, a subaltern of twenty-one, that he actually thought it was protection the Colonel's

daughter wanted. Till she slipped going up a hill, and fell into his arms, pressing her legs and hip to his muscle-stiffened thigh, the two of them clenched so hard that they almost rolled downhill together, but rushed instead to the plateau above the barren plain. There he took her, while she cried bitterly, and clawed blood from his back and arms. (213)

Through the use of figurative language—specifically, the metaphor of a "ripe mango"—Dyer analogizes Mary to the subcontinent. Like a luscious piece of Indian fruit, she is ready to be plucked and devoured by the voracious colonial male. Moreover, the novel draws a structural parallel between Mary and the native male, both of whom are represented as objects of the violence of colonial masculinity. Dyer's ferocious consummation of his desire has all the subtlety of a rape. And like the native men who taunt him, Mary, in the general's perception, is complicit in her brutalization, goading him into assaulting her. The rape itself gets legitimized and sanctified by the colonial patriarchy through the act of matrimony.

The novel renders Dyer even more perverse by exposing his concern over Alice's safety as arising from his incestuous desire. In the middle of the firing he dwells on his niece's physique: "He'd never seen a girl as slight and frail as that child. Her hips were hardly broader than a boy's. Her legs were so delicately fine and thin—he could circle her calves with his hand" (214). The attention to Alice's hip measurement implies that Dyer wonders at her physiological capacity to accommodate either the male organ or a child, making her into the object of heterosexual, male, reproductive desire. As the description of Dyer encircling his niece's calves attests, he is unable to visualize her body without fantasizing about touching it. Dyer's anxiety over the safety of Englishwomen and his construction of native men as a threat to colonial women, according to Wolpert's fictional interpretation, is a projection of his own desires to enact violence against British women. By showing how discourses of Dyer's innocence were structured on gendering the victims of native violence as British women, while concurrently making them the object of Dyer's desire, Massacre at Jallianwala Bagh acknowledges the difficult position that Anglo women occupied within the colonial hierarchy, as the beneficiaries of colonial privilege on the one hand and as victims of British patriarchy on the other. At the same time, by imagining the sexual fantasies that Dyer was having during the slaughter, Wolpert suggests that the massacre was yet another assertion of Dyer's potency over the natives.

Even though the novel psychologizes Dyer's motives in carrying out the massacre in the Jallianwala Bagh, it clears a small space for the articulation of a larger critique of the colonial system. Wolpert draws on the representation of Dyer as "foreign" which was current among Dyer's detractors and contrasts it with the quintessentially British aspects of his character. As Sir William Hunter waits to make Dyer's acquaintance, he reflects on the "nightmare visions evoked by the written testimony, which had prepared him for the scent of brimstone, horns, and a tail; for the frightfulness of a Prussian butcher of Belgian babes; or at least the blustering bombast of an Irish bully" (4). Here Hunter aligns the colonial perversities of the massacre with the stereotypic attributes of the German and Irish national characters. Yet when he finally meets Dyer, he is struck by Dyer's "ordinary" Britishness:

> Much to William's surprise [Dyer] was soft-spoken, and as the preliminary interrogation proceeded he was amazed to note that the General seemed quite human, even civilized. He looked so typically British, the big-jawed ragged cliff of a face with its graying shrubbery under the nostril ledge, a brow as nobly broad as any peer's—it was almost a face to trust, to respect, a general's manly visage. . . . How could [Hunter] possibly be faced instead by an ordinary British brigadier? (4)

Because the very terms of the concept "British" are related in topographical metaphors, however, Wolpert's critique of colonialism can progress no further. Dyer's physiognomy takes on the characteristics of the British landscape itself, evoking its cliffs, shrubs, and ledges. Thus, without any apparent irony, the novel embodies "Britishness" as manifest in the corporeality of the Anglo male, without instead probing those institutions that interpellated Dyer's colonial subjectivity.

|||||

Divergent interpretations of Dyer have continued to circulate in narratives about colonial outrages up to the present.[22] The singular focus on Dyer in these narratives has paradoxically universalized him into a discursive archetype that signifies two different meanings: he is both a deadly aberration of the colonial rule of law who mistakenly interprets his duties, and at the same time the loyal colonial servant who is scapegoated for his dedication to his fellow colonials. Contrary to such interpretations which marshal the ideology of rogue-colonial individualism to cast him as an anomaly, I have tried to demonstrate that General Dyer's actions are paradigmatic of the peculiar logic of colonialism and its reliance on deadly force. Interpellated by the military through an educational apparatus which stressed practical training in counterinsurgency and the study of military law, General Dyer must be understood as the logical product of the British colonial system. That colonialism was based on dominance without hegemony, Guha emphasizes, renders suspect the whole rhetoric of the colonial rule of law used to individualize Dyer and to distance him from the colonial project. Guha asks,

> But what rule of law? What rule of law where the law did not even remotely issue from the will of the people; where Indians, denied the right to vote for most of the duration of British rule, were allowed, during its last thirty years, only a restricted franchise which took decades of struggle and incalculable amounts of physical and spiritual pain to increase, between the Act of 1919 and the Act of 1935 (an inflated estimate of) three per cent of the adult population to fourteen per cent? What rule of law where the 'law', during the first hundred years of the raj (out of a total of one hundred and ninety), was merely a body of executive orders, decrees, regulations; where, during the next three quarters of a century, all legislative institutions at the central and provincial levels of government were composed either entirely of officials and official nominees or the latter supplemented, for a relatively short period at the height of British constitutional magnanimity, by a handful of Indians elected on the basis of restricted franchise? . . . What rule of law where the execution of the laws, made for the people but not by them, was so often characterized by double standards—one, until the end of the nineteenth century, for the whites and other for the natives, and during the remainder of British rule, one for the administrative elite, British and Indian, and the other for the rest of the population? (Dominance 275–76)

As Guha's rhetorical questions point out, the discourse of the rule of law can only have meaning within the context of a state formation that draws its legitimacy from a universal adult franchise. In order for the law to be "maximally effective and productive of positive results," according to Gramsci, it "will have to be freed from every residue of transcendentalism," "from every absolute," and "from every moralistic fanaticism" (*Prison* 246). The debates about the Jallianwala Bagh massacre in the House of Commons represent, on the contrary, the spectacle of politicians delivering fine speeches and pointless declarations saturated with the pious and empty moralism of the colonial rule of law. In those debates, the construction of Dyer through rogue-colonial individualism represents him as at best a hero, forced by unfortunate circumstances into an action that only the enemies of the British Empire would impugn, and at worst a pathological monster, taking out his own murderous aggressions on an innocent assembly of unarmed Indians. Between these extremes, and because of the ambiguities I have indicated between, for example, martial and common law, Dyer emerges as an anomaly, a scandal, a figure who must at least be "retired" from the benign operations of the Empire and its peaceful "rule of law."

FEMINIST-NATIONALIST INDIVIDUALISM:

MARGARET COUSINS, ACTIVISM,

AND WITNESSING

While chapter 1 analyzes the ideology of rogue-colonial individualism that underwrote the British colonial regime and its discursive and military forms of power, this chapter turns to a consideration of the ideology of feminist-nationalist individualism and its manifestation in various suffrage organizations, in Ireland and India, which operated within a broadly nationalist framework. The chapter centers on the figure of Margaret Cousins, an Irish suffragette who emigrated to India in 1915 and became an eloquent commentator on Indian women's political struggles. Rather than impose the full text of colonial femininity onto the lives of Indian natives, Cousins was able to theorize a politics of "witnessing" that worked to respect and guarantee the authority of the Indian woman to document her own social situation and formulas of resistance. Cousins's feminist activism in Ireland, as she herself recognized, uniquely prepared her to develop a politics of feminist solidarity with South Asian women. Her formation and development as an activist—as narrated in her duography *We Two Together*, written with her husband, James Cousins—illustrate how her conceptions of agency were shaped both by the specificities of her geopolitical locations and by her social identity as a colonized subject in Ireland and as a western woman in the subcontinent.[1] Within the Irish context, Cousins understood agency to be an active intervention against the patriarchal reproduction of gender relations that perpetuated the political subordination of Irish women to British and Irish men. Her activism in Ireland, which was focused on securing women's franchise within the framework of constitutional nationalism and the passage of home rule legislation, tended to be performative: she often engaged public audiences in face-to-face encounters or staged actions scripted to elicit press coverage of the suffrage movement. Within the Indian context, however, Cousins's feminist work encompassed a broader range of social and political issues, including purdah, dowry, female education, child marriage, the remarriage of widows, and the national question. Her conception of her own agency, in this context, was discursive, taking the form of writing in solidarity with the Indian women's movement, by acting as a "witness" to it, and strategically directing her arguments in support of the Indian women's social and political agenda to an external western audience.

Yet in spite of these differences between the feminist activist cultures in both locations, Cousins's conception of agency was consistently "anchored in the practice of thinking" herself "a part of feminist collectivities and organizations" (Alexander and Mohanty xxviii). As a founder of feminist organizations such as the Irish Women's Franchise League (IWFL), the Women's Indian Association (WIA), and the All India Women's Conference (AIWC), she had a feminist praxis always grounded within larger collectivities whose activities were directed at attaining political objectives. "To talk about feminist praxis in global contexts," M. Jacqui Alexander and Chandra Talpade Mohanty note, "would involve shifting the unit of analysis from local, regional, and national culture to relations and processes across cultures" (xix). Such analysis demands situating the local in relation to larger, cross-national processes and entails a "corresponding shift in the conception of political organizing and mobilization across borders" (xix). According to Alexander and Mohanty, feminist praxis stands to gain "responsibility, accountability, engagement, and solidarity" from this kind of critical move (xix). A critical assessment of Margaret Cousins's writing has a continuing usefulness because she provides an early model of how a geopolitical analysis of the lived experience of activism can make possible feminist solidarity across colonial sites, and hence helps to create an alternative archive that is at once feminist, activist, and transcultural.

This chapter represents another example of the multisited research method of "follow[ing] the life or biography" advocated by George Marcus. In contrast to its use in tracing General Dyer's career trajectory, which revealed the circulation of colonial military and administrative personnel and disclosed some of the structural links in the Empire, its value for following Margaret Cousins's life history from Ireland to India is to propose alternative networks of resistance, both informal and highly organized, among nationalists and feminists globally. In suggesting an alternative circuit of anticolonial activist exchange between disparate colonial sites within the British Empire, the methodological imperative to follow the biography also illustrates what Stuart Hall calls the "theory of articulation." An articulation is a type of connection that can make a unity of two distinct elements under certain historical conditions; the nature of this unity, or linkage, is not "necessary, determined, absolute, essential" or transhistorical (Hall 141). Hall maintains that the theory of articulation "enables us to think how an ideology empowers people, enabling them to begin to make some sense or intelligibility of their historical situation, without reducing those forms of intelligibility to their socio-economic or class location or social position" (141). Tracking Cousins's movements across the Empire, in the context of her participation in various social movements, permits the articulation of India and Ireland within the specific historic conjuncture of the colonial state and organized resistance to it.

Rather than insist that Cousins's status as a gendered female colonized subject in Ireland imbued her with some sort of "epistemic privilege" to declaim against both the British colonial state and indigenous forms of South Asian patriarchy, I emphasize that it was Cousins's *analysis* of the Irish colonial formation, and her understanding of her singular position as a Protestant woman with nationalist allegiances within it, which allowed her to develop modes of solidarity with the Indian women's movement. As Paula Moya remarks, while there may be no "*a priori* link between social location or identity and knowledge . . . experience in its mediated form contains a 'cognitive component' through which we can gain access to knowledge of the world" (136–37). Experience, in other words, is constituted by "our theoretically mediated interpretation of an event" (Moya 136). Hence the experience of repression does not in and of itself provide a catalyst for organizing and activism (Alexander and Mohanty xl). "It is, in fact, the *interpretation* of that experience within a *collective* context," Alexander and Mohanty rightly insist, "that marks the moment of transformation from perceived contradictions and material disenfranchisement to participation in women's movements" (xl; emphasis in original).

The paralysis that attends some contemporary feminist debates on cultural appropriation, identity politics, and activist imperialism is avoided in the formulations by Moya and by Alexander and Mohanty of the relationship between social identity, experience, and agency.[2] Indeed, the feminist anxiety that surfaces in discussions of identity politics and dominant appropriations of marginalized subject-positions—evident in the perennial question "Who can speak with critical authority for others?"—seems to be an anxiety about the nature of feminist solidarity with women who inhabit different social identities.[3] The category of solidarity, while often bandied about in the feminist critical lexicon, is rarely defined in concrete terms; perhaps this is because questions of identity and critical authority are generally abstracted from specific kinds of feminist praxis—even in discussions which acknowledge that women have a differential access to power based on their social location. I follow Aijaz Ahmad's lead in defining solidarity as a deliberate affiliation with specific forms of praxis within collectivities of individuals who themselves act from determinate social and political positions (152). Cousins's ability to harness her activist experience in Ireland and retool it to fit the geopolitical and social conditions of women in India presents an exemplary instance of international feminist solidarity.

Nonetheless, Cousins's feminist struggle against the patriarchal hegemony of the colonial state was itself marked by the traces of that formation on the Indian nationalist movement which opposed that state. The mainstream Indian nationalist movement, of which the AIWC was a part, drew on rhetoric that was inflected with the idioms of patriarchy, bourgeois class consciousness, and Hinduism, projecting a nationalist subject who was primarily male, middle-class, and Hindu. The Janus-faced quality of nationalist discourse has a crucial bearing on how nationalists understood gender relations within the nationalist project. As Deniz Kandiyoti notes, insofar as nationalist discourse "presents itself both as a modern project that melts and transforms traditional attachments in favour of new identities and as a reaffirmation of authentic cultural values culled from the depths of a presumed communal past," it "opens up a highly fluid and ambivalent field of meanings which can be reactivated, reinterpreted and often reinvented at critical junctures of the histories of nation-states" (378). The personal status of the "modern citizen," particularly the gendered female nationalist subject, becomes one site through which tensions between modernist and conservative, antimodernist strands in nationalism are mediated. As secular Indian nationalists attempted to establish the indigenous and patriotic roots of their modernizing projects, so too did members of the AIWC justify their participation in the nationalist and women's movements by invoking a gendered rhetoric of patriotism and self-sacrifice for the nation. AIWC members often legitimized feminist and nationalist activism by utilizing metaphors of Hindu domesticity in ways that left unchallenged the gendered and class-inflected discourse of distinct social spheres. "A pervasive feature of such 'feminism,'" Kandiyoti explains, "was that rather than presenting itself as a radical break with the past, which it did in fact represent, it often harkened back to more distant and presumably more authentic origins" (379).

Cousins's attempts to write the histories of the Irish and Indian women's movements through the generic conventions of autobiography, albeit one with a dual subject-author, additionally betray an uneasiness with the gap between individual social agency and collective action. As Rachel Jennings asserts, "the conventions of radical autobiography assume an ontological oneness between the subject and . . . her political associates," in that the writing subject presents her activist experiences as both normative and representative of the experiences of others in the movement (11). The imperative to narrate the personal and private aspects of the self is thus simultaneously coded as the expression of a public and collective sociopolitical body to which the subject belongs. The collective sociopolitical body is, however, itself a rhetorical formulation based on the subject's selection of certain individuals to include in the account of the movement, a process which necessarily excludes the contributions of others from her narrative. In Cousins's text, feminist-nationalist individualism is constituted discursively through the construction of Cousins herself as at the center of suffragette activism in Ireland and through the conspicuously understated role in the movement that she assigns to other principal agents, particularly Hannah Sheehy-Skeffington. Yet this construction of herself as the locus of feminist activism is not a stable one throughout *We Two Together* and is recontextualized through the rewriting of herself in relation to shifting geopolitical locations. The narrative impulse to write the history of the Indian women's movement, which, as Cousin herself recognized, must deemphasize her contributions to authenticate its project, runs counter to the autobiographical convention of foregrounding the radical, individual subject as the necessary cause of historical change and agent for it.

FEMINISM AND NATIONALISM: THE IRISH CASE

In her groundbreaking study *Feminism and Nationalism in the Third World*, Kumari Jayawardena succinctly summarizes the double bind that feminists in colonized territories face from their male compatriots across the ideological spectrum: "It has variously been alleged by traditionalists, political conservatives and even certain leftists, that feminism is a product of 'decadent' Western capitalism; that it is based on a foreign culture of no relevance to women in the Third World; that it is the ideology of women of the local bourgeoisie; and that it alienates or diverts women, from their culture, religion and family responsibilities on the one hand, and from the revolutionary struggles for national liberation and socialism on the other" (2).[4] As Laura E. Lyons insightfully notes, the construction of "feminism" as a "foreign" ideology denies women "the ability to have and to act on their own political beliefs" by insinuating that they are "parroting" the modernizing impulses of the elite native bourgeoisie or "following the lead of women outside Ireland" ("At the End of the Day" 279).[5]

The Irish debate between feminists and nationalists assumed a particular urgency in the first two decades of the twentieth century as the two movements intensified their organizing efforts against the British colonial state. Many Irish nationalists felt that the colonial relationship between Britain and Ireland had largely contributed to the degraded status of Irish women and that national liberation alone would guarantee political equality for women. The independence struggle, for these nationalists, necessarily took priority over other issues such as women's suffrage and tenant rights. For instance, Countess Markievicz exhorted Irish women to stay focused on the national question and to avoid the distractions of reform issues. "Fix your mind on the ideal of Ireland free, with her women enjoying the full rights of citizenship in her own nation," she urged, "and no one will be able to sidetrack you to use up the energies of the nation in obtaining all sorts of concessions . . . that for the most part were coming in the natural course of evolution" (quoted in McKillen 58). The temporal axes of Markievicz's entreaties, couched in the vocabulary of social Darwinism, are oriented simultaneously toward the distant past of Celtic Ireland and the near future of the Republic post-independence. Ridding Ireland of the corruption constituted by British colonialism required projecting the more egalitarian gender relations of the Celtic period into the future of the independent state.

The discursive skirmishes between nationalists and suffragettes crystallized around the activities of the IWFL, founded by Hanna Sheehy-Skeffington and Margaret Cousins in 1908 as an activist alternative to Anna Haslam's nonmilitant organization, the Irish Women's Suffrage and Local Government Association. IWFL members employed a wide range of tactics in their aim to secure the parliamentary vote for women, including giving open-air speeches, lobbying Irish M.P.s, heckling unsympathetic Irish and English politicians, and publishing articles and pamphlets. Several of their tactics, such as window breaking, were patterned on the activities of the militant British suffragette organization the Women's Social and Political Union, whose work Cousins followed through its weekly paper *Votes for Women* (*We Two Together* 163). While the IWFL tracked the activities of the British organization, it maintained its own organizational autonomy. According to Cliona Murphy, "Although the Irish movement for women's suffrage asserted solidarity with the aims—and often the means—of the British movement, and did receive verbal backing from London, its substantive connection to the British movement amounted to little more than its connections with the American or Australian movements" (Murphy 7).[6]

Perhaps it was the IWFL's willingness to draw on the experiences of British suffragettes, whose national affiliations were after all colonial, which drew criticism from republican women antagonistic to the organization's formation. In the pages of *Sinn Fein*, Countess Markievicz attacked what she perceived as the IWFL's ties with the English women's movement.[7] Noting that English women could afford to work on a single issue, because they had a parliament in which they could be represented, Markievicz argued that the IWFL's struggle to gain representation in an "alien Parliament" was misguided, and she urged Irish women to broaden their agenda by placing the fight for a free Ireland before all else (Levenson and Natterstad 25). Her attacks on the IWFL were often condescending and trivialized their activities in relation to the nationalist cause: "We hear a great deal just at present of a League that is being started in Dublin called the Irish Women's Franchise League. This League appears to be a very vague organisation, but we see no reason why, when its members have gained a little experience, it should not become something definite and something useful to Irishwomen, and—bar consequence—useful to Ireland" (quoted in Levenson and Natterstad 24). The strident nature of her criticism of the IWFL even moved Arthur Griffiths, the editor of *Sinn Fein*, who was generally unsympathetic to women's suffrage, to issue a disclaimer to her article: "We shall not condemn [the IWFL] or any body which tends to awaken civic and national consciousness in Irishwomen" (quoted in Levenson and Natterstad 25). Though Markievicz, who was later president of Cumann na mBan (a women's auxiliary to the Irish Volunteers) for seven years, continued to have public disagreements with the IWFL, she eventually supported their work when they entered their militant window-shattering phase (MacCurtain 55).[8]

Suffragettes remained suspicious of nationalist claims like Markievicz's that British colonial domination was the major cause of women's social and political oppression. Writing in *Bean na hÉireann*, the print organ of the women's republican organization Inghinidhe na hEireann, Hanna Sheehy-Skeffington challenged the nationalist assertion that the condition of women was more equitable in Celtic Ireland. "Some Celtic enthusiasts hold the average Irishman very high above petty sex spite and prejudice and quote Irish traditions of womanhood in support of the theory. One learns, however, to distrust this thriftless Irish habit of living on the reputation of its ancestors, especially when one is faced with the problems of Ireland today" (quoted in McKillen 56). Disputing the notion that the ideology of "petty sex spite" was a colonial imposition, Sheehy-Skeffington insisted on acknowledging native manifestations of patriarchy and on grounding discussions of gender equality in contemporary conditions.

Many IWFL members did not perceive feminism and nationalism to be ideologically antithetical. In fact, Cousins and Sheehy-Skeffington were acutely cognizant of the colonial context of the campaign for votes for women, recognizing that Ireland required, in Cousins's words, "a scheme for a militant suffrage society suitable to the different political situation of Ireland, as . . . a subject-country seeking freedom from England" (*We Two Together* 164). The colonial relationship between Britain and Ireland had the potential to overdetermine the hierarchy of a joint activist effort, by assigning leadership roles to English women and subordinate ones to Irish women within the suffrage movement. Neither

Cousins nor Sheehy-Skeffington had any "desire to work under English women leaders"; Cousins emphatically declared, "we could lead ourselves" (164). She explained: "Our work was to see that votes for women was incorporated in the Home Rule Bill for which Ireland was fighting" (164). Both women considered themselves Irish nationalists and believed, in Cousins's words, that "anything which improved the status of women would improve, not hinder, the coming of real national self-government" (185).

Both Cousins and Sheehy-Skeffington, then, refused to disarticulate the issue of suffrage from that of nationalism. For them the colonial context informed the sociopolitical status of Irish women, necessitating that they insert the suffrage issue into the debate on home rule. These efforts provoked stubborn resistance from some nationalist quarters, as Sheehy-Skeffington described:

> It is remarkable, and a discovery that all rebels make in their time, how watertight the minds of rebels can be. Here were good Irish rebels, many of them broken in to national revolt, with all the slogans of Irish revolution and its arsenal of weapons—Boycott, Plan of Campaign, Land for the People, and so forth, the creators of obstruction in Parliament—yet at the whisper of Votes for Women many changed to extreme Tories or time-servers who urged us women to wait till freedom for men was won. (Owens and Sheehy-Skeffington 12–13)

Assessing the interaction and impact of feminist and nationalist organizations, such as the IWFL, Cumann na mBan, and the Irish Women's Workers Union, Beth McKillen concludes that these two emancipatory movements exerted a reciprocal influence on one another. As both movements gained momentum in the second decade of the twentieth century, nationalists paid greater attention to women's demands for electoral representation and suffragettes became more vocal in their support for an independent Irish republic.

ORGANIZING AND COUNTER-FEMINIST OPPOSITION IN IRELAND

Cousins's account of the IWFL's formation and activities, till her abrupt departure for Liverpool and then India in 1913, offers a grassroots theory of feminist organizing, whose major strategy was to disrupt what Tom Foster terms the "spatial logics" of gender. Because women were identified primarily with the private sphere and the institution of the family, and men with the public sphere of civil and political discourse, the IWFL sought to advance the issue of votes for women by taking their campaign to public spaces such as Phoenix Park. Barred from some public gatherings, the suffragettes often relied on their husbands and other male sympathizers to press their cause. Such a periodic dependence on male allies suggests that women's discourse could not enter the public realm unless it was somehow attached to men. Indeed, resistance to the suffragettes was often articulated through a patriarchal discourse which drew on the literal and discursive signifiers of domesticity.

The IWFL's constitution included a declaration of its objectives and the methods that its members would use in their organizing efforts:

1. Action entirely independent of all political parties.
2. Vigorous agitation upon lines justified by the fact that women at present have no voice in the making of laws under which they live.
3. The organizing of women to enable them to give full expression to their desire for political freedom.
4. Education of public opinion. (quoted in McKillen 53)

Cousins's description of the IWFL's agenda in *We Two Together* more explicitly emphasizes the nationalist context of the suffrage struggle and acknowledges the organization's willingness to operate outside the colonial rule of law:

The aim of the Irish Women's Franchise League was to obtain the parliamentary vote for the women of Ireland on the same terms as men then had it, or as it might be given to them. Its policy was to educate by all forms of propaganda the men, women and children of Ireland to understand and support the members of the League in their demand for votes for women, and to obtain pledges from every Irish Member of Parliament to vote for Women Suffrage Bills introduced in the British House of Parliament, and to include Women Suffrage in any Irish Home Rule Bill. The forms of propaganda of the Irish Women's Franchise League were to be both constitutional and non-constitutional, as dictated by political circumstances. (*We Two Together* 165)

What characterizes Cousins's description is the flexibility of the league, a recognition by its members that their tactics should be adapted to the prevailing political situation. Given that the organization "quickly attracted a body of about 800 women from other suffrage organizations," its willingness to engage in nonconstitutional forms of activism seems to have appealed to many women who had perhaps become disillusioned with the effectiveness of more cautious tactics (McKillen 54).

The IWFL had a central office in Dublin, housed in the Antient Concert Rooms building (the seat of many nationalist and Irish revivalist activities), and it hoped to establish local chapters throughout Ireland (*We Two Together* 165). Though Cousins does not directly say so, the IWFL's early organizers appear to have envisioned the central office as playing a major role in the local chapters. Voluntary IWFL organizers would leave Dublin to "tour the country and form Branches of the League," with each of the local chapters paying an "annual subscription to the central funds" (165). She also neglects to mention any discussions within the Dublin office of attempts to encourage women around the country to form league branches on their own. Nor does Cousins explain the funding arrangements between the central office and local chapters, raising a number of questions. For example, did the local chapters receive a portion of their subscriptions back to offset their operating expenses? Were these funds converted to resources, such as pamphlets and buttons, that were then distributed to the local chapters? Or did the subscriptions simply cover the Dublin office's operating costs? IWFL members seem to have believed in the political efficacy of a top-down structure, with the central office providing guidance to local chapters.

In Dublin, IWFL members inserted the issue of votes for women into public discourse by taking their campaign into public spaces. They often gave open-air speeches, borrowing the English suffragettes' logistical planning of this kind of event. "Experience had taught the English suffragettes the convenience, economy, mobility and reliability of speaking from four-wheeled lorries without horses," Cousins related. "The lorry made a strong, raised, steady, dignified platform" (166). Typically these open-air events had three speakers, two women and one man, and did not require much advance publicity. Cousins stated: "We did not ask people to come to us. We had the lorry placed where the people themselves were accustomed to gather and they never failed to come and listen and ask questions at the end of the hour" (167).

Though Cousins has more explicit statements on the IWFL's goals elsewhere in her text, we can extract a theory of grassroots organizing from details such as the use of horseless lorries, or wagons, for plat-forms. In her description of the open-air speeches, we can read the league's refusal to confine political activities to sanctioned spaces such as meeting halls. Open-air events had the advantage of accommodating a larger number of people than an indoor location would allow and enabled these events to attract a more diverse range of ages and classes, provided that everyone had equal access to public space. The question-and-answer period following the presentations enabled spectators to interact with the speakers, illustrating that IWFL members were willing to engage in debate with those unsympathetic toward women's suffrage and that they understood how effective political organizing can maxi-mize contact between activists and others. Additionally, apart from se-curing the lorry and determining the choice of speakers, the open-air speeches required little in the way of logistical planning and support.

The dual imperatives of carrying out massive propaganda campaigns and establishing local branches of the IWFL led its members to under-take speaking tours around the country. The women generally traveled in pairs. They often had difficulty finding lodgings, securing meeting loca-tions, and getting announcements for meetings printed at short notice (167). Persuading a local resident to preside over the meeting was some-times impossible. Cousins attributes these difficulties to an unsympa-thetic press, which out of its loathing for the English suffragettes had painted them in broad strokes as " 'wild women,' 'hooligans,' " and " 'unsexed females' " (167). From town to town, the reception accorded to league members was unpredictable, as Cousins recalled:

> At Castlebar, in County Mayo, a band of irresponsible men tried to ruin our meeting by singing songs to drown our voices. But after regaling us with "Put me on an island where the girls are few," there was a moment's quiet, and Meg Connery asked them if they would really like such an island. They were so pleased with her repartee and her plucky spirit that they quieted down and became quite sensible. At another country meeting rowdies brought flour with them and threw it towards us on the platform. Commotion ensued among the au-dience. We could not make ourselves heard. One of the elders of the town chided them with, "Can you not give the young girls a chance to spake?" We won them round; but we found "apple-pie beds" laid out for us in the hotel. (167)[9]

The counter-feminist tactics deployed by antisuffragettes in this anecdote operate on a semiotic continuum of both literal and discursive signifiers of domesticity. Flour functions as a literal signifier of gendered female labor circumscribed within the social space of the kitchen. As a principal ingredient in pastry dough, flour also provides a link in the semiotic chain of counter-feminist discourse: the short-sheeted beds which await the suffragettes after a hard round of organizing figuratively evoke another sign of food and domesticity, the "apple pie." Opposition to feminist activism, as this example demonstrates, sought to recontain women in the private sphere by drawing on signs of feminine domesticity.

Such attempts to contain suffrage work within the discourse of domesticity were informed by the fear that electoral representation for women would both masculinize women and herald the demise of the family. The press characterization of the suffragettes as "wild women," "hooligans," and "unsexed women" constructed them as agents of moral turpitude who had upset the natural order of social relations by adopting masculine behavior. Antisuffrage leaflets distributed during an IWFL demonstration outside the United Irish League's national convention, for instance, gendered suffrage activism as manly, wittily punning on Cousins's name: "Irish women condemn the *masculine conduct* of Sheehy-Skeffington and Cousins. Beware of the English Pankhursts and their *Irish Cousins*" (quoted in Levenson and Natterstad 34; emphasis mine). According to Hanna Sheehy-Skeffington, masculinist opposition to suffrage came from all quarters, left and right:

> The Press, both National and Conservative, official Sinn Fein, the clergy on the whole (organized religion generally) were opposed to the militant movement, primarily because revolt of women for their own emancipation is always frowned on by organized males, and partly because the Churches are opposed to any change. Organized Labour wanted women to help them press for Adult Suffrage, ridiculing Women's Suffrage as 'Votes for Ladies.' Some Socialists feared that women, if given the vote would prove clerically-minded. (Sheehy-Skeffington and Owens 17)

The theme on which rhetorical attacks against the suffragettes predictably centered was the breakdown of the home. Sheehy-Skeffington offered the example of the bishop of Limerick, Dr. O'Dwyer, who "fulminated against Votes for Women on the usual lines in a Lenten Pastoral, warning his flock against this insidious enemy of the Home" (17). And John Dillon, a leader of the Irish Parliamentary Party, portentously told a deputation of women that "Women's Suffrage" would result in no less than "the ruin of our Western civilization. It will destroy the home, challenging the headship of man, laid down by God" (quoted in Sheehy-Skeffington and Owens 19).

At issue in such opposition to women's suffrage was the desire to preserve the primacy of male power within the family structure conceived of as the most basic social unit of western civilization. League members operated within a patriarchal logic similar to that of their opponents and often invoked their status as wives and their domestic skills to challenge popular characterizations of the suffragettes as mannish and "unsexed females." IWFL husbands were exhibited on the stage and circulated among the audience, authenticating the marital credentials of the women and conferring upon them the respectability associated with that peculiar institution. In his account of the Irish suffragette movement in *We Two Together*, James Cousins provided one example of how he dispelled any suspicions about Margaret's marital status and domestic skills. As Margaret spoke on a lorry, he milled among an audience "to catch its sentiment" and heard a woman "happily engaged in interjecting comments such as Irish crowds always enjoyed" (*We Two Together* 196):

WOMAN (towards the speaker who of course was out of earshot, a matter that never deters born hecklers): "What *you* want is a husband." (Laughter from the small section of the crowd around her).

J. H. C. (unknown of course): "I believe, ma'am, the lady is very happily married—which I hope you are." (Loud laughter. A gleam from the eye of the woman. The voice of the speaker in the distance).

WOMAN (after a pause, unable to resist temptation): "You ought to be at home cooking for your husband, if you have one." (Laughter).

J. H. C.: "If I'm not wrongly informed, ma'am, the lady, though she has her own servant, is a very good cook. I hope *you* have arranged as good a meal for your husband as she has for her's." (Loud laughter, and a glare from the woman. Another pause while the soft-voiced speaker continues).

WOMAN: "What you should be doin' is sewin' or darnin' instead of standin' there talkin'." (Laughter).

J. H. C.: "She has as much right to be standing there talking as you have to be standing there talking, and in any case *she's* talking sense. And I think I'm not far wrong in saying that the very nice dress she has on she made with her own hands for this occasion—which maybe is more than you can say about your dress." (Chuckles and craning of necks to get a better view of the principals in a promising verbal fight).

WOMAN (with exasperation and innuendo, the last refuge of the defeated): "You seem to know a divil of a lot about the woman."

J. H. C. (almost casually, but with a trace of triumph): "I do know quite a lot about her ma'am. She happens to be my wife." (*We Two Together* 197)

The heckler tries to undermine the suffrage cause by depicting it as the site of misplaced domestic zeal that could be better utilized in the service of a husband and household. Cooking and sewing, in her opinion, constitute more appropriate labor for IWFL members than giving political speeches. Ironically, James Cousins's rhetorical retaliation functions within a logic of heteronormativity similar to that of the heckler, because it affirms Margaret Cousins's status qua wife and attests to her culinary and tailoring talents. His verbal dexterity in parrying the heckler's discursive thrusts—and thus in winning the crowd's approbation—depends upon marking a class distinction between the two women. Attributing a lower-class vernacular to the heckler, James Cousins casts doubts on the woman's ability to minister to her husband's domestic comforts and observes that notwithstanding Margaret's skills in this area, his own wife can afford a servant to discharge such duties. The apparent humor of this incident, as evidenced by the numerous parenthetical references to "laughter" throughout the passage, derives from James's agility in reversing the charges of inept housekeeping and directing them against the heckler, and his success in establishing Margaret's superior class position vis-à-vis the woman.

INTERPELLATING THE HETEROSEXUAL SUBJECT

Yet the assumption that the logic of heterosexuality which underwrote both counter-feminist discourse and the IWFL's tactics was a natural way of ordering sex and gender relations is belied by Margaret Cousins's often poignant account of her courtship with James. In sharp contrast to his tender reminiscences of their engagement, her narrative emphasizes her disappointment in James, who failed to measure up to her romantic "ideal" of a "tall," "dark" professor, "with a beautiful voice," and her struggle to feel affection for him in the face of scarce opportunities for marriage (*We Two Together* 85). "I did not fall in love," Margaret Cousins confides, "I had to be dragged up into it" (86):

> Often I asked myself why it was that in that first year of knowing him I had such a dislike for him. I cried with disappointment the night after he proposed to me. But I knew he was good and clever and full of the highest ideals. Also I was queerly humble about myself and strangely worldly-wise. With three lovely younger sisters I thought this was probably my only chance of marriage. I must not rashly throw it away. I knew he was a poet; and I loved poetry. Perhaps a poet might work out as well as a professor. I decided to give him a trial. . . . For six months I forced myself to suffer his company so that I might, as I told him, "learn what he was really like." But scandal began to wag its tongue about us. So I agreed to an engagement, but made the provision that I reserved the right to break it at any moment. (87)

The social pressure to get married persuades Margaret to give her beau a chance even though she initially feels distaste for him. It is the fear of scandal which leads her to formalize her relationship with him and consent to an engagement. In the period preceding their betrothal, she assiduously works to overcome her dislike of her fiancé, remarking that "[it] had taken me half of our three year engagement to grow content with Fate's choice for me" (88). She adds:

> In those first years I used to analyse my lack of emotional care whether he turned up or not as I continued my piano practice and he happened to be later than our time of appointment. And now, so near the fatal or heavenly day of marriage I still had some region of indifference or coldness or uncertainty about the future in me which I was rather ashamed of as being unworthy of him, and not the fictional sort of emotionalism that a bride is expected to have. (88)

The vocabulary of fatalism evident in these reflections illustrates the conflicted nature of Cousins's self-narration in relation to marriage: on the one hand, she represents herself as a passive victim of marital circumstance in her references to "fate," and, on the other hand, this passivity stands in stark relief to her active determination and hard work to feel affection for her diminutive suitor.

Margaret's apprehensions regarding James were not assuaged during the apprenticeship she served in her natal home learning to be a wife.

> The six months previous to our marriage was a testing time for me. I had to leave Dublin and retire to the bosom of my family to be taught how to cook, to collect a trousseau, and learn household management. . . . The home atmosphere had been for years one of continuous babies, growing parental friction, a queer mixture of autocracy, kindliness, love of music and beauty, an irrational kind of religious faith, a sense of congestion. One could see everywhere what a lottery marriage had been; how many blanks had been drawn? What was my guarantee for life-long happiness in such an inescapably close relationship? (88)

Characterizing this apprenticeship as an endurance test, Cousins gains an understanding of both the unproductive and productive aspects of marriage. One aspect of being a wife entailed cooking, acquiring clothes and linens, and managing servants and budgets, all of which are activities that were considered unproductive labor because of their repetitive nature and their failure to produce a commodity. The second aspect of being a wife consisted of the productive labor of reproducing children, which in the Gillespie home had increased the tension between the spouses. Cousins's skepticism about the institution of marriage as a kind of "congestion" which was an "inescapably close relationship" is bound to her analysis of the household labor and reproductive labor that it involved.

But if her sojourn with her natal family had successfully interpellated her as a wife in terms of the training it offered her in cooking and household management, nothing had prepared Cousins for the physical intimacy of marriage. She records her horror at her discovery of sexual relations:

> It was providential that there were so many interests claiming my attention in those first years. I remember that I grew white and thin during our first married year. People thought this was due to my being a vegetarian. But I knew it was due to the problems of adjust-

ment to the revelation that marriage had brought me as to the physical basis of sex. Every child I looked at called to my mind the shocking circumstances that brought about its existence. My new knowledge, though I was lovingly safeguarded from it, made me ashamed of humanity and ashamed for it. I found myself looking on men and women as degraded by this demand of nature. Something in me revolted then, and has ever since protested against, certain of the techniques of nature connected with sex. Nor will I and many men and women of like nature, including my husband, be satisfied, be purified and redeemed, life after life, until the evolution of form has substituted some more artistic way of continuance of the race. (108–9)

Cousins views heterosexual intimacy with loathing, associating it with shame and the animalistic imperative to reproduce the species. So traumatized is Cousins by "the revelation . . . of the physical basis of sex" that it becomes the primary lens through which she perceives her early marital experiences: thus, her quotidian activities are welcome distractions from the horror of her newly acquired sexual knowledge and every child becomes a signifier of its debased sexual origins. Her emphatic declarations that she has "revolted" and "protested against certain of the techniques of sex" suggest that she decided not to have sexual intercourse with her husband. The cryptic references to her spouse, their lack of "satisfaction" with the "shocking circumstances" of conception, and their certainty that more aesthetically pleasing methods of perpetuating humanity will present themselves imply that Margaret Cousins disarticulated marriage from normative heterosexual sexual practices, opting for a decorporealized form of intimacy instead.[10]

While Cousins remains silent on the topic of marital sex throughout the rest of the duography, neither admitting to engaging in it nor declaring sexual abstinence as a guiding principle of her marriage, the fact that she did not bear any children raises the possibility that she challenged the reproductive orthodoxies of marriage. What her narrative indisputably does establish, however, is her determination to marry James, in the face of her initial dislike for him, because of the ideological pressures of patriarchy. Cousins's account of her courtship with James thus contrasts starkly with the dominant registers of feminist individualism theorized by Gayatri Spivak, who writes, "what is at stake, for feminist individualism in the age of imperialism, is precisely the making of human beings, the constitution and 'interpellation' of the subject not only as individual but as 'individualist'. This stake is represented on two registers: child-bearing and soul making" ("Three Women's Texts" 263). Childbearing is represented as "domestic-society-through-sexual-reproduction ca-thected as 'companionate love'" and soul making is articulated as "the imperialist project cathected as civil-society-through-social-mission" (263). In Cousins's narrative of her engagement, the veil of "companionate love" is stripped aside, laying bare the sexual reproduction of domestic society.

HECKLERS AND HATCHETS:
MALE ALLIES AND ENGLISH SUFFRAGETTES

In addition to legitimizing the status of league members, men were enlisted for other purposes as well, such as heckling unsympathetic politicians during speeches. Male hecklers would be dispersed among the audience and call out slogans such as "Give votes to women!" at timed intervals. Since such heckling tended to be associated with mili-tant female suffragettes, the presence of male hecklers helped disarm the audience by providing a public show of male support for women's en-franchisement; this implicitly refuted the common tendency to equate a stance in favor of women's rights with an anti-male bias. Such public support could help shift the conservatism of a discourse that had cast the suffrage movement as consisting of disgruntled, man-hating women to one which emphasized women's rights to citizenship.

Sometimes men had access to meetings from which women had been banned altogether. When Prime Minister Herbert Asquith, a Liberal, decided to visit Dublin in 1912 to rally support for his Home Rule Bill, the IWFL announced they would find some means of protesting his opposi-tion to women's suffrage (We Two Together 186). Leah Levenson and Jerry Natterstad describe the public reaction in the press to the suffragettes:

> Letters began to appear in the Evening Telegraph, signed with pen names like "Home Ruler," warning suffragettes not to demonstrate during the visit. One, signed "A Home Ruler Woman," threatened that if Francis Sheehy-Skeffington "and his suffragist friends begin their dirty tricks and surprises, they may expect to receive at the hands of

Nationalists more than what they bargained for." Another, signed "Milesius," urged the police to "use whips on the shoulders of those unsexed viragoes." An *Evening Telegraph* editorial stated that any attempt to disturb the prime minister's visit would be considered a declaration of war on the Home Rule movement and warned "Mr. Sheehy-Skeffington and the little band who share his views" to keep their hands off Mr. Asquith. (40)[11]

Organizers of the meeting feared for Asquith's safety and decreed that no women would be allowed to attend. With the help of Dudley Digges, an actor visiting Countess Markievicz at the time, Francis Sheehy-Skeffington disguised himself as a cleric and gained entrance to the speech (Levenson and Natterstad 42). Margaret Cousins recalled hearing from her husband:

> He allowed Asquith to get well launched into his speech, and all seemed to go smoothly without horrid suffragette interruption. But at an appropriate point in Asquith's speech a clear sharp man's voice rang out: 'Give votes to women. Stop forcible feeding of women prisoners. Put votes for women in the Home Rule Bill.' Pandemonium overtook the meeting. Voices shouted, 'It's Skeffy.' The respectable clergyman was handed over to infuriated stewards and ejected from the building. (*We Two Together* 187)

Barred from attending the meeting, league members chalked the pavements outside with the announcement that they "would hold an open-air meeting beside the Custom House, the nearest suitable ground to the Theatre Royal," the site of Asquith's speech (187). The crowd, according to Margaret Cousins, "was definitely antagonistic":

> The only time in our suffrage decade when I had seen hat-pins in women's hands as weapons was on that occasion amongst low-class women who stood in front of the lorry and shouted us down. I watched a poor-class youth with a stone in his hand. In a moment he threw it towards me as I tried to gain the attention of the crowd. Then the idea got into the crowd's head that it should push the lorry out of its place. As they proceeded to do so more stones were thrown at us. The police ordered us to come down from the lorry. There was nothing else to do. They closed round our little band and started us walking towards O'Connell Street, to catch a tram they indicated. We had

to walk along the side of the River Liffey. The crowd surged round us and started pushing. It looked and felt at some moment as if they would push us into the river. But the police held firm and overcame their weight. They whistled as we reached the electric tram-line. We were shoved by the police into the first tram that came along, and they followed us into it. A shower of stones from the defeated crowd broke the windows of the tram. (187–88)

Though Cousins remarks on the crowd's unusually high level of hostility, she does not attempt to explain it. But public ire against the suffragettes had been raised by events of the previous day. While John Redmond accompanied Asquith around Dublin, his ear had been grazed by a small hatchet. The press attributed the attack to the English suffragette Mary Leigh, a member of the Women's Suffrage and Political Union, who had traveled to Dublin to heckle Asquith during his trip. Headlines screamed: " 'The Virago and the Hatchet' and 'Hatchet Outrage' " (quoted in Levenson and Natterstad 41). There are several interpretations of the incident. In an interview in 1965, Mary Leigh claimed that when Asquith's carriage reached Nassau Street, she ran up to it and dropped a small hatchet at his feet. Attached to the hatchet was the message: "This is a symbol of the extinction of the Liberal Party for evermore" (quoted in Levenson and Natterstad 40). Sheehy-Skeffington, however, presented a different version, writing that Leigh threw the hatchet which "skimmed between Asquith and Redmond and grazed the latter's ear" (Sheehy-Skeffington and Owens 22). Still another interpretation comes from Marie Johnson, a member of the Irish Women's Suffrage Society, who wrote years later: "A small axe struck John Redmond on the head. The cry was all over the place that it was one of the militant leaders from England, but it was not so, it was thrown by Helena Moloney [sic], a very extreme Republican, simply anti-British" (quoted in Levenson and Natterstad 41). That same evening Leigh, along with another English suffragette, Gladys Evans, had unsuccessfully tried to burn down the Theatre Royal where Asquith was scheduled to speak on the following day.

Asquith's visit and the public's antagonism to the suffragettes provided an instance of the national liberation struggle colliding with feminist demands. As the letters to the *Evening Telegraph* indicate, home rulers were ready to rally behind Asquith's bill. The presence of English suffragettes and their role in the affair only exacerbated tensions between home rulers and the Irish suffragettes. The English suffragettes' visible meddling in activities widely publicized by the IWFL served to discredit the league's nationalist position. As Inderpal Grewal points out in her important study *Home and Harem: Nation, Gender, Empire, and the Cultures of Travel*, "middle-class Englishwomen were interpellated as feminist through imperialist subject positions" (14). While Grewal cautions against viewing the imperialist politics of English suffragettes as identical with those of upper-class and bourgeois Englishmen, she explains that "the habitus" of the English suffrage movement was structured by the dichotomy of colonial values that blinded them to the links between racial and class hierarchies which underwrote colonial culture (67).[12] This blindness often led many English suffragettes to support imperialism explicitly, or through the more implicit colonial rhetoric of the benevolent ethical imperative to improve and reform the natives. Though Leigh and her companions Gladys Evans and Lizzie Baker were acting on their own initiative, in the public's eye they were closely identified with Irish suffragettes. Cousins's failure to mention these events is strange, given that as a secretary to the IWFL she had to issue a public disclaimer of the attack and attempt at arson. The *Irish Independent* (July 20, 1912) and the *Evening Telegraph* (July 19, 1912) published her statement denying that the league had any knowledge of the English women or connection with them. "Beyond unity of demand," Cousins explains, her organization had no association with English suffrage groups (quoted in Levenson and Natterstad 42).

TEXTUAL GAPS AND THE CONSTRUCTION OF THE SELF

In their article "De/Colonization and the Politics of Discourse in Women's Autobiographical Practices," Sidonie Smith and Julia Watson historicize western autobiographical practices, noting that the "Enlightenment 'self' [generally male] sees its destiny in a teleological narrative" that foregrounds the " 'individual' and 'his' uniqueness" (xvii). The male subject of these accounts, Smith and Watson argue, produces a politics which is simultaneously one of "centripetal consolidation and centrifugal domination" (xvii). The process of construction in the West results in a coherent, self-actualized subject that often derives "his" legitimacy and impulse toward self-representation from "a specific history of privilege" based on an elite economic, gender, cultural, national, and religious identity (Smith and Watson xvii).

Shifting the autobiographical subject from the colonial to the native does not necessarily dislocate these dominant narrative paradigms. Given that decolonization is always a complex, multifaceted process, involving both the deformation and reformation of identity, the autobiographical production of natives can become the site for ideological contradictions and contestations, as the native subject rehearses narrative representational paradigms from the metropole. Smith and Watson elucidate:

> Entry into the territory of traditional autobiography implicates the speaker in a potentially recuperative performance, one that might reproduce and re/present the colonizer's figure in negation. For to write 'autobiography' is partially to enter into the contractual and discursive domain of universal "Man," whom Rey Chow calls the 'dominating subject.' Entering the terrain of autobiography, the colonized subject can get stuck in "his meaning." The processes of self-decolonization may get bogged down as the autobiographical subject reframes herself through neocolonizing metaphors. (xix)

While Cousins resists the construction of feminist individualism through the discursive modalities identified by Spivak as "companionate love" and "social mission," her narrative bears the traces of the western autobiographical tradition. Estelle C. Jelinek offers a gendered reading of western autobiography, anticipating Rey Chow's work, in her claim that male writers represent their lives in idealized terms which enable them to project their narratives and experiences as universal (14). Such narratives are characterized by the male subject's tendency to exaggerate, mythologize, and monumentalize his adventures. These aspects of the self-representation of western male subjectivity are evident in the ideology of feminist-nationalist individualism, and in Cousins's construction of herself as the primary agent behind the Irish suffrage movement, particularly in its more militant window-shattering and hunger strike phase, without recognizing the crucial contribution of Hanna Sheehy-Skeffington.

The significant gaps in Cousins's narrative of the Irish suffrage movement cohere around her failure to mention Sheehy-Skeffington's activities, which also included breaking windows, being imprisoned, and going on a hunger strike. Together, these lacunae constitute Cousins as the prototypical suffragette subject who was one of the earliest to embark on the militant path. For example, Cousins narrated how she and two other suffragettes shattered the windows of Dublin Castle by banging them with lead-tipped umbrellas on January 28, 1913, to protest the second reading of the Liberal Home Rule Bill of 1912, which excluded women's franchise (*We Two Together* 188). Sentenced to a one-month prison term as a result of her protest, Cousins credited herself as being one of "the first women prisoners [to go to jail] on behalf of women's demands for their sex in a Home Rule setting" (188). Yet Sheehy-Skeffington had earned this distinction eight months before, on June 13, 1912, as part of an IWFL contingent which had broken the windows of the General Post Office, the Customs House, the Land Commission Office, and the Ship Street Barracks (Levenson and Natterstad 37). While serving the last week of her prison sentence in July of that year in Mount-joy, Sheehy-Skeffington had gone on a hunger strike to show her solidarity with Mary Leigh and Gladys Evans, who were given harsh sentences for their role in the events surrounding Asquith's visit.[13] Claiming that the "hunger-strike was then a new weapon," Sheehy-Skeffington applauded IWFL members for being "the first to try it out in Ireland" (Sheehy-Skeffington and Owens 23). While the hunger strike had its origins in Celtic Ireland, the suffragettes reintroduced it to modern Ireland as a political weapon.[14] Cousins, however, neglected to mention Sheehy-Skeffington's imprisonment or hunger strike, though her own experiences are recounted in great detail.[15]

Cousins's memories of militant suffrage activism were subject to ideological processes which inflated her own importance, marginalized the contributions of other suffragettes, and exaggerated some incidents while minimizing or suppressing others. Her account of window breaking, imprisonment, and hunger strikes cast these actions as central to the Irish nationalist and suffrage movements, whose political significance echoed throughout the Empire. Though Sheehy-Skeffington had preceded her by eight months, Cousins's description of shattering the windows of Dublin Castle and of her arrest defines these events as originary moments in the Irish suffrage movement and anti-colonial movements internationally:

It appeared to us to be necessary that some extreme militant action should be carried out which would assure world-wide publicity of our protest against the exclusion of women from the Bill. Three of us volunteered to break the windows of Dublin Castle, the official seat of English domination. The sound of breaking glass on January 28, 1913, reverberated round the world and did what we wanted. It told the world that Irish women protested against an imperfect and un-democratic Home Rule Bill. We (Mrs. Connery, Mrs. Hoskins and myself) were marched from the Castle to College Street police sta-tion, next door to the Vegetarian Restaurant, each between two po-licemen who, at our request, did not hold our arms or handcuff us, but allowed us to walk freely as they accepted our word that we would not try to escape. We were the first women prisoners on behalf of women's demands for their sex in a Home Rule setting. It was some-thing new to Ireland. (188)

The women's protest, in Cousins's estimation, signals the entry of Irish activism into political modernity. Writing her story in the forties, after Irish women had gained the franchise and male nationalists like Terence MacSwiney had adopted the hunger strike as a political weapon, Cousins could lay claim to helping establish a modern Irish political tradition. The belated nature of traditional autobiographical practice, in which the subject reflects on the significance of past experiences from the perspec-tive of her present-writing self, facilitates the scripting of such an origi-nary narrative of protest and activism.

To legitimize her claim that militant suffrage activism initiated a modern epoch of protest, Cousins had to represent her organizing ef-forts as extraordinary. She attributed her skills in organizing to her physical, emotional, and social makeup. Her construction of herself as the activist subject par excellence emphasizes her physical stamina, her strong work ethic, and her courage:

I was born with an extra store of physical energy, a strong constitu-tion, ability to sleep soundly anywhere, to digest almost anything, and hardly to know headache or toothache. I possessed unending natural curiosity to know as much as I could about everything and everybody around me. . . . I always wanted to change things into better shape. I was always ready to be a pioneer in making the change. I liked men. I liked women. I liked people in groups. I even enjoyed crowds. It was natural for me to give myself out fully in the service of anything in which I was interested. I never shirked hard work. I never asked any co-worker to do more or other than I was myself ready to do. . . . As for mental equipment: I always thank my stars for my natural courage. Adventure on all planes called to me, possibly because I hardly knew fear. . . . Danger, the unknown, a test, an examination, a trial, a fight, have always stimulated me and raised my coefficient of capacity. (53)

The love of change, people, hard work, adventure, combined with a robust constitution and abundant courage, are offered here as Cousins's meta-explanation for her agency. The originary impulse behind her activism, in other words, is represented as a natural—indeed, biological—effect of her temperament. In her opinion, these natural attributes are augmented by good writing skills and extensive activist experience, dating back to her formative teenage years:

I always had ease in writing letters and in putting ideas on paper. I began being a secretary when I was thirteen, and continued the service to society after society till, at sixty, I was elected President of the All-India Women's Conference, which I had created a decade previously. The thankless job of collecting funds for philanthropic causes has dogged my footsteps. It has been my good luck always to be a voluntary worker for such causes; which was well, as my impersonal enthusiasm for work made me its servant, not any self-interest like monetary necessity or personal ambition. (53–54)

A profound sense of democracy informs Cousins's activism and her engagement with social movements. "I had the lucky heritage of being at home with anybody anywhere, from royalty to scavenger, from duchess to dustman," she declared, "I am fundamentally aware of our equal human-ness" (54). A commitment to humanism, rather than the desire for financial gain or personal fame, Cousins insisted, propelled and sustained her participation in social movements.

The disavowal of "personal ambition" here, in the larger context of the narrative gaps regarding Hanna Sheehy-Skeffington's contributions to the Irish suffrage movement, demonstrates how feminist-nationalist individualism permeates even the most self-conscious accounts of activism and agency. In Cousins's narrative, the subject is constituted and in-

terpellated as individualist, to paraphrase Spivak, on the basis of a discursive absence of suffragette competitors, such as Sheehy-Skeffington,
cathected as a self who becomes the source of Irish activism's matura-
tion into modernity.

FROM POTATO MISSILES TO HUNGER STRIKES

In her seminal study of writing and organized national liberation movements, *Resistance Literature*, Barbara Harlow distinguishes prison memoirs from conventional autobiography, arguing that prison memoirs
"are actively engaged in a re-definition of the self and the individual in
terms of a collective enterprise and struggle" (120). "The prison memoirs of political detainees are not written for the sake of a 'book of one's
own,'" she notes, "rather they are collective documents, testimonies
written by individuals to their common struggle" (120).[16] *We Two Together*
records Margaret Cousins's experiences of prison in England and Ireland, where she served one-month sentences in both Holloway and
Tullamore Jails. Her reactions to detention contrast remarkably with one
another: the differential rendering of her prison experiences is enacted
on the registers of the individual and collective. The trope of the individual, figured as the isolated subject of penal discipline, permeates
Cousins's account of her incarceration in Holloway Jail. At Tullamore Jail
in her native Ireland, however, the suffrage collectivity emerges as the
primary unit of subjectivity and she represents her detention in literary-
history terms very similar to those theorized by Harlow as paradigmatic
of prison memoirs.

If feminist-nationalist individualism poses a challenge to collectivity
through its imposition of a historiographical paradigm that reduces
certain insurgent practices to individual founding figures, its far more
devastating consequences, as Cousins's account of Holloway demonstrates, can be the outright dismantling of the individual's identification
with the collective altogether. From this vantage, Cousins's subsequent
emphatic emphasis on collectivity—her refusal to individuate the historical record in her account of Tullamore—might be read as the dialectical
response to her experiences in Holloway, where feminist-nationalist individualism is traumatically recoded for Cousins as isolation and aliena-
tion from Irish and British suffrage organizations.

Along with six other members of the IWFL, Cousins had traveled to

London in November 1910 to participate in a deputation to the prime minister, four hundred women strong, organized by the Women's Social and Political Union. The suffragettes sustained injuries from the police in their unsuccessful attempts to gain an interview with the prime minister. Organizers then decided to break the windows of the houses of cabinet ministers in protest. The Irish contingent descended on the home of Augustine Birrell, chief secretary for Ireland. Armed with potato "missiles" purchased on the way to Birrell's residence, the women launched these at all the windows within their reach (We Two Together 177). Since they were able to accomplish their mission without getting arrested, the Irish suffragettes decided "to carry on the fight" the next night by breaking the well-guarded windows of Asquith and Lloyd George, which had remained intact during the previous night's offensive. They successfully broke Lloyd George's windows at 10 Downing Street with shards of a broken flower pot (We Two Together 178). As a result of this action, Cousins was sentenced to her first monthlong prison term, which she served in Holloway Jail.

Cousins's account of her experiences at Holloway illustrates one of the primary limitations of feminist-nationalist individualism in its ability to undermine collective modes of social organization by disarticulating the individual subject from a group affiliation. This aspect of feminist-nationalist individualism is evident in Cousins's account of her incarceration at Holloway and demonstrates the "essentially conservative mode" of narration inherent in autobiography, which, according to John Beverley, shows that "individual triumph over circumstances is possible in spite of 'obstacles' " (23). In outlining the daily routine and the physical details of prison life, Cousins represents herself as a subject in isolation, who is disciplined by the prison apparatus:

> My memories of that month sum themselves up as a species of living death because of the solitariness of the confinement. My watch had been taken from me as well as all trinkets. We could not hear any bells or clocks sounding from outside, and the arrival of three meals (pushed through a locked aperture) as the only means of knowing the time of day was one of my chief trials. The heat of the cell from hot-water pipes was suffocating. To obtain relief and ventilation we broke the window panes with the heels of our shoes. The pillow was so hard that it turned up my ears, so I stuffed it with a thick petticoat. As a

vegetarian I was given an extra quantity of milk at each meal, no tea or coffee for the month, a piece of a kind of brown bread at each meal; and vegetables were limited in kind: the only cutlery was a blunt tin knife and a spoon, no fork. We were allowed any number of "improving" books sent in by friends. I read Buck's "Cosmic Consciousness," Swedenborg's "Heaven and Hell," all Vivekananda's books (sent in by Lady Sybil Smith), re-read Anna Kingsford's "Clothed with the Sun," More's "Utopia." I used to get very tired of reading, and my safety-valve was in embroidering a table-centre the materials for which I had pushed into my suitcase as an after-thought at the last minute of packing at home. No writing materials were allowed. There was a short church service daily which each prisoner was expected to attend. I always went because I could see my companions then, though no conversation was possible. I deeply rebelled against the spy-hole in the locked door, and felt degraded by being known and spoken to only as a number. The daily hour of exercise was spent in walking behind one another in complete silence round and round a narrow path in a high-walled enclosure. (*We Two Together* 180–81)

Cousins's narrative of Holloway illustrates how prison, as a repressive state apparatus, attempts to prevent organized dissent within its walls by subjecting prisoners to regimentation, surveillance, and solitary confinement. These tactics were effective in thwarting a collective response to prison conditions by the suffragettes. For Cousins prison becomes a series of physical hardships that must be individually overcome (as in the too-hard pillow) or endured (as in the diet). While Cousins singles out her sense of temporal disorientation resulting from the confiscation of her watch by prison authorities, she does not seem to recognize alternative methods of tracking time, rooted in the communal experiences of mealtimes, the church sessions, and the common exercise hour. Although she uses the pronoun "we" throughout her description, she neither grants her fellow prisoners any individual subjectivity, nor ascribes to them any collective agency. From her account, the suffragettes did not establish covert ways of communication with one another, a prerequisite for the development of a collective response to resist prison conditions.

Apparently the disciplinary mechanisms of the prison apparatus were successful in disarticulating the imprisoned suffragettes from collective action. Detained because of their ability to organize collective opposition to state electoral policies, the suffragettes, according to Cousins, understood themselves as the isolated subjects of incarceration. She summed up her prison experiences with the terse statement, "One loses one's power of will and initiative in incarceration" (*We Two Together* 181). The apparent perception of the loss of political agency, in this instance, might also be a function of geography. At Holloway jail, IWFL members were separated from their Irish support networks, family and organizational. Indeed, the Irish women had to rely on the material and psychological support of the Women's Social and Political Union, of whose internal dynamics they had little knowledge. The absence of sympathetic family members on the outside to raise public awareness of their imprisonment, along with the difficulty in communicating with the central league office, which could have issued them directives, increased the isolation of the Irish prisoners.

Cousins's account of her one-month incarceration in Tullamore Jail, in Ireland, in January and February 1913, can be read as a dialectical response to her experiences at Holloway inasmuch as it emphasizes the collective nature of the prisoners' refusal to submit to the objectification and discipline of the prison apparatus. From the initial one-night incarceration in Mountjoy Jail, which preceded their transfer to Tullamore, Cousins and her companions actively resisted the prison authorities' attempts to regiment them by refusing to be searched, to disrobe, or to give their thumbprints (*We Two Together* 189). Continuing this spirit of defiance while in Tullamore Jail, the suffragettes developed successful strategies to change their classification from common criminals to that of political prisoners. They declared their intention to go on a hunger strike for political status during their court trial and decided to give the authorities a week to comply with their demands. Though the women had not formally been accorded political status, the prison authorities at Tullamore treated them with respect, addressing them by name rather than number, and housing them within separate rooms in the jail hospital. Other comforts included a fireplace in each room, an "iron bedstead, clean warm bed-clothes, a chair, a table, a writing slate and pencil, some 'moral' books, eatable food of a poor kind, and the right of association in labour and exercise" (190). In addition, the prisoners were allowed to wear their own clothes instead of prison uniforms. James Cousins reported that the chairman of the Prisons Board told him, "The prisoners were having all the facilities of political prisoners but it was not announced" (209). The chairman added, "We have to cod [sic] the public" (209). The middle-class status rather than the political status of the suffragettes, however, probably explains the privileges they received, which were not ordinarily granted to prisoners classified as "common criminals."[17] These privileges enabled the prisoners to keep physically fit, maintain their morale, and organize their strike during the common work and exercise period. "We enjoyed one another's company," Cousins said, "and worked up courage to face the possible fast" (190).

While the suffragettes went on hunger strike they continued to drink water. The prison authorities, aided by male doctors, monitored the prisoners' physical condition by routinely weighing them, testing their blood and urine, and analyzing their vomit (Murphy 103). In their reports on the hunger strike, these officials dwelt on the psychology of the suffragettes, emphasizing their mental "abnormality," and trivialized the protest by reducing it to a weight-loss plan. J. Stewart, a medical officer for many of the women prisoners, for instance, characterized Madge Muir's "mental condition" as "not normal[,] she is given to lying. . . . She is most abusive (to me at least without any cause) she is at times sulky and reticent and before committal it is alleged that she was partly attired in male clothes" (quoted in Murphy 103). Psychological normality, for Stewart, as the rumor about Muir's cross dressing reveals, is crucially linked to his understanding of normative gender behavior. Muir's rumored clothing choices are presented as a kind of sartorial duplicitousness that parallels her tendency toward deceitfulness and lying. Together these different forms of deception, for Stewart, signify a larger deception which centers on Muir's refusal to conform to her proper gender identity. The state authorities additionally trivialized the women's political protest by casting the hunger strike as physiologically beneficial for the heavier suffragettes. Describing the physical effects of the hunger strike on the women, the governor of Tullamore wrote: "The statement that Mrs Ryan lost a full stone in weight is grossly exaggerated. She lost 4 lbs, Mrs Walsh 6 . . . . Mrs Palmer 1 1/2. . . . Before the hungerstrike Mrs Palmer was getting quite fat" (quoted in Murphy 103).

The suffragettes' campaign for political status was not tightly coordinated between those inside and outside the prison. Because the suffragettes were only allowed visits from "spiritual advisers" who "were not permitted to give any outside information or to take any" news out of prison, communication between the prisoners and their supporters consisted of informational updates coded as prayers. According to Cousins, one innovative clergyman circumvented the restriction against communication by strictly following the letter of the law, if not its spirit:

> On his first visit to me, when we were famishing to know what steps our friends were taking to get our status made right, he was as tight as an oyster. I knew he was full of news and I was frantic to get at it. But he was loyal to his duty. Before leaving me, after a short empty conversation, he exercised his right to pray with me; and what he could not tell me he could, without restriction, tell to "God!" His prayer was something like the following: "O God! bless the efforts that are being made by the friends of these noble women to secure them honourable status or release; and influence the Lord Lieutenant to grant the request that has been made in the widely signed memorial to His Excellency." (*We Two Together* 190–91)

Having informed the suffragettes of efforts made on their behalf outside of prison, it remained for the priest to tell the public that the prisoners had gone on a hunger strike. He communicated this message through code, relying on the Bible to convey the information. A mysterious letter along with a telegram received by James Cousins confirmed public rumors of the hunger strike:

> "I have just received the enclosed. The only meaning I can take out of it is that the hunger strike has been begun and that this (Wednesday) is the third day. Sorry if I am correct." The enclosure was a telegram from which the office of origin and names of sender and addressee were carefully obliterated, and passed on the letter's suggestion of hunger strike. The wire said:

MATTHEW SIX SIXTEEN AND GENESIS ONE THIRTEEN PASS ON.

Obviously it was a code covering a secret. A Bible was dug out and I turned up the texts given, with the following result:

MOREOVER, WHEN YE FAST, BE NOT AS THE HYPOCRITES, OF A SAD COUNTENANCE. AND THE EVENING AND THE MORNING WERE THE THIRD DAY

The crucial words were "fast" and "third day." I got in touch as quickly as possible with Skeffy, and, since he was a born news-vendor, the press of the world knew next day that the three suffragettes in Tullamore Jail in which men prisoners for the cause of Irish freedom had won the rights of politicals, had gone on hunger strike on February 3, since no response had been received to the petition to the Lord Lieutenant. (210–11)

The efficacy of political protest depends in part on public knowledge of it and thoughtful media coverage of the relevant issues. Knowledge of the suffragettes' hunger strike was disseminated through a loose network of associations which included the church and the press. As Louis Althusser notes, both the church and the press have functioned in bourgeois capitalist formations to uphold the authority of the state by acting as the ideological state apparatuses through which hegemony is materialized. In Althusser's model, resistance is localized within such formations: while these formations rely on ideological state apparatuses to insure the consent of the population and on repressive state apparatuses to discipline challenges to the state through the use of force, at the individual level discrete figures struggle within the constraints imposed on them by their institutional settings. The priest's role in disseminating the information of the protest, along with the coding of news of the suffragettes' hunger strike in biblical allusions, illustrate how ideological state apparatuses like the church can be sites of localized, individual resistance to the state. Armed with news of the strike, the Irish Citizen launched a discursive assault on the intransigence of prison authorities regarding their refusal to grant the women political status and rallied public support around the suffragettes.

The public show of support for the suffragettes contributed to the success of their hunger strike, which gained them political status after a week of protest. Perhaps it is because this protest was successful that Cousins's narrative of her Tullamore incarceration emphasizes the collective agency of the suffragettes. The differential treatment of political agency in accounts of her prison experiences in Holloway and Tullamore Jails—cast as individual endurance in the British setting and collective resistance in the Irish one—suggests that her strategies for resisting the disciplinary prison regime at Tullamore were a dialectical response to the political paralysis that she experienced at Holloway. The collective resistance of the suffragettes at Tullamore was certainly facilitated by solidarity work carried out by those outside the prison apparatus, even if only through informal associations, demonstrating that human rights activism on behalf of political prisoners can be crucial to the morale of prisoners and the success of their protest of prison conditions.

COUSINS'S THEORY OF WITNESSING

Several months after her release from Tullamore Jail on February 27, 1913, Margaret Cousins embarked on a journey that would take her to Liverpool and eventually to India. The Cousinses' abrupt departure from Ireland on June 2, 1913, at a time when the suffragette, home rule, and labor movements were rapidly gaining momentum, helps explain how their part in the Irish women's movement slipped into obscurity. The dramatic series of events launched by the Easter Rising of 1916, culminating in partition and civil war, eclipsed the earlier work of Margaret Cousins which had contributed to those efforts. Cousins had participated in a movement which provided models of militancy to Irish nationalists, according to Margaret MacCurtain (*Mother Ireland*). She had helped build a movement that would achieve universal adult suffrage in the Free State Constitution of 1922 for all men and women over twenty-one years of age.

Cousins's narrative of the IWFL's formation and activities bridges the gap between theory and practice by providing a series of entertaining anecdotes which intersperse the IWFL's goals with basic information on how actions were carried out. It is worth noting that some of this information can still be useful to activists today. For example, in one instance Cousins explains that the cost of publicizing events or meetings was greatly reduced by substituting chalked messages on sidewalks for printed notices. While Cousins's account of the Irish suffrage movement casts her as its primary originator, her account of the Indian women's movement is strikingly different in its narrative features and in the secondary role that it assigns to her contributions to that movement. The sections on Indian women's suffrage in *We Two Together* never achieve the dramatic intensity of those on Ireland. Although this might be explained by two factors—Cousins's dual authorship with her husband, and the nonmilitant nature of the Women's Indian Association and the All India Women's Conference, both of which restricted themselves to socially acceptable activities such as lobbying politicians, writing articles, and speaking at sanctioned events—I will argue that Cousins's complex understanding of historiography and historical agency more decisively explains her differential treatment of the Indian women's movement.[18] It is this understanding which enabled her to develop a sophisticated theory of witnessing that labored to recognize Indian women as political agents, capable of making and recording their struggle against colonialism and patriarchy.

By the early 1940s Cousins had concluded that regardless of her desire to take part in what she termed "the struggle against such foreign imbecility" in India, she should refrain from doing so. "I had the feeling that direct participation by me was no longer required," she noted, "or even desired, by the leaders of Indian womanhood who were now coming to the front for some national service that was not far below the horizon" (*We Two Together* 740). At this juncture, with the Quit India movement gaining momentum, Cousins's decision implicitly acknowledges two points: first, that as part of the old guard, she had to make way for a younger generation of women; and second, that the struggle for national liberation had to be fought by Indians alone. We may question the wisdom of the latter formulation, given that struggles have many fronts and given the important role that solidarity groups have played at other times, for example in pressing for sanctions against South Africa under apartheid, or in preventing an outright invasion of the stalwart nation of Nicaragua by the United States during the Sandinista era. But in the context of Cousins's times, her recognition that her efforts could be construed as an orientalist form of activism is quite remarkable, as is her willingness to play down her contributions to the movement to clear a discursive space for Indian activists. Her willingness to narrate herself as peripheral to the Indian women's movement significantly differs from the central role that she accorded herself in the Irish suffrage movement in relation to Sheehy-Skeffington.

In her later years, Cousins felt that her contribution to the struggles for Indian independence and Indian women's rights would better take the form of writing. In the preface to her *Indian Womanhood Today*, published in 1941, she elaborates a theory of "witnessing." Describing her hesitation to revise and republish *The Awakening of Asian Womanhood* (1923), Cousins noted:

For the very passage of time had brought my Indian sisters into publicity as their own historians, and I cannot hope to give a more comprehensive view of the Indian women's movement to solve its problems than have the 30 women leaders all of Indian birth in Kitabistan's former informative publication "Our Cause," edited by Shyam Kumari Nehru. But when the old saying "Spectators see most of the game" kept popping into my mind I realised that the circumstances of the first half of my life might have their own value in giving weight to evidence of the unbelievably rapid emergence of India's women of all castes and communities into the positions of honour they now hold, albeit the masses are still in the darkness of illiteracy, child marriage, poverty, and political subjection to a foreign race and government. I know only too well the "vague and ignorant thinking" which generally prevails in India and in other countries about the high character and inherent ability of the women of India as well as about their chains of out-of-date customs, and I saw that it was my duty as well as my privilege to add this service of "witness" to whatever else I may have been permitted to do in my identification of my life in India with that of my Indian sisters, who have given me such affection, and from whom I have learnt so much of the Values of the Eternal. (6–7)

Cousins's opening contains echoes of the colonial paradigm of casting natives as children who will eventually mature to the responsibilities of self-government, given enough time, under the benevolent guidance of the colonial patriarchy. But her use of the term "sister" to describe her relationship to Indian women distances her from the colonial paradigm based as it was on the parent-child metaphor. For Cousins, writing allows movements to accomplish two things: first, to engage in self-critique, and second, to persuade nonparticipants of the justice of the cause. In this passage, the functions are further distinguished on the basis of "national origin." Indian activists are to produce the movement's self-criticism, while non-Indians are to assume the task of educating an international public. Cousins leaves Shyam Kumari Nehru's "Our Cause" to fulfill the first function, describing this text "as a comprehensive view of the Indian women's movement *to solve its problems*" (*Indian Womanhood Today* 6; emphasis mine). For herself, Cousins visualizes the role of a witness who can explain the movement to the unconverted.

As delineated by Cousins, these functions follow different trajectories. Writing produced by Indian women is directed at activists within the movement to work out ideological and tactical differences. Writing produced by "witnesses," Western women like Cousins (the qualification "like" is important), is directed at outsiders—in India and abroad—who must be persuaded to champion the movement's agenda. The Western background of the witness, as the result of the unfortunate pervasiveness of racist colonial ideology, grants her text a legitimacy with Western audiences that a text by an Indian counterpart would not have. Margaret's racial and national identity legitimated her authority, much as James's gender identity and nationalist sympathies legitimated his account of the Irish suffrage movement. Indeed, *Indian Womanhood Today* is written for Western consumption; numerous details of women in other countries establish a comparative framework for western readers. For instance, challenging English and American claims that Indians are unfit for self-government on the basis of how they treat their women, Cousins notes:

> Only those who are entirely ignorant can bring up these arguments since the General Election of February 1937, in India, which brought over eighty Indian women into the expanded legislatures. To-day women's political position gives India the second place in the world for the number of women elected to the legislatures of the countries—the United States of America being first, with one hundred and forty eight in its State legislatures and two in its Senate. It is true that about 130 women are in political power in Russia, but the Constitution of that country is so different from all others and so unique in its attitude to women that it may be treated as an exception; and thus India is seen as second in world rank. (78–79)

Her preface specifically identifies her audience as a Western one. "Such a varied life has given us a wealth of friendship and experiences as rarely falls to Westerners in this land," Cousins declared, "and in this book I shall strive to share my blessings with readers whose circumstances have not given them the first-hand material by which to clarify their thinking and evaluate the present condition of the Indian women's movement and its probable lines of future development" (9).

Though Cousins allows Western women to play the role of witness, she does not authorize all of them to take on this "privilege." Rather they must be qualified, like her, to speak on Indian themes. Her own background, Cousins believed, makes her well suited to the duty of witnessing:

> The circumstances of my birth in Western Ireland of Protestant Unionist parents, though I myself became convinced of the justice and necessity of Home Rule for Ireland even if it in effect transferred power to Roman Catholic hands; the first half of my life being spent in Ireland in the forefront of causes of Freedom and Culture—Music, Poetry, the Irish Literary Theatre, the Home Rule Movement, and intensively in the last ten years there, the Woman Suffrage Movement, filling the early married life of Dr. Cousins and myself, all caused me to come to India twenty-five years ago peculiarly well equipped to attune myself with the conditions of India. . . . Being Irish, in India neither as a Christian missionary, nor as a British Government servant, nor for any political propaganda, and having already studied and gained much from Indian philosophies—Vedic, Buddhist, and Islamic,—it was easy for me to evaluate strong and weak points in present-day contemporary Indian civilisation. (7–8)

In this passage, Cousins delineates a number of qualifications that authorize her to bear witness: her Irish background, which gives her firsthand knowledge of English colonial oppression; many years of experience as an activist in Ireland; a long familiarity with India based on twenty-five years of residence in the country; no formal affiliations with any ideological state apparatuses such as the government or church; and her having been a student of Indian culture.

Cousins established these five criteria in response to Katherine Mayo, who was a U.S. citizen, and the publication of her scurrilous meditation on the status of Indian women, *Mother India*. Mayo was a pro-imperialist feminist whose earlier work *Isles of Fear* argued that the United States should not give up the Philippines. In *Mother India*, first published in May 1927, Mayo continued her pro-imperialist diatribe, insisting that the poor treatment of Indian women justified continuing British intervention in Indian affairs. In Mayo's text, reprinted five times by the end of August 1927, she blamed all of India's "material and spiritual" problems—such as "poverty, sickness, ignorance, political minority, melancholy, ineffectiveness [and] a subconscious sense of inferiority"—on the Indian male's "manner of getting into the world and his sex-life thenceforward" (22). Locating the sexual pathology of Indian men as the origin of wide-scale poverty on the subcontinent, Mayo ignored the ways in which the colonial economy systematically underdeveloped the region. She also went on to document the devastating effect of child marriage on Indian females.

The book provided the British with moral fodder for their denial of Indian self-rule. In London the *New Statesman and Nation* wrote that *Mother India* demonstrated "the filthy personal habits of even the most highly educated classes in India—which, like the degradation of Hindu women, are unequalled even among the most primitive African or Australian savages" (quoted in Joshi and Liddle 31). The article ended on a moralistic note: "Katherine Mayo makes the claim for swaraj (self-rule) seem nonsense and the will to grant it almost a crime" (quoted in Joshi and Liddle 31). As Uma Chakravarti asserts, colonial ideology often makes the status of native women into a signifier of cultural depravity; "[t]he 'higher' morality of the imperial masters could be effectively established by highlighting the low status of women among the subject population," she explains, "as it was an issue by which the moral 'inferiority' of the subject population could simultaneously be demonstrated" (34).

Cousins herself undertook a lecture tour in the United States to refute the "exaggerations" of Mayo's text, which had done, in her estimate, a "disservice" to India (*Indian Womanhood Today* 134). Cousins stated indignantly: "I had the privilege myself of speaking in thirty-four large American cities in 1929 refuting from my own intimate knowledge of Indian life and conditions the untrue generalizations [Mayo] made against the Indian people which sensation-mongers lapped up as gospel truth, when instead it was insidious poison" (134–35). The five criteria for witnessing, laid out by Cousins would, Cousins hoped, make superficial analysis like Mayo's impossible to replicate.

As demonstrated by her criteria for witnessing, Cousins conceived of identity in broader terms than those based on the experiential filiative register of her Protestant Unionist background. Her analysis of the British colonial formation in Ireland, as well as her long engagement with activism, positioned her to develop modes of solidarity with the Indian women's struggle that did not replicate the dominant paradigms of Western social reform which constructed the native as the passive object of British benevolence. Rather than impose the text of colonial femininity onto Indian women, Cousins accorded political agency to native women, recognizing that they could record their own struggles. Her writing on the Indian women's movement was formulated as an expression of solidarity with Indian women. In contrast to her presentation of self and the ideology of feminist-nationalist individualism in her narrative of the Irish suffrage movement, in which she identifies her activism as inaugurating a modern era of Irish activism, Cousins narrated her participation in the WIA and AIWC as marginal to the success of the Indian women's movement.

In spite of her attempts to underemphasize her role in the Indian women's movement by representing her efforts as purely discursive in relation to Indian women's activism, Cousins's contributions to the movement are legible in the very pages of her solidarity accounts. For example, the Indian publishers of her *The Awakening of Asian Womanhood* (1922) had this to say about the difficulty of extracting a manuscript from her: "The makers of history have no time to be writers of it—till afterwards. The author of this book is so busily engaged in one department of history-making in India that it has taken the publishers two years to get the materials for it from her" (*Awakening* v). Cousins's duties as the joint secretary of the WIA and editor of its print organ *Stri Dharma* show the artificiality of her dichotomy between the roles of Western witness and Indian activist. Her book consists of articles previously published in the *Times of India, New India, Stri Dharma, Tomorrow,* and *Britain and India.* Her publishers explained the origins of the articles in this manner: "The contents of this book have come into existence, not as cold reminiscent history, but as living and immediate despatches in the form of newspaper and magazine articles written during the campaign in India for the bringing of the direct power of women into all departments of public life" (*Awakening* v–vi). As the publisher's note makes clear, participating in the movement for Indian women's suffrage included, for Margaret Cousins, writing on its behalf.[19]

ORGANIZING IN INDIA: THE WIA AND THE AIWC

Notwithstanding Cousins's attempts to narrate her participation in the Indian women's movement as peripheral to it, her initiative in organizing a series of "tea-parties" is what resulted in the formation of the WIA. As the origins of the WIA within a middle-class society milieu might suggest, the ideology of the WIA and its offshoot, the AIWC, tended toward gender, religious, and class conservatism. Both organizations subscribed to the social space distinction that Partha Chatterjee identifies as the "inner" and "outer," "*ghar* and *bahir*, the home and the world" ("Nationalist Resolution" 238). This division of social space was gendered insofar as the first term of each pair was associated with the spiritual domain of women, the second term with the "profane activities of the material world" figured as the "domain" of men (238–39). Moreover, the discourse of religiosity attached to the domain of women, within the home and ghar, was itself overdetermined by an idiom of Hinduism through the invocation of a "golden age" of gender relations during the Vedic period. That the conceptual parameters of the WIA and AIWC were circumscribed by a restricted logic of gender and religious identity indicates the bourgeois ideology of both groups and their inability to theorize the gendered subject as other than middle-class.

The "tea-parties" organized by Cousins evolved into the Abala Abhivardini Samaj (Weaker Sex Improvement Society), "an inferiority title that took" her "some time to get used to" (*We Two Together* 299). The Samaj confined its activities to "ladies' afternoon classes" in English, badminton, and rattan weaving, a craft picked up by the enterprising Cousins on a visit to Burma (*We Two Together* 299–300; Forbes, "From Purdah to Politics" 223). Eventually in 1917, the organization merged with a Tamil Women's Association to become the Women's Indian Association (Forbes, "Caged Tigers" 528). According to Kamalabai L. Rau, another founding member of the WIA, the organization sought to educate women by making them "conscious of their place in the growing society of the land" (quoted in Forbes, "Caged Tigers" 528). Another founder of the WIA, Dorothy Jinarajadasa, used the network of Theosophical lodges, to which she and Cousins belonged, to organize branches of the WIA.[20] The central office in Madras had specific responsibilities in four areas: establishing institutions, educational work, data collection, and petitioning. Boasting an office and library staffed by a secretary, the headquarters in Madras was willing to open orphanages and shelters, provided that local branches would take over the administration of these institutions (Forbes, "From Purdah to Politics" 227). Tracing the growth of the WIA, Geraldine Forbes writes: "From the small beginning, local organizations began to discuss and pass resolutions on topics such as votes for women, prevention of child marriage, and inheritance rights for women. These demands were then presented to the appropriate officials in the government" ("Caged Tigers" 528). Consciousness raising and lobbying became the twin foci of the WIA. Stri Dharma, under Cousins's editorship, publicized these activities and debates within the WIA, becoming an important link between the local branches of the organization.

A series of articles published in the pages of Stri Dharma led to the formation of the All India Women's Conference (AIWC) in 1927. A. L. Huidekoper, another Irish woman who had been a teacher at Bethune College, wrote some articles calling on women to respond to E. F. Oaten's challenge delivered to a prize-giving ceremony at the college in early 1926. The director of public instruction of Bengal, Oaten had urged women to speak their mind on education, saying:

> You have asserted yourselves in the field of politics. How long is it before you assert yourselves in the field of secondary and higher education? How long are you going to tolerate a man-made syllabus, a man-made system, a man-made examination and a controlling authority in which women have no influence as the dominating arbiter of your educational destinies? . . . We must have the cooperation of women to help us remedy what is wrong in women's education. I would urge that women who alone can help us adequately, should tell us with one voice what they want and keep on telling us till they get it.
> (quoted in Basu and Ray 4)

In response to Oaten's challenge, Cousins sent out an appeal to women to formulate their educational demands. Unlike the Irish Women's Franchise League which had a top-down structure, the AIWC as conceived by Cousins was more of a grassroots organization. Believing that women's educational needs varied across the subcontinent, she called on women to organize at the local level, with the idea of devising local solutions to educational problems. Each of these local conferences was to send several delegates to the All India Women's Conference, where the delegates would collectively synthesize local proceedings and arrive at "an authoritative and representative memorandum by women on educational reform which would be published widely and sent to all Indian educational authorities" (quoted in Basu and Ray 5).

Fifty-eight delegates representing twenty-two constituent conferences, along with two thousand spectators, assembled at Fergusson College in Poona for the AIWC's first session in 1927 (We Two Together

448; Basu and Ray 7). The delegates passed a series of resolutions on education, defining it in broad terms "as training which will enable the child and the individual to develop his or her capacities to their fullest extent for the service of humanity" (*We Two Together* 448–49). This definition led the delegates to consider the "physical, mental, emotional, civic and spiritual development" of children in their formulations of suggestions (449). They drafted resolutions on school curriculum, the need for compulsory primary education and compulsory medical exams, a demand to establish schools for the disabled, and a call for the use of the vernacular as the medium of instruction.[21] Resolutions targeted especially toward women's education demanded that the age of consent be raised to sixteen and that the government create facilities for girls in purdah. The conference also supported a resolution recommending that all girls' education should emphasize the ideals of motherhood, the making of a beautiful home, and training in social work (*We Two Together* 449; Basu and Ray 8).

The latter resolutions, aimed specifically at women's education, reveal the social space distinction of ghar and bahir, the home and the world, that underwrote the AIWC's and the mainstream nationalist movement's conceptions of gender. Purdah, which signifies the seclusion of South Asian women from the public world and literally means "curtain," was a significant aspect of the gendering of social space. According to Hanna Papanek, the purdah system regulates the "interaction between women and males outside certain well-defined categories" (3). While generally associated with Muslims, purdah is also an important feature of the Hindu social system. Papanek explains the following differences between purdah in the two religions: "Muslim purdah restrictions do not apply within the immediate kin unit, but only outside it, while Hindu purdah is based on a set of avoidance rules between a woman and her male affines. Muslim seclusion begins at puberty, Hindu seclusion strictly speaking begins with marriage" (3). For Hindus, purdah takes the form *within the home* of averting the eyes, lowering the head, and covering the hair in front of older male in-laws. For Muslims, purdah is manifest in assuming the veil, which includes a range of sartorial practices varying in degrees of bodily coverage, *outside the home*. In both religious traditions, purdah is a metaphor for modesty, describing "a whole continuum of custom," such as wearing the all-encompassing burqah (robe), remaining secluded within the home, and honoring unspoken rules of sex-segregation, that was followed by approximately one third of the female population during the twenties (Forbes, "Indian Women's Movement" 66).

Given the restrictions placed on female mobility, purdah was and continues to constitute the social space demarcation between home and world. Chatterjee describes the normative assumptions underwriting this division:

> The world is the external, the domain of the material; the home represents our inner spiritual self, our true identity. The world is a treacherous terrain of the pursuit of material interests, where practical considerations reign supreme. It is also typically the domain of the male. The home in essence must remain unaffected by the profane activities of the material world—and woman is its representation. And so we get an identification of social roles of gender to correspond with the separation of the social space into ghar and bahir. (Chatterjee, "Nationalist Resolution" 238–39)

The essentialist view of women informing the social space distinction is naturalized in statements from the AIWC in its early years. The organization justified different systems of education for men and women on the grounds that "women were not meant by nature to take part in the struggles of life or to compete with men in the domain particularly his own" (quoted in Forbes, "From Purdah to Politics" 227). Because of women's "special nature," they were better suited to social work. To this end, the AIWC suggested courses to develop women's inherent capacities, in Geraldine Forbes's words, "for self-abnegation, self-restraint, self-sacrifice, catholicity of outlook, and justice" ("From Purdah to Politics" 226–27). The AIWC's construction of "femininity" closely tallied with that of the nationalist version of it, emphasizing the female virtues of "chastity, self-sacrifice, submission, devotion, kindness, patience and the labours of love" (Chatterjee, "Nationalist Resolution" 247).

The AIWC's championing of social work allowed middle-class, upper-caste women to leave the home and widen their experiences while sanctioning their activities under a conservative rhetoric of difference. Because of their inherent capacities, AIWC members maintained, women would be able to discharge their duties to society without neglecting their domestic duties (Forbes, "From Purdah to Politics" 227). Indeed, the public sphere would become an extension of the private one as society became transformed metaphorically into the home, of which the woman was the most capable administrator.[22] Cousins voiced this opinion in an article titled "Indian Womanhood: A National Asset." She urged women to offer

> their own free services to their Motherland with their own distinctive views concerning the solution of national problems. The Nation is but the larger household. The motherhood-spirit is wanted in its administration. Men are not mothers and fathers combined! Let them not arrogate all public services to themselves but leave opportunities for public service as well as private service open to women. Now, when schemes of self-government are being developed, let no artificial man-made barriers and restrictions be placed in the way of woman's free entry into the political, religious and social life of the country. She may not be ready yet for it, but the path must not be in a state of blockade and of vested sex-prejudice when she reaches the point at which her spirit and influence of motherhood overflows from the private life to the mothering of the national family. (*Awakening of Asian Womanhood* 24–25)

It is the construction of "femininity," once "invested with a nationalist content," Chatterjee argues, "which made possible the displacement of the boundaries of 'the home' from the physical confines earlier defined by the rules of *purdah* (seclusion) to a more flexible, but culturally nonetheless determinate, domain set by the *differences* between socially approved male and female conduct" (Chatterjee, "Nationalist Resolution" 247; emphasis in original). A crucial aspect of this process was the invocation of the woman as mother, which conferred respectability on women activists even as it desexualized them, leaving them less open to the pressures of *sharam*, the cultural concept of shame.

The ideology of the home and the world was neither created by the AIWC nor restricted to it, and it appeared in mainstream nationalist discourse as well. In fact, the boundaries between the mainstream women's movement and the nationalist movement were porous, since many of the leaders of the AIWC and the WIA came from prominent nationalist families, facilitating the establishment of informal networks among the women's organizations, which restricted their membership exclusively to females, and nationalist organizations. Moreover, individual members of the AIWC and the WIA were active in nationalist politics. Geraldine Forbes assesses the relationship between the Indian women's movement and the nationalist struggle in the following terms: "over the years situations and events caused leaders of these [women's] organizations to vacillate, redefine their aims, amend by-laws, argue with each other, and finally end up with organizations which were somewhere between separate and autonomous women's associations and women's auxiliaries of the Indian National Congress" ("Indian Women's Movement" 56).

Given that the membership of the women's movement and the nationalist organizations often overlapped, it is not surprising that both movements should have had similar attitudes toward gender and the social space distinction. Mahatma Gandhi's notions of female education, for instance, were underwritten by this ideology. In *India of My Dreams*, he wrote:

> In framing any scheme of women's education this cardinal truth must be kept in mind. Man is supreme in the outward activities of a married pair and, therefore, it is the fitness of things that he should have a greater knowledge thereof. On the other hand, home life is entirely the sphere of women and, therefore, in domestic affairs, in the up-bringing and education of children, women ought to have more knowledge. (quoted in Jayawardena 96)

Gandhi appropriated essentialist elements of this ideology in his theory of *satyagraha*, noncooperative nonviolence, believing "the female sex is not the weaker sex; it is the nobler of the two: for it is even today the embodiment of sacrifice, silent suffering, humility, faith and knowledge" (quoted in Jayawardena 95). He felt that women were better suited to practice satyagraha than men, because of their greater capacity for self-sacrifice: "Woman is more fitted than man to make ahimsa (nonviolence). For the courage of self-sacrifice woman is any way superior to man" (quoted in Jayawardena 97). Drawing his models of ideal womanhood from Hindu mythology, Gandhi promoted Sita, the long-suffering wife of the epic *Ramayana*, as the model for Indian women (Jayawardena 96). But as Barbara Ramusack points out, Gandhi's gendering of satyagraha "tended to reinforce traditional stereotypes of ideal feminine qualities that subordinated the individual to the group" (Ramusack and Sievers 61).[23]

In spite of its communal overtones and the disempowering models of ideal womanhood that it offered, Cousins adopted Gandhi's formulation of satyagraha. In *Indian Womanhood Today*, she states:

> It is in the sphere of idealism that India is most uniquely holding up a new technique as the only possible alternative to war, namely, Satyagraha, non-violent non-co-operation. It is essentially a technique suited to womanhood whose whole nature and function is to create and not to destroy life. No trend in the life of world womanhood is so sinister, so fraught with future evil results, as the twisting of womanhood from the "ministering angel thou" type sung by poets of the past, into the maker of death-dealing armaments. It is, therefore, significant that organised womanhood in India has so boldly and openly ranged itself under the banner of Non-violence, and that the Congress women, the women of the villages, are in this time of world war showing themselves able to sacrifice all they hold dear to proclaim their faith in non-violence which is the ideal of all the Saviours of the world, an ideal found in all sacred teachings. (187–88)

In this passage, Cousins avoids overt references to Hinduism by vaguely identifying nonviolence in broad theological terms and eschewing the naming of specific religions or sacred texts. The sensitivity that she demonstrates here is undercut, however, by passages elsewhere in which she explicitly evokes Hindu mythology. Her book *The Awakening of Asian Womanhood* advances arguments for women's rights by repeatedly alluding to a golden age of Indian society, located during the Vedic period, in which men and women were equal. Mining Hindu mythology, she points to the evidence of women's high status in the mythic figures of Damayanti, Draupadi, Savitri, and Sita, who, she insists, commanded respect in the past. "The stories," Cousins pontificates, "perpetuate the fact that in those 'good old times' women received the same opportunities for education and self-expression as did the men, and that a free and untrammelled natural comradeship existed between men and women in India until the time of the Muhammadan invasion" (*Awakening of Asian Womanhood* 85–86). As Uma Chakravarti insightfully notes, the women's question was overdetermined by the orientalist and nationalist invention of a Hindu-Aryan identity which scripted "the myth of the golden age of Indian womanhood as located in the Vedic period" (28). While Cousins deflated the paradigm of companionate love in her account of her own courtship and marriage, this ideal nevertheless serves as the palimpsest for both

Cousins's and the Indian nationalist construction of the golden age. According to Chakravarti, the golden age myth saw men and women as autonomous subjects whose marital bonds, primarily constituted by affection, were actualized through religious ritual:

> The men were free, brave, vigorous, fearless, themselves civilized and civilizing others, noble, and deeply spiritual; and the women were learned, free, and highly cultured; conjointly they offer sacrifices to the gods, listening 'sweetly' to discourses, and preferring spiritual upliftment to the pursuit of 'mere' riches. Additionally they represented the best examples of conjugal love, offering the supreme sacrifice of their lives as a demonstration of their feeling for their partners in the brief journey of life. This was to be an enduring legacy. (46)

The nationalist construction of ideal womanhood, located in the distant past, functioned as a counter to the contemporary humiliation of women (Chakravarti 30).

Given her belief in a Vedic golden age, it should come as no surprise that Cousins blamed the deterioration in women's condition on the "Muhammadan invasion," which she felt was specifically responsible for purdah. After the invasion, she claimed, "everything changed for Indian womanhood" (*Awakening of Asian Womanhood* 86):

> Muhammadanism has a different philosophy of life and the hereafter from Hinduism. It secludes its women from the sight of all men save the husband; only to a veiled woman does it pay respect, and all its married women are so strictly guarded that not even to draw water from her well may a Muslim woman leave the zenana. Naturally when these people spread conqueringly over the land, carried away by the lust of war and power, they, like all militarist people in their moment of victory, came under sway of their passions, and finding Indian women going about freely, and judging them by their own *purdah* standards, thought them loose women, and used them accordingly. Their rule lasted five centuries, and during that time the Hindus of the North were driven in self-defence to introduce the *purdah* and early-marriage system.

Cousins seems insensitive to the political implications of her arguments, as demonstrated by use of the term "these people" to describe Muslims. The Muslim entry into India, for her, signals a rupture in a nostalgic narrative of equality. Cousins's belief in the myth of the golden age depends on suppressing the caste system, generally dated to the Aryan invasions, which initiated the Vedic period. Moreover, notwithstanding one important qualification, her willingness to attribute the Hindu practices of purdah and child marriage to the lust of conquering Muslim men echoes Mayo's assertion that the Indian male's sex drive is the root of all of India's social evils. For Mayo, the Indian male's sex-drive is the origin of *all* of India's problems, whereas for Cousins the Muslim male's sex drive is the origin of *two* Indian problems, namely purdah and child marriage.

Cousins's analysis of purdah was not unique: it was a standard interpretation of female seclusion among some Hindu circles. Both Hindu and Muslim progressives denied that rigid purdah originated with their religions. As evidence Muslims pointed to Muhammad's time, when women had unlimited movement and did not wear the veil (Forbes, "Caged Tigers" 531). Hindus constructed a golden age in which men and women were equal, based on the speeches of female characters in the Vedas. According to Forbes, "The abuses of the system were regarded as the result of 'custom,' further explained by some as imitation of Muslim court customs, as imitation of Hindu customs, or as necessary to protect women during the Muslim invasions. . . . Hindu feminists began to see purdah as a custom brought to India by Muslim invaders and a cause of women's fall from the high position they held during the 'Golden Age' " ("Caged Tigers" 531). As tensions mounted between India's two main religions, Muslims feared that they would become marginalized in an independent India governed by a Hindu majority and grew increasingly protective of their religious identity. Interpretations of purdah would prove divisive among Indian women who focused on identifying its religious origins rather than on vociferously challenging its practice. "Muslim feminists admitted that the Koran contained passages about female modesty, but denied that Indian-style purdah could be blamed on Islam," Forbes explains. "What had been the feminist issue of the nineteenth century had by the third decade of the twentieth century become an issue which divided Hindu feminists, with their insistence on a particular interpretation of the 'Golden Age', from Muslim feminists, who had grown protective of their religion" (531).

Just as the AIWC universalized Hindu identity, projecting it as an ideal through the invention of a gender-egalitarian past, so too did the organization universalize bourgeois-class identity by refusing to analyze how social-class position had a differential impact on the condition of women. The seemingly progressive nature of the AIWC's bottom-up structure is belied by the composition of its membership and leadership, which primarily drew from women educators, doctors, lawyers, middle-class housewives, and members of the Indian royal houses. Membership in the organization did not extend to subaltern women or have an impact on their issues in any positive fashion. The class composition of the AIWC is reflected in its priorities: for example, its concern with purdah was a middle- and upper-class issue, since the lower classes relied on female labor to add to the family income and consequently did not practice purdah. The organization's acceptance of the ideology of distinct social space and its attempts to accommodate purdah, moreover, helped its professional members to obtain jobs in separate institutions, without having to compete against men.

In fact, the activities of the AIWC sometimes harmed lower-class women. At the third annual session of the conference in 1929, for instance, members took up the condition of women industrial workers and passed a resolution calling for "the absolute prohibition of women labour in underground mines" (Basu and Ray 84). This resolution cost women miners their jobs and forced them back into the home. Judging from the correspondence of Rajkumari Amrit Kaur, the AIWC vice-president in 1935, this action elicited protest from British labor organizations. She responded with typical upper-class benevolence, arguing that women workers required protection till they could organize themselves. Kaur's letter to the Open Door Council of London, dated February 13, 1935, reads:

> While realising to the full the dangers of "over protection" in the case of women workers, our Association feels very keenly that owing to the evils of child marriage and the consequent ill-effects on the health of children and the appalling illiteracy among women as also the terrible conditions under which, generally speaking, our women have [to] work that until such time as they are educated and organised enough to speak for themselves we must ask for a certain amount of necessary protection for them. We should like to assure you that we shall not as far as lies in our power, allow "protection" to mean the denial of human rights to women but we would, at the same time, ask you to

bear in mind that conditions of life in India are wholly different from Europe and it is very difficult for us to get things altered as quickly as we would fain wish to have them altered. (quoted in Basu and Ray 116–17)

Kaur's letter figures lower-class women as suffering the effects of child marriage, poor health, and illiteracy. If, as Eva Cherniavsky has remarked, subalternity marks a condition outside of literacy, for Kaur it necessitates the representational intervention of upper-class women who have greater epistemic privilege and insight into the conditions of lower-class women, by virtue of their South Asian location, than European women. The AIWC's perception that lower-class women were not capable of speaking and politically representing themselves is further evidenced in its limited view of women's suffrage. Because the organization felt universal suffrage "may not be practicable in India" "for some time," they pushed for franchise on equal terms with men (One Who Knows 16). Between 1921 and 1929 all the legislative areas, as a result of lobbying by women's organizations, "conferred the symbol and instrument of equal citizenship with men on women who possessed equal qualifications—a certain amount of literacy, property, age, payment of taxes, length of residence" (Cousins, Indian Womanhood Today 32). These qualifications were impossible for lower-class women to meet.

The AIWC's elitist tendencies are also reflected in the president's having been appointed by Cousins rather than elected by the body as a whole. In justifying her decision to name the Maharani (or "Queen") Saheb Chimnabai Gaekwad of Baroda as the president of the first AIWC session in 1927, Cousins emphasized the Maharani's social-class background: "[The AIWC was] a democratic body, but we meant to represent all the people, from highest to lowest, and to lift the lowest towards the highest. We needed a leader of social eminence, experience, warm interest in the women's cause, ability and personality. This pointed to Her Highness the Maharani of Baroda" (We Two Together 447). Her conception of democracy is based on an explicit class hierarchy: the Maharani's royal background and prominence are sufficient qualifications for the presidency of the conference.

The elitist tendencies apparent in the origins of the AIWC continue to plague it to the current day. In an appendix to a history of the AIWC based on records and interviews with many members, Aparna Basu and Bharati

Ray record a long list of members' grievances. The following complaints appear in a list of twenty:

1. The AIWC is an organisation for the upper class elite who talk superficially at meetings but put nothing into action. At the same time a majority claim it is a middle class organisation.
2. Annual and half-yearly meetings are more tourist programmes and holidays rather than serious sessions where work is done.
3. The older generation is keen on holding high positions and hogging the limelight and is reluctant to give room to the next and younger generation.
8. Society ladies should visit rural villages and slums and educate these women on their legitimate rights instead of running masala and papad units.
14. Urban members hold responsible positions. Rural members are not allowed to come forward. (*Women's Struggle* 156–57)

These complaints suggest that upper-class, urban, senior women are reluctant to relinquish leadership positions within the organization. That the AIWC is even now dominated by women from elite social-class backgrounds illustrates that feminist collectives can struggle against hegemonic power structures and still be marked by those very same structures (Alexander and Mohanty xxxviii). Both the AIWC and the WIA established branches all over India and by the mid-1930s their combined membership totaled over ten thousand women (Forbes, "Indian Women's Movement" 54). While the organizations universalized middle-class, Hindu identity and subscribed to the nationalist division of distinct social spaces, their efforts nonetheless saw to it that the Indian Constitution would guarantee women complete political equality under the law. This success was followed by other legislative ones that abolished social restrictions against women, such as the Sarda Act (1929), the Special Marriage Act (1954), the Hindu Marriage and Divorce Act (1955), the Hindu Minority and Guardianship Act (1956), the Hindu Adoption and Maintenance Act (1956), and the Suppression of Immoral Traffic in Women Act (1956) (Basu and Ray 142). Many of these laws were laxly enforced and relatively few women took advantage of their new legal status. Yet the legal infrastructure established by the AIWC was a necessary step for the improvement in women's lives, since it provided women with state support to redress gender-related grievances. In addition to its legislative efforts, the AIWC also helped to create new institutions designed to improve women's conditions, such as the Lady Irwin College for Home Science in Delhi (which now offers undergraduate and graduate courses in a variety of disciplines), the Family Planning Centre (now the Family Planning Association of India), Save the Children Committee (now the Indian Council of Child Welfare), the Cancer Research Institute, and the Amrit Kaur Bal Vihar for cognitively disabled children (Basu and Ray 142).

Cousins's articulation of feminist-nationalist individualism emphasizes different aspects of that ideology in relation to her differential conception of feminist agency in Ireland and India. In her account of Irish suffrage, Cousins imposes an individualist paradigm on the collective history of the Irish women's movement by claiming for herself the role of its founder and originator. In her account of the Indian women's movement, however, she deindividuates her seminal role as an initiator and organizer of that movement, to clear a discursive space in which Indian women can emerge as practitioners and theoreticians of Indian feminist historiography. The limitations of feminist-nationalist individualism, in the South Asian context, are not evident so much in the construction of the feminist activist subject as an individualist per se but in the universalization of the nationalist subject as quintessentially middle-class and Hindu.

Writing the history of the feminist-nationalist activist subject requires that she constantly rewrite herself in relation to shifting colonial and organizational contexts. As Biddy Martin and Chandra Mohanty note, the rewriting of the self "is an interpretive act which is itself embedded in social and political practice" (210). Between the poles of the experiential and the theoretical resides, for Cousins, a subjectivity continuously negotiating its identity in terms of the individual agent and a larger feminist collectivity. Yet Cousins's differential treatment of subjectivity in Ireland and India is not without its own internal contradictions. In India, Cousins embraced the sexual codes of companionate marriage through her subscription to a specifically Hindu version of Indian nationalism that she had explicitly rejected in Ireland as a model for her own marriage. While her willingness to advocate for Indian women's suffrage on the basis of restoring some prelapsarian, gender-egalitarian, Vedic Golden Age can be read as an articulation of respect for the Indian women's movement's indigenous members, it also bespeaks an orientalist romance with norms of Indian femininity. Cousins's invocation of Hindu mythology in the service of a feminist-nationalist project suggests a tension between reporting on the ideology of a movement and agitating as one of its partisans, based on a kind of conversion experience by an enamored "student of Indian culture." Such a tension raises larger questions about the nature of solidarity work and the ostensibly fine distinctions that arise between being a witness and becoming assimilated, or what is more pejoratively referred to in colonial discourse as "going native."

The decentered practice of feminist witnessing requires both building on the earlier work of women like Margaret Cousins who conceptualized feminist agency in relation to international structures of domination and overcoming some of the limitations of feminist-nationalist individualism which informed these earlier activist efforts. It requires theories of subject formation that dialectically position individual subjectivity in relation to larger social collectives and a practice which is simultaneously based on a historically situated analysis and attentive to the multiple structures of domination, including ethnic, sectarian, and economic ones, which are constitutive of women's experiences.

This chapter presents a case study of heroic-nationalist individualism in the writing of Kalpana Dutt, a member of Jugantar, one of several organizations which engaged in the armed struggle in the 1920s and 1930s against colonialism. Offered as a retrospective tribute to her comrades in the organization, written after she had served six years of a life sentence, been released, and converted to communism, Dutt's *Chittagong Armoury Raiders Reminiscences* articulates and also attempts to critique heroic-nationalist individualism. Dutt grapples with the central contradiction that motivated Jugantar: its promulgation of an ideology of heroic-nationalist individualism for the resistance movement that constructed *individual* nationalist subjects within an idiom of Hindu masculinity and directed their political agency toward the *collective* liberation of South Asians from colonialism.

The constitutive features of heroic-nationalist individualism, as expressed by the Bengali terrorist movement, can be mapped at both the individual and collective levels. At the collective level, heroic-nationalist individualism was premised on the idea that the use of political violence against British officials and native collaborators was the most effective means to resist colonial rule. The native elite, moreover, was best equipped to lead the armed struggle, which emphasized a notion of "blood sacrifice" that itself was modeled on the Irish Easter Rising of 1916. Heroic-nationalist individualism scripted terrorist acts, especially assassinations, as public spectacles which showcased the bravery of individual nationalist combatants in order to mobilize other South Asians in the anticolonial struggle. At the individual level, this ideology was manifest in the construction of the nationalist subject as an upper-caste male *ksatriya* (warrior) who functioned to challenge the degrading British stereotype of the Bengali *babu*. The incontrovertible bravery and physical strength of the nationalist subject, established through her or his willingness to confront danger in terrorist activities, served to counter the colonial caricature of the Bengali male as effeminate, bookish, and altogether ridiculous, a caricature used by the colonial authorities to discredit nationalist aspirations.

Indian nationalist discourse and the ideology of heroic-nationalist individualism are of course highly gendered and, more specifically, inflected with Hindu elements. As in many other nationalist movements, the land itself became a highly gendered signifier within the discourse of the Indian independence movement. Combining a passive, long-suffering persona with a vengeful, bloodthirsty one, India was simultaneously rendered by nationalists as the mother and as the Goddess Kali. India was embodied as a woman, represented in the conventional tropes of violation, shame, and honor of nationalist discourse. She required the heroic sacrifice of her sons to purge her of the shame of foreign domination and to restore her violated honor. Dutt draws on this conventional representation of the violated motherland throughout her reminiscences and also employs the recurring trope of moral decline. Her description of her comrades is suffused with a nostalgia that laments the passing of a "golden age" when Chittagonian youth embodied heroism in the service of the anticolonial armed struggle. In contrast to an earlier age of heroism, according to Dutt, contemporary Chittagong is marked by a fall, a state of "degeneracy," characterized by the rule of thugs, war profiteers, and sexual traffic in women. Women become the signifier, in her text, of the moral depravity wrought by colonialism.

Against such pervasive moral turpitude, Dutt claims, the ideology of heroic-nationalist individualism is ultimately inadequate: it must be superseded by an ideology that emphasizes a notion of the social contract based in an organizational structure—namely the Communist Party—which is able to direct the efforts of anticolonial activists toward a broad-based mobilization of the populace. Cautioning against perceiving nationalist movements in too monolithic terms, Barbara Harlow notes that while "resistance organizations and national liberation movements represent a collective and concerted struggle against hegemonic domination and oppression," they are marked by "their own internal contradictions and debates" (*Resistance Literature* 29). Harlow argues that it is the "self-critical controversies that sustain the movements' active agency in the historical arena of world politics" and "need to be theoretically elaborated and given their full 'historical and sociological weight' " (29). In spite of Dutt's acknowledgment of the limitations of heroic-nationalist individualism, her text is saturated by an internal contradiction between individualism and more collective types of identity, and this contradiction manifests itself in a tension between narrative form and ideological content. Even though Dutt recognizes the shortcomings of heroic-nationalist individualism relative to communist ideology, she relies on a formal narrative structure which valorizes the figure of the individual by organizing her narrative into short anecdotal biographies of her fellow combatants in the movement. The biographical genre has implicit within it an ideology of individualism, because it is predicated on the notion of a coherent, self-evident, self-conscious, and commanding subject, constructing "textually for the reader the liberal imaginary of a unique, 'free,' autonomous ego as the natural form of being and public achievement" (Beverley 23). The narrative organization of Dutt's book is entirely consistent with the terrorists' strategy of foregrounding individual bravery, through highly visible public acts, over mass mobilization. Conspicuously absent in the account are details pertaining to collective action and group dynamics, in spite of Dutt's exhortations regarding the importance of class-based organizing efforts. Moreover, *Chittagong Armoury Raiders Reminiscences* contains very little explicit information on the terrorist movement's material practices and provides few rationales for their actions.

Wrestling with the limitations of the armed struggle and heroic-nationalist individualism, Dutt implicitly engages with one of the central problematics of Indian nationalist historiography identified by Ranajit Guha as the study of the

> *historic failure of the nation to come to its own*, a failure due to the inadequacy of the bourgeoisie as well as of the working class to lead it into a decisive victory over colonialism and a bourgeois-democratic revolution of either the classic nineteenth-century type under the hegemony of the bourgeoisie or a more modern type under the hegemony of workers and peasants, that is, a "new democracy." ("On Some Aspects of the Historiography of Colonial India" 43; emphasis in original)

The failure of the Indian bourgeoisie to actualize itself politically is reflected in the discursive absences that characterize the "speaking subject of 'Indian' history" (Chakrabarty 230). Indeed, heroic-nationalist individualism in *Chittagong Armoury Raiders Reminiscences* gets articulated not so much through a construction of what Dipesh Chakrabarty calls an "endlessly interiorized subject" who reveals the private aspects of the bourgeois self; rather, the individualism in Dutt's account is represented through discrete portraits of the public life of her fellow combatants. In this regard, her account instantiates Chakrabarty's claim that "the themes of 'failure,' 'lack,' and 'inadequacy' . . . ubiquitously characterize the speaking subject of 'Indian' history," in that the speaking subject of Indian history is primarily rehearsed as a public self who is unwilling to acknowledge the more private features of her or his experience (230). The "modern individual"—who in Europe is constituted by " 'public' and 'private' parts of the self" by virtue of the discourse of citizenship—commingles "with other narratives of the self and community that do not look to the state/citizen bind as the ultimate construction of sociality" (232). Chakrabarty observes that these narratives often present an "antihistorical consciousness," entailing "subject positions and configurations of memory that challenge and undermine the subject that speaks in the name of history" (232). In Dutt's text, sociality is figured through alternative narratives of self and community which draw from Hinduism, caste identity, and South Asian patriarchy; these native constructions of the modern individual, while themselves the product of the dialectical nature of colonial experience, inform the discourse of the Bengali terrorist movement and heroic-nationalist individualism.

Given the anecdotal character of Dutt's text and its lack of theoretical self-consciousness regarding its potential historic mission as a manual for collective aspects of anticolonial struggle, the discursive challenge of *Chittagong Armoury Raiders Reminiscences* necessitates a critical reading of its narrative gaps. Such a reading would insert historical knowledge of the material practices of Jugantar and their theoretical justifications through the categories of gender, collective agency, and organizing. This chapter analyzes the articulation of heroic-nationalist individualism, along with its limitations, within the context of Jugantar's strategies, their theoretical legitimizations, the gender ideology underwriting the armed struggle, the material practices of women in Jugantar, and the structure of the organization.

THE QUESTION OF VIOLENCE

Frantz Fanon's handbook for the role of the native intellectual in national liberation movements, The Wretched of the Earth, significantly opens with the following line: "National liberation, national renaissance, the restoration of nationhood to the people, commonwealth: whatever may be the headings used or the new formulas introduced, decolonization is always a violent phenomenon" (35). Decolonization attempts no less than to "change the order of the world" by instigating a "program of complete disorder" against the colonial status quo (36). This obvious point regarding the violent nature of the process of political transformation instigated by an anticolonial nationalist project is worth reflecting on in the context of South Asia; popular representations of the Indian independence movement in the West, such as Richard Attenborough's Gandhi (1982), are overdetermined by a construction of Mahatma Gandhi as a saintly individual and a corresponding emphasis on nonviolence as the singular political strategy responsible for the success of the struggle. Yet the term "nonviolence" is something of a misnomer in that it recognizes the victims and perpetrators of violence selectively, based on identitarian grounds. Violence gets named as such when its agents are natives and its victims are British. It does not get named as violence, however, when its agents are either British personnel or colonial state policy, and when its victims are natives. In actuality, overt and covert forms of violence permeated the British colonial state and the Indian independence movement. Whether it was General Dyer's massacre at the Jallianwala Bagh or machine guns fired out of British helicopters at native crowds during the Quit India movement in 1942 or the mass population transfer brought about by partition and the attendant one million deaths, the Indian independence struggle was saturated by overt forms of violence. Covert violence also characterized British colonialism and the nationalist movement more generally: for instance, altered distribution networks and the transformation of the indigenous economy to meet the industrial and military requirements of the metropole often had devastating consequences for Indians, as the Bengal famine of 1943 illustrates. Given that millions of people died as a result of colonial policy and overt forms of colonial aggression, the Indian independence movement cannot be accurately characterized as nonviolent.

If the term "nonviolence" is used to occlude native victims of violence, denying them the status of subjecthood, the term "violence" is often employed, as Guha explains, to pathologize natives as disposed to "spontaneous" and "unpremeditated" outbursts of irrational fury, generally figured in metaphors "assimilating . . . revolts to natural phenomena" ("Prose of Counter-Insurgency" 45–46). He notes that while the dominant narrative presents instances of insurgency and armed revolts as "anarchic," "instinctual," and "external" to subaltern consciousness, armed rebellion is generally the last resort of people who have exhausted constitutional and legal means to redress their grievances. People have far too much to lose in challenging the state's monopoly on force—in point of fact, they risk losing everything, including their lives—to embark on "such a project in a state of absent-mindedness" (45). The representation of the use of political violence by natives as confirmation of the native proclivity toward barbarism and savagery derives from the binary oppositions of colonial discourse. The disarticulation of Indians from "civilization," a primary feature of colonial discourse, renders them as inherently violent, a representation which reinforces both the repressive and the ideological apparatuses of the colonial state.

Such a self-justification zealously guards the colonial state's monopoly on the use of force and is generally evident in the discursive containment of insurgency by characterizing it as "terrorism." According to Richard E. Rubenstein, "political terrorism is sui generis" because it is "a specific form of violence distinguishable from both crime and warfare, although bearing a family resemblance to both" (22). The agent of violence in both crime and warfare has her or his identity defined relative to a notion of citizenship and the state. With criminal violence, the subject is coded as deviating from the ideals of citizenship and thus disrupting the state's operations of law and order. In warfare, however, the subject becomes the paradigmatic ideal citizen, not only willing to kill in the name of patriotism but also, as Benedict Anderson has observed, to die on behalf of the "limited imaginings" of the nation (16). The agent of insurgent nationalist violence, however, exists outside the category of citizenship and derives her or his identity in opposition to the colonial state structure. Neither deviant citizen nor an ideal one, she or he deploys violence, and risks death, in the name of a nation which is not yet actualized and is coming into being through the anticolonial struggle.

As Timothy Brennan reminds us, "the violence that comes from defending one's identity or livelihood as opposed to one's privileges is not the same" (165). The transformation of repressive political structures necessitates distinguishing between those who employ violence to protect their social and economic privileges and those who employ it to secure their basic human rights and civil liberties; in other words, it is important to differentiate between the colonial state's use of violence in the interests of a ruling elite and the use of violence by insurgency movements. Yet the discourse of antiterrorism generally refuses such a distinction by relying on a categorization of political violence that draws on one of two similes: terrorism-as-crime or terrorism-as-war (Rubenstein 22). The terrorism-as-crime simile denies the possibility that terrorism, armed struggle, and mass mobilization are linked in a continuum; it assumes that terrorism will not evolve into a mass movement (31). Rubenstein argues: "To assert that a violent act is essentially criminal is to have concluded that it is *not* integral to a process of legitimate political transformation" (33). In contrast, the terrorism-as-war simile views terrorist activity as a justifiable method of warfare and embodies a prediction that guerrilla warfare, "fought by a vanguard with limited, largely passive civilian support," will eventually be transformed "into a conventional war or revolution that mobilizes the masses to defend their interests directly" (28). As the organization progresses from individualistic modes of violence toward armed struggle—also known as "sustained or escalated terrorism" by those in power—the focus of rebel attacks may shift from symbols of authority to more strategic economic, military, and political targets (29). Indeed, the Jugantar's decision to conduct an armory raid instead of assassinating individual British officials signals such a shift.

In South Asia, the term "terrorism" is not automatically pejorative and has different valences that are context specific. Bengali terrorists have attained the status of folk heroes who are highly revered in northern India. Yet they are most often referred to as "terrorists," illustrating that when the signifier "terrorist" is applied to forms of armed resistance to British colonial rule, it loses its negative connotations.[1] The terrorists perceived themselves as part of a vanguard which would mobilize large numbers of people in the anticolonial struggle by virtue of their example of heroic sacrifice and referred to themselves as "revolutionaries," drawing on the simile of terrorism-as-war. In the Indian nationalist context, both usages, "terrorists" and "revolutionaries," complicate the association of terrorism and crime so prevalent in the West. Throughout *Chittagong Armoury Raiders Reminiscences*, Dutt generally refers to her fellow combatants as "revolutionaries," except for in one instance in which she calls them " 'terrorist' revolutionaries" (9). Significantly, this usage occurs in a passage devoted to converting followers of the movement to communism while in "the cold, silent recess of the prison-cell" (8). The term " 'terrorist' revolutionaries" simultaneously challenges the simile of terrorism-as-crime while maintaining a distinction between terrorism and mass organization.

Because heroic-nationalist individualism has a limited understanding of class and collective action, and because the term "terrorist" in the Indian nationalist context is not pejorative, I have chosen to follow popular, north Indian usage in referring to participants in the movement as "terrorists" with, of course, the above qualifications on the use of political violence.

RE-ENACTING THE RISING: EASTER 1916
AND THE CHITTAGONG ARMOURY RAID

On April 24, 1916, the day after Easter Sunday, about fifteen hundred members of the Irish Volunteers, the Citizen Army, Cumann na mBan, and the Irish Republican Brotherhood occupied parts of Dublin and issued the Proclamation of a nonsectarian Irish Republic underwritten by socialist and feminist principles. Led by such notable figures in the Irish nationalist, labor, and cultural revival movements as Countess Markievicz, James Connolly, Padraic Pearse, and Thomas MacDonagh, the Rising was conceived initially as a widespread rebellion that would be constituted by an armed insurrection in Dublin and guerrilla warfare in the countryside, backed by weapons supplied from Germany and the United States. However, when a German arms shipment was intercepted shortly before the planned date of the Rising and one of its leaders, Roger Casement, was arrested, the success of the insurrection grew dubious. Prospects for victory became even more vexed when Eoin MacNeill, chief of staff of the Irish Volunteers, issued orders countermanding the insurrection on gaining knowledge of it for the first time. With confusion reigning among the ranks of the Irish Volunteers and a dearth of arms, the military council in charge of planning the Rising became convinced that as a military maneuver the insurrection would fail. Yet the council believed that the insurrection could be valuable in symbolic terms as a "blood sacrifice" which would galvanize and inspire the population in the armed struggle against British rule. The British government, with superior weapons and artillery and larger numbers, suppressed the revolt within a week. The final tally of casualties included about 116 soldiers, 16 policemen, 64 republicans, and 254 civilians dead and more than 2,600 people injured (Curtis 278). The Rising did not have much initial popular support. But the colonial government's ruthless efficiency in conducting secret courts-martial and executing the rebels and fifteen of their leaders between May 3 and 12, 1916, outraged the Irish public and bestowed on the insurrection a symbolic importance which would resonate in the Irish nationalist imaginary and define it as a pivotal moment in the struggle for an independent Ireland.[2] Pearse's prediction, written from his cell in Kilmainhain jail while awaiting execution, proved remarkably prescient: "We shall be remembered by posterity and blessed by unborn generations" (quoted in Evans and Pollock 97).

The Easter Rising also reverberated in the nationalist imaginary of the Bengali terrorist movement which monitored nationalist activities in Ireland. By the early thirties, multiple links between Irish and Indian nationalists had been established textually and through face-to-face meetings between participants in both movements. Although it is difficult to ascertain the extent of these links, or the degree of their formality, at least several scholars have remarked on their existence. In her excellent history *The Cause of Ireland*, for instance, Liz Curtis reveals that at the beginning of the twentieth century, Egyptian, Indian, and Irish nationalists made each other's acquaintance at various socialist conferences and sometimes trained jointly in the use of weapons (315). She also notes that Irish republican sailors transmitted political communications between Indians at home and in exile (316). During the twenties, Indian newspapers such as the nationalist paper the *Forward* featured regular columns on developments in the Irish nationalist movement (Gordon 338).

It was mainly the dissemination of news about Irish nationalist activities through textual sources that enabled Irish nationalists to provide, to their Indian counterparts, paradigms for resistance to colonial rule, such as the hunger strike. As C. Sehanabish attests, Sinn Fein leaders like Terence MacSwiney, who died while on a hunger strike in 1921 during the Anglo-Irish war, exerted a strong influence on Bengali nationalists. Reflecting on the impact of MacSwiney's death among nationalists in the region, he remembers:

> It was widely reported in our papers about this Irish revolt of 18th April—that Ireland, so near England, almost a stone's throw, but even then they could retain power. The hunger strike was a peculiar weapon used by both Irish and Bengali revolutionaries. Maybe we were influenced by them. MacSwiney died after 72 days of hunger-strike; and when Jatin Das died here after 63 days, one of the things I remember was the telegram from Mrs. Mary MacSwiney, wife of the great leader: "Ireland joins India in grief and pride over the death of Jatin Das. Freedom shall come." (quoted in Masani 114)

While the hunger strike was a tactic derived from Irish models, specifically that of Irish suffragettes, as used by political prisoners seeking to gain political status or protest their conditions of incarceration it also evoked Hindu cultural practices and the gendered discourse of Indian nationalism. Married Hindu women traditionally fast on certain religious days to guarantee the health of their husbands and sons. The body of the hunger striker stood as a symbol of the body politic, ill and emaciated under colonial rule. Simultaneously, however, fasting became a ritual method of restoring the health of the body politic. And as in the discourse of nationalist politics more broadly, this tactic gendered India as a suffering woman.

For members of Jugantar, paradigms of Irish resistance were circulated primarily through biographies of Irish nationalists which Surjya Sen, the leader of the terrorist movement, prescribed as reading materials for the combatants. Biographies of James Fintan Lalor, Dan Breen, Michael Collins, and Eamon de Valera were especially popular.[3] Yet it was the Easter Rising, in which none of these figures had played a central decision-making role, that most gripped the nationalist imaginary of the Bengali terrorist movement. After Jugantar's leaders—Surjya Sen, Ananta Singh, and Ganesh Ghosh—were released from detention under the infamous Bengal Criminal Law Amendment Ordinance in 1928, they engaged in a period of self-reflection on the efficacy of their previous campaign of assassinating colonial officials, concluding that an armed insurrection modeled on the Easter Rising would provide a heroic example of resistance to mobilize the populace to resist colonial rule.[4] As one of the participants, Lokenath Bal, noted, "The bloodstained memory of the Easter Revolution of the Irish Republican Army touched our young minds with fiery enthusiasm" (quoted in R. C. Majumdar, *History of Modern Bengal* 263). The terrorists planned an ambitious program to raid police and military installations, destroy communications facilities, and attack British social centers. By cutting communications they hoped to prevent the government from getting reinforcements. Like the military council of the Irish Rising, the Bengali terrorists realized that their struggle had little chance of succeeding militarily, but they believed in the symbolic importance of their insurrectionary gesture. Dutt explains that "they thought their short but heroic legend would be blazoned forth all over the land and inspire new generations to fight for the freedom of their motherland" (1).

Calling themselves the Indian Republican Army after the Irish Republican Army, sixty-four Bengali terrorists commemorated the anniversary of the Easter Rising, on April 18, 1930, by launching simultaneous attacks on the police armory, the Auxiliary Force armory, the Post and Telegraph Office, and the European Club at Chittagong (Tripathy 46). They succeeded in capturing a large number of pistols and rifles, as well as a few Lewis guns for which ammunition was however lacking (R. C. Majumdar, *History of Modern Bengal* 273). They damaged the Post and Telegraph Office—cutting off telegraph communication—derailed a train, paralyzed the armed police force, and gained control of Chittagong for four days (Tripathy 46). On April 22, 1930, British reinforcements arrived and attacked the Bengali terrorists on Jalalabad hill. The insurgents' rifles proved no match for the machine guns of the colonial army, and as a result a large number of Indian fighters died. At this point the Indian Republican Army changed its strategy, deciding to carry on a protracted guerrilla struggle instead of fighting till death. The combatants fled to the forests, where they continued the guerrilla campaign for several years (Gordon 248). Surjya Sen eluded capture till 1933; he was tried and hanged in 1934 (248). With the execution of Surjya Sen and the imprisonment of other key leaders, the Indian Republican Army, Chittagong branch, dissolved.

Lacking the temporally and geographically compressed dramatic intensity of the Easter Rising, the Chittagong Armoury Raid did not assume the symbolic importance in the Indian nationalist movement that the Easter Rising achieved in the Irish nationalist movement. Yet its participants certainly gained regional fame, becoming modern-day folk heroes, for their courage and sacrifice rendered in the name of the Indian nation.

NARRATING HEROIC-NATIONALIST INDIVIDUALISM

The project of facilitating the transformation of the Bengali terrorists into regional folk heroes in Dutt's *Chittagong Armoury Raiders Reminiscences* is enacted by four major narrative strategies that combine historical, literary, and mythological discourses. Her invocation of the generic features of comedy, her use of Western literary references, her allusions to Indian myths, and her shifting point of view simultaneously portray the terrorists in mythic terms and paradoxically legitimize that status by relying on the authenticating strategies of the eyewitness testimonial. All these literary strategies emphasize the extraordinary bravery, physical strength, and intellectual coolness under pressure of her fellow combatants. Organized around individual characters in the movement—of the thirteen chapters of her tale, eleven take their names from fellow combatants—her text is less a collective narrative of group action than a tribute to brave individual men and women.

The mythologizing project crucially legitimizes itself by drawing on conventions of historiography that present Dutt's text as a participant's account. The title itself, *Chittagong Armoury Raiders Reminiscences*, sets up two narrative expectations, establishing the Chittagong Armoury Raid of 1930 as a central textual event and suggesting that the story will be narrated by actual participants. But the book does not deliver on these discursive expectations either in its historical focus or in its choice of narrators. Though the introduction of the book focuses on the armory raid, the rest of the text covers a range of events dating from the release of a number of terrorists from prison in 1928, to the Bengal famine of 1943, to the provincial elections of 1945. Dutt mentions these events as anecdotes that bear on the moral character of the individuals whom she profiles. Moreover, she herself did not participate in the armory raid, since she was studying in Calcutta at the time (Dutt 10). In fact, she was not an active member of Jugantar until her return to Chittagong during her college holidays, some three weeks after the armory raid. Contrary to the expectations set up by the title, *Chittagong Armoury Raiders Reminiscences* is a nonparticipant celebration of the experiences and characters of the individuals who took part in the raid.

In addition to the title, the participant status of the account is further suggested through the narrative point of view, which changes throughout the text. None of the combatants speak for themselves; rather, their experiences are discursively mediated through Dutt's representations of them. The heroic-nationalist individualist paradigm underwrites both the organization of the text, since most of the chapters are focused on an individual combatant, who is constructed as a death-defying hero by virtue of her or his physical stamina and capacity to endure pain. The narrative voice freely alternates between the first person and third person omniscient. Describing Ambika Chakravarty's injury during the battle of Jalalabad hill, for example, Dutt writes:

> He had been shot through the head. His comrades left him for dead. He fainted and then later the cool night breeze slowly brought him back to consciousness. He was still terribly weak, could not move an inch without howling with pain. He himself had grave doubts whether he was still alive. It was highly unlikely, perhaps he had become a ghost? He tried out experiments—moved his hand ever so slowly, touched his forehead and felt an acute pain. Ah! He still had a sense of pain! The pain was real all right and not at all ghostly—may be he was still alive. Then he tried to pick himself up, ever so cautiously. But then he tumbled downhill right into a pond below. He revived after gulping down some water and started walking towards the town, he hobbled along, stopping every now and then for breath. (32)

Writing in the third person omniscient perspective, Dutt adopts Chakravarty's point of view in this passage, attributing ruminations to him on the supernatural which, from an epistemological perspective, she cannot possibly know. Yet she begins this section in the first person by admitting that "there were several leaders of the Chittagong armoury raid whom I had never actually seen. Ambikada was one of them" (31). If Chakravarty did not describe his ordeal to Dutt, then who furnished her with the details that figure in her account? She does not say, failing to name the sources that ordinarily authenticate historical discourse. Dutt's lack of explicit sources, together with the ambiguity surrounding her use of narrative perspective, blur the distinctions between historical and mythological discourses in her text. The changes in narrative perspective seem to bestow upon her book the authority of an eyewitness account, by giving the impression that Dutt was actually present at the events she describes. Given these shifts in perspective, together with the title of the work, it is not surprising that some scholars have mistakenly assumed that Dutt participated in the Chittagong armoury raid. Both Kumari Jayawardena (*Feminism and Nationalism in the Third World*) and Vijay Agnew (*Elite Women in Indian Politics*) incorrectly identify her as a participant. Agnew even claims that Dutt "led the Chittagong Armoury Raid" when "she was only 18" (63).

The larger tragedy of the armory raid and its aftermath, which ended in the deaths of so many of the youthful terrorists, is offset in Dutt's narrative through the insertion of comic episodes from the struggle that typically thematize escape. At one level, the terrorists escape from the authorities by eluding capture, and at another, more existential level, they escape from death itself. In the section on Mani Dutt, who is also known as the "Lecturer," Kalpana Dutt describes an incident in which three of the terrorists, who have gone underground, tentatively venture into town. Some cart drivers begin to harass them. Suspecting that an informant has betrayed them to the cart drivers, Lecturer decides on a course of action:

> He challenged [the cart drivers] and he started going at them with both fists. He held them at bay and asked us to run for it. It was awkward, we had to run down the main street with a torch in one hand and a revolver in the other. Meanwhile the cartdrivers started shouting: "thief! thief!" After we had got a good start on them, Lecturer let them go and sprinted to join us and started yelling "thief! thief!" himself. At this, people thought the "thieves" were ahead of us and tried to run further ahead and we were beyond suspicion ourselves. In the confusion, we struck down an alley and were safe. (57)

Anecdotes such as this one highlight the terrorists' ability to think and act under great pressure and emphasize their cleverness. In addition, these stories provide moments of humor in the narrative by casting the authorities and their native collaborators as comic dupes of the terrorists.

But although these narrative moments help to humanize the terrorists and render them likable by highlighting their quick-wittedness, Dutt also characterizes them as extraordinary by invoking literature, Western popular culture, and Hindu mythology. Refusing to acknowledge a difference between historical and mythological discourses, her character sketches often compare particular comrades to literary and religious heroes. In one instance, she likens Surjya Sen to Doctorda, the terrorist protagonist of Sarat Chandra's novel *Pather Dabi* (12). And in another instance, Ananta Singh becomes "Robinhood," "a legend, a symbol of freedom and fearlessness" (Dutt 17). Indeed, her first glimpse of Singh is narratively framed in terms of a legend about masculine strength and heroism:

> The famous Ramamoorthy circus had come to Chittagong. I was a small girl then. The family went along to see it. Elephants walked over the chest of a giant of a man. A heavy, strong armed giant held back a car whose engine was running fullspeed. I used to get thrilled by it all. An Englishman broke a hefty set of chains tied to a car—they were thick and strong! Then the white giant threw out his chest—Tarzan-fashion—and challenged Chittagonians to dare come and repeat his performance. An unknown youth took up the challenge. He walked up and broke the chain while the audience watched with bated breath—was he not foolhardy to try? I had heard then that his name was Ananta Singh. (17)

This anecdote begins with examples of superhuman strength that seemingly defy rational explanation. It then introduces "the white giant," a veritable "Tarzan," as part of this superhuman continuum. The challenge by the "white giant" sets up two notable oppositions. The challenger and his opponent embody differences in age and nationality. While the "giant" is an "Englishman," his opponent is an Indian "youth." In meeting the Englishman's challenge, the youth symbolically defeats Tarzan. This defeat can be read as a repudiation of the Tarzan myth, the ultimate white male colonizer's fantasy of "going native," in which the actual (African) native has been eliminated altogether in favor of the pristine innocence of nature.[5] Chittagong's own Ananta Singh rises to challenge the physical supremacy of the Englishman, proving that the English can be defeated, even on their own terms.

At the same time, however, the incident links the young Singh with a

Hindu mythic past in which public challenges and displays of masculine strength loom large. Singh joins the youthful ranks of Rama and Arjuna. In the *Ramayana*, Rama rises to King Janaka's challenge by lifting, bending, and stringing Shiva's enormous bow in front of an awed audience. Similarly, in the *Mahabharata* Arjuna is the only one who can meet the challenge of Draupadi's public *swayamwara*—an ancient ceremony in which an upper-caste woman garlands her choice of a husband—where competitors are required to "string a bow kept on a pedestal and shoot five arrows at a revolving target above by looking at its reflection on a pan of oil below" (R. K. Narayan 32). Both contests reward the victors with marriage. Rama wins Sita as his bride, and Arjuna gains Draupadi as a spouse (though he ends up sharing her with his four brothers, on account of filial duty and as a result of a semantic misunderstanding). Given the gendering of South Asia as a female in nationalist discourse, in Singh's case the female prize becomes India herself.

Dutt's fellow combatants, as evident from her quotations, also muster Western literary references in the service of heroic-nationalist individualism to create discursive parallels between themselves and British military heroes. Dutt quotes extensively from her comrade Ganesh Ghosh's poem "The Chittagong Brigade," which echoes Tennyson's "The Charge of the Light Brigade." Though it is impossible to reconstruct Ghosh's original text from her fragments, we can arrive at the significance of the excerpts that Dutt quotes and see how these fit into the larger project of mythologizing the terrorists by evoking associations which would resonate with a metropolitan readership. In the following passage, italics demarcate Ghosh's text from Dutt's:

"*Steadily*
   Step by step
      Forward marched
         To the grave,
            To the field of fame
         Forward marched
           The youths brave."

Then he wrote: *The fifty-eight marched on for four days, over the hills—without food, without sleep—haggard but determined. They pushed on under the blazing April sun, without any cover—over the bleak, waterless hilly wastes. The water-bottles were hot like pieces of live charcoal. Couldn't shoulder the rifles.*

They were sizzling hot.

Then—*"Tegra opened martyrdom's gate"*, he wrote. Tegra was the first to fall before machinegun bullets. He was Loknath Bal's younger brother. Then others—many others—were mown down. (27–28)

Significantly, the excerpts that Dutt quotes and their focus on the physical elements of the environment such as the blazing sun, the waterless hills, and the heat differ strikingly from representations of nature in the Bengali folk tradition, where nature and physical elements function within three interpretive frameworks: the natural, the religious, and the sexual. In Ghosh's poem, however, the allegorical elements inhere in the personification of nature as the enemy, which threatens the terrorists with dehydration and unbearable heat and becomes their agent of death. Allegory operates through a geopolitical semiotics, with nature signifying the repressiveness of the British colonial state.

Written as it is in English, "The Chittagong Brigade" draws less on a Bengali literary tradition than on an English one, echoing Tennyson's poem, composed in 1854 in response to the deaths of English soldiers in the Crimean War. Because of a confusion over orders during the war, a brigade of six hundred British cavalrymen charged some entrenched batteries of Russian artillery in what became a senseless slaughter of British troops. As a result, three fourths of the horsemen lost their lives. Tennyson ends his poem with the following stanza:

When can their glory fade?
O the wild charge they made!
All the world wondered.
Honor the charge they made!
Honor the Light Brigade,
Noble six hundred! (Abrams et al. 1176)

Ghosh's last stanza is a creative transformation of Tennyson's piece:

When can their glory fade
O, the brave fight they gave
Honour the Chittagong brigade
The noble fifty-eight. (28)

Ghosh strategically echoes Tennyson so as to give the terrorists the same status of national heroes that Tennyson gave to the British soldiers during the Crimean War. Ironically, Ghosh draws on a British poem about the British army to establish the bravery of Indians resisting British colonial rule. There is further irony given that Tennyson's poem is also a critique of the bad military leadership and political foolhardiness which led to the massacre of the Light Brigade, as shown by his use of the line "Someone had blundered" in his poem.

The various textual strategies deployed by Dutt in *Chittagong Armoury Raiders Reminiscences*, such as its multiple literary, religious, and historical allusions and its shifts of narrative perspective, both authenticate her text as a participants' account and help transform her comrades into regional mythic figures in northern India. Indeed, she often attributes stories about the terrorists to "the people," suggesting that her comrades have already attained mythic status in the region. P. C. Joshi, the general secretary of the Communist Party of India from 1935 to 1947 and Dutt's husband, agrees with this assessment. In the preface to the first edition of the book, he writes: "To read these reminiscences is to understand what made the leaders of the group legendary figures and the humblest of them household names where they were born and worked" (v). A constitutive feature of heroic-nationalist individualism, then, is the discursive construction of the nationalist subject as a heroic figure, authenticated by history and certified by her or his resemblance to popular-culture icons, whose capacities include the intellectual agility, courage, and physical stamina to challenge the colonial state.

PERFORMING TERRORISM

Because terrorist acts function as performances that showcase the courage of individual nationalist subjects, heroic-nationalist individualism conceives of political violence in symbolic terms. Until 1928 Jugantar concentrated on targeting British officials, policemen, and collaborators for assassination. Because these groups were symbols of the colonial state and its collaborators, the terrorists sought through assassination to alert both the government and South Asian society at large that the nationalist struggle and Indian independence were imminent. In other words, just as nationalist terrorism was primarily directed at disrupting the routine operations of the colonial state, so too did it attempt to convey to the general populace that the constituted authority was no longer entrenched and unchallenged. As Baljit Singh has remarked, the symbolic importance of terrorist acts derives from their resonance with three groups: the populace, the regime in power, and the resistance organization itself (8). Terrorism affects each group differently: the populace by creating local heroes willing to risk their lives for the collective good; the colonial state by destroying its military capability and challenging its psychological hold over the populace; and the resistance organization, by sometimes promoting internal stability and growth (Singh 8).

Jugantar's political assassinations exhibit these characteristics. Reflecting on the assassinations that took place in Bengal during the nationalist period, Tara Ali Baig comments: "Looking at terrorism today, I can't help feeling that was a rather polite kind of terrorism. There was no question of bombing groups of innocent people. There were definitely targeted individuals" (quoted in Masani 115). Before 1924 most of Jugantar's assassination targets consisted of Indians who belonged to the police department, which had waged an active campaign against the terrorists (Laushey 24, Nath 39). Indians who were not officials of the government were also selected as targets if they fell into one of three categories: police informants, witnesses who testified against the terrorists in court, and terrorists within the organization who had betrayed fellow members (Nath 39). Some of the terrorists, Shaileshwar Nath observes, conceptualized the assassination of traitors as a form of "divine dispensation, inasmuch as, the English merely tried to serve their own country whereas the Indians were traitors to their Mother" (40).

After 1924 Jugantar decided to target Europeans, generally government officials, for assassination. From 1931 to 1932 Jugantar's targets included police inspectors, district magistrates, and a sessions judge. Unsuccessful attempts were made to assassinate Dacca's divisional commissioner, the governor of Bengal, and the commissioner of police of Calcutta, Sir Charles Tegart, notorious for his torture of terrorists (Tripathy 46). Nath describes another seemingly curious aspect of these assassinations: "most of the murders were committed in broad daylight and in the most crowded localities" (40). Bina Das attempted to assassinate the governor of Bengal, Sir Stanley Jackson, in broad daylight in the middle of Calcutta University's Convocation ceremony. Santi Ghosh and Suniti Choudhury assassinated the district magistrate of Comilla on his veranda in the middle of the day. All three women were arrested immediately after their acts. A good deal of the power of these assassinations

as symbolic acts derived from their public performance and the willingness of individual terrorists to take responsibility for them.

For Indian nationalists, terrorist activities as public performances
were also an intervention in the racialized discourse of the Bengali babu,
a figure much denigrated by colonial authorities. The highly educated
Bengali community challenged British conceptions of Indians as generally childlike and primitive (Islam 7). Colonial authorities attributed a
childish naïveté to Indians, finding evidence for this stereotype among
communities that appeared to fit easily into this category: peasants,
"tribal" groups, and the princely classes, who were viewed as childishly
self-serving (7). As Philip Mason, a former colonial official, admitted:
"British officers in colonial situations always . . . like the simple, unspoilt
people" (quoted in Allen 199). The educated classes, especially Western-
educated Bengalis, were dismissed as comic imitations of Westerners
and were virulently caricatured in the figure of the Bengali babu: a small,
dark-skinned, effeminate, male intellectual who had an imperfect command of English. *Hobson-Jobson*, the dictionary of British India's patois,
describes "baboo" as "often used with a slight savour of disparagement,
as characterizing a superficially cultivated, but too often effeminate, Bengali . . . . The word has come often to signify 'a native clerk who writes
English'" (Crooke 44). In Charles Allen's *Plain Tales from the Raj*, former
colonial officials describe "the fashion" of denigrating "the *babu* type":

> 'We used to make fun of them, very unfairly, because they were in-
> terpreting rules which we had made.' *Babu* jokes, based on the En-
> glish language either wrongly or over-effusively applied, were a con-
> stant source of amusements for all 'Anglo-India'. Coupled with the
> denigration of the *babu* was a traditional distrust of the Bengali—
> 'litigious, very fond of an argument'—who was frequently seen as a
> trouble-maker: 'He doesn't appeal to many British people in the same
> way as the very much more manly, direct type from upper India.' (37)

This stereotype was so pernicious that it has remained current in the
post-Empire. In an interview that appeared in the *Souvenir Chowkidar*
(1986), the Raj revival writer Pat Barr asks Geoffrey Moorhouse, the
author of *Calcutta*, "whether some Bengalis might resent having the story
of their capital so well told by a foreigner who never even lived there"
(Llewellyn-Jones 42). Moorhouse replies: "They disagreed with some of
it naturally, *Bengalis always argue*. But they like the book" (Llewellyn-Jones

42; emphasis mine). Several years later, the *Chowkidar* in fall 1989 assured its readers that "a Bengali without a point of view is like a fish out of water" (Llewellyn-Jones 81). The term "Bengalis" is a regional and cultural marker, signifying people whose ancestors are from Bengal and who have a common language and culture. In these examples, all Bengalis have been cast as babus, highly opinionated and consequently slightly ridiculous.

The stereotype of the Bengali babu belonged to a gendered colonial discourse of racial typologies, as the British division of Indians into the martial and nonmartial races attests. In *Plain Tales from the Raj*, former colonial officers identify the martial races as Gurkhas, Sikhs, Punjabi "Mohammedans," Jats, Dogras, Garhwalis, and Mahrattas (Allen 199–200). Lewis Le Marchand's characterization of the Gurkha soldier is typical of the discourse on the martial races, emphasizing as it does the innate simplicity, blind obedience, and tremendous courage of these men. The Gurkha, in Le Marchand's view, is "very proud, very gay, very simple. He's as brave as a mountain lion and he'll obey any order you like to give" (quoted in Allen 200). While the British valorized those races they had designated as martial ones, they denigrated the races they deemed nonmartial such as the Bengalis. In this regard, the performance of terrorism was crucial to establishing the Bengali nationalist subject as a political agent with military capabilities.

The Bengali terrorist movement, in other words, internalized the discourse of the martial races, which also resonated with traditional Hindu notions of caste. Ashis Nandy argues that the British concept of the martial races—"the hyper-masculine, manifestly courageous, superbly loyal Indian castes and subcultures" which "mirrored the British middle-class sexual stereotypes"—resurrected "the ideology of the martial races latent in the traditional Indian concept of statecraft" (7). This concept of statecraft was closely linked to the ksatriya (warrior) caste, whose duties traditionally included governance and the protection of the state. Aurobindo Ghosh, who was a terrorist before becoming a yogin in 1910, valorized the ksatriyas as the caste that would be the agent of Indian independence. In helping to produce much of the ideological and cultural foundations of the terrorist movement, Ghosh drew on Hindu literature, particularly the *Bhagavad Gita* from the *Mahabharata*, to legitimize the use of violence as a strategy of resistance. In *The Doctrine of*

Passive Resistance, Ghosh sanctifies violence as a ksatriya's *dharma,* or moral duty. He writes:

> The morality of the Ksatriya justifies violence in times of war, and boycott is a war. . . . Aggression is unjust only when unprovoked; violence, unrighteous when used wantonly or for unrighteous ends. . . . The sword of the warrior is as necessary to the fulfillment of justice and righteousness as the holiness of the saint. . . . To maintain justice and prevent the strong from despoiling, and the weak from being oppressed, is the function for which the Kshatriya was created. "Therefore" says Sri Krishna in the *Mahabharata,* "God created battle and armour, the sword, the bow and the dagger." (quoted in Gordon 120)[6]

The terrorists' actions can be understood in part as an attempt to establish masculine notions of bravery through individual public acts of violence that accord with ksatriya martial values. Analyzing the data available for the first phase of terrorism in Bengal, Leonard Gordon notes that 90 percent of the terrorists came from high castes; they were *brahmins, kayasthas,* and *vaidyas* (146). Of the eleven people whom Dutt profiles, the majority are brahmins and from the kayastha caste. An important aspect of heroic-nationalist individualism, then, was the public performance of assassinating Europeans and native collaborators and of staging dramatic raids with little chance of military success, to challenge the British stereotype of the Bengali babu as cowardly and effeminate.

ENGENDERING THE ARMED STRUGGLE

As the internalization of the discourse of the martial races evidences, the terrorists accepted the colonial culture's ordering of manliness as greater than womanliness, which was in turn superior to femininity in men (Nandy 52). To this extent, they did not break out of the binary logic of colonialism. When the assassins were women, however, binary notions of gender became more complicated. If Indian men established their manliness by publicly assassinating European men, the assassination of European men by Indian women served to undermine European manhood. Indian women had long been considered backward and submissive in comparison with their European counterparts. The female terrorists were potent examples that Indian women could challenge British authority, by inverting the colonial ordering that equated strength with the masculine and the colonizer and weakness with the feminine and the colonized. The British government's treatment of women in the mainstream nationalist movement often emphasized this ordering. F. C. Hart, a former policeman who served in the Special Branch, describes one encounter with female satyagrahis:

> A number of women laid themselves down on the ground right across the street and held up all the traffic. When the Superintendent of Police arrived on the scene he was at first nonplussed. If they had been men he could have sent in policemen to lift them out bodily, but he daren't do it with women. So he thought for a bit and then he called for fire hoses and with the hoses they sprayed these women who were lying on the ground. They only wore very thin saris and, of course, when the water got on them all their figures could be seen. The constables started cracking dirty jokes and immediately the women got up and ran. (quoted in Allen 206)

In this example, the superintendent of police has marshaled the Indian cultural concept of sharam to the authorities' advantage. Sharam, or shame, is a powerful concept used to control Indian women which is closely linked to notions of sexual chastity and has come to signify sexual impropriety of some sort. The term can be employed to cover a whole range of behavior. By exposing women's bodies to the public gaze, the British authorities violated traditional norms of female propriety, according to which women covered their bodies as a sign of their chastity. The authorities' shrewd manipulation of sharam effectively quashed the women's political protest.[7]

Though the female terrorists' actions symbolically emasculated European men, they did not theorize their actions in feminist terms. For instance, Bina Das, who unsuccessfully attempted to assassinate Sir Stanley Jackson, the governor of Bengal, during the convocation ceremony at Calcutta University in 1932, explained her act in the following manner:

> I had been thinking—is life worth living in an India, so subject to wrong and continually groaning under the tyranny of a foreign government or is it not better to make one supreme protest against it by

offering one's life away? Would not the immolation of a daughter of India and of a son of England awaken India to the sin of its acquiescence to its continued state of subjection and England to the iniquities of its proceedings . . . . All these [sufferings of the people] and many others worked on my feelings and worked them into a frenzy. The pain became unbearable and I felt as if I would go mad if I could not find relief in death. I only sought the way to death by offering myself at the feet of my country and invite the attention of all by my death to the situation created by the measures of the Government, *which can unsex even a frail woman like myself, brought up in all the best tradition of Indian womanhood.* (quoted in Forbes, "Ideals of Indian Womanhood" 64; emphasis in original)

Das's explanation does not describe the relationship between India and England as simply that of victim and victimizer. Rather she holds both countries culpable for England's continued rule over India. By describing herself as a "daughter of India" and Jackson as a "son of England," Das implicitly couches the relationship between both countries in a familial metaphor. As members of the same generation, Jackson and Das are siblings, whose deaths will become symbols that will "awaken" the English and Indians to the injustice of colonial rule. Das's use of the familial metaphor rewrites the relationship between the two countries implied by E. M. Forster's *A Passage to India.* Forster's positioning of the colonial encounter within a perverse relationship—with suggestions of sexual assault—between an Indian man and an Englishwoman became a trope for later writers of the Raj. Paul Scott literalized this trope by initiating *The Raj Quartet* with the rape of an Englishwoman by a number of Indian men. Scott's "story of a rape" is a symbol of "two nations in violent opposition locked in an imperial embrace of such long standing and subtlety it was no longer possible for them to know whether they hated or loved one another" (Scott 1).

But the sibling metaphor employed by Das does not altogether break with the sexual implications of Forster's narrative. Das simultaneously envisions Jackson's death as well as her own by "immolation." This reference to immolation conjures up the practice of *sati,* the immolation of a Hindu woman on her husband's funeral pyre. Satis are venerated as minor deities for expressing the ultimate devotion to their *pati-vrata,* the husband-God. Lata Mani argues that the debate around sati was part of a

larger process of "reconstituting" indigenous tradition under colonial
rule: "in different ways, women and brahmanic scripture become inter-
locking grounds for this rearticulation. Women become emblematic of
tradition, and the reworking of tradition is largely conducted through
debating the rights and status of women in society" (90). Sati was prevalent among upper-caste Bengalis, who were major participants in the
rearticulation of tradition. The area around Calcutta had the highest
concentration of upper caste satis in the early nineteenth century (Mani
88). Das says that she has been "brought up in all the best tradition of
Indian womanhood," a tradition which at one time included sati.[8] Her
subtle reference to sati metaphorically makes Jackson her husband. But
if he is metaphorically her husband, he is also her brother, rendering
their relationship incestuous and, by implication, "unnatural." Their
relationship is symptomatic of the perversity of the times, in which the
repressive measures of the Government have "unsex[ed] even a frail
woman like" Das.

Das's assassination attempt, according to Geraldine Forbes, was intended "to rouse people to action because Bina was an Indian girl driven
to an unnatural act by the British Raj" ("Ideals of Indian Womanhood"
65). For all of Das's protestations that the violence of her action is
antithetical to female nature, her Hindu cultural background and that of
the Bengali terrorists are replete with strong, violent, female figures.
Shakti is the female power principle embodied in the Goddesses Kali and
Durga, who are both manifestations of Shiva's spouse Parvati and highly
venerated in Bengal. Rama Joshi and Joanna Liddle describe Kali as "a
malevolent destroyer, the manifestation of a terrible sinister force, black
anger, implacable and bloodthirsty" (54). The gods created Kali to save
them from their more powerful enemies. After completing her task, she
continued her rampage of killing until her husband Shiva appeased her
by lying down in front of her (55). In her malevolent aspect Kali demands
blood sacrifices (55). In her more benevolent manifestation as Durga,
she is figured as a female warrior riding a tiger, with weapons in most of
her multiple arms. Shakti came to symbolize the "Motherland in different stages and conditions" (Mahajan 223). V. D. Mahajan elaborates
this point:

> Jagatdhatri—riding a lion which has the prostrate body of an elephant
> under its paw, represented the Motherland in the early jungle clearing

stage. This is, says Bankim Chandra, the Mother as she was. *Kali* the grim goddess dancing on the prostrate form of Shiva, the God— *Durga*, the ten-headed [sic] goddess, armed with swords and spears in some hands riding a lion, fighting with demons this, says Bankim Chandra, is the mother as she will be. (223)[9]

The early terrorists drew on these potent Hindu symbols of women warriors for inspiration. Barindra Kumar Ghosh, the younger brother of Aurobindo Ghosh, and Bhupendra Nath Dutt, the brother of Swami Vivekananda, started the political journal *Jugantar*, from which the later terrorists took their name. "Jugantar" literally means "a different age." In the context of the nationalist struggle, it can be translated as "a new age." (Indeed, the *Samsad Bengali/English Dictionary* adds "an epoch making revolution" to these definitions.)[10] Ghosh and B. N. Dutt published the journal from 1906 to 1908, when the authorities shut it down under the Newspapers (Incitement to Offences) Act (R. C. Majumdar, *Revolutionary Movement in Bengal* 7). With a circulation of around seven thousand in 1907, *Jugantar* was taken seriously by the British, as the *Sedition (Rowlatt) Committee's Report* indicates: "Its character and teaching entirely justify the comments of the Chief Justice, Sir Lawrence Jenkins, quoting and adopting the following words of the Sessions Judge of Alipore. 'They exhibit a burning hatred of the British race, they breathe revolution in every line, they point out how revolution is to be effected' " (7). *Jugantar* exhorted its readers to sacrifice themselves at the altar of India, to take a life before giving one's life. Some examples of their rhetoric include the following statements:

We will bathe in the enemy's blood and with it dye Hindustan. (quoted in Mahajan 232)

Look there, the terrible sword glowing with blood is swirling. Look there, the guerrilla bands are swarming the country; they are plundering the arsenals; there, the vacant throne of the demon is being washed away by the waves of the Bay of Bengal. (quoted in Mahajan 232)

Will the Bengalee worshipper of Shakti shrink from the shedding of blood? . . . The worship of the goddess will not be consummated if you sacrifice your lives at the shrine of Independence without shedding blood. (quoted in Mahajan 239)

In these passages, India becomes the Goddess Kali herself, who demands a blood sacrifice. In constructing India this way, the terrorists sanctified—through Hinduism—the violence that they visited on the British. The terrorists' use of Hindu rhetoric paralleled Gandhi's mobilization of Hindu discourse in his campaign of nonviolence. And though unintended in both cases, this language had the consequence of excluding Muslim participation in the movement. The Bengali terrorists counted few Muslim participants among them, even though Bengal had a significant Muslim population at the time.

The apparent contradiction of having a strong, powerful goddess represent a subjugated country was partially resolved by having India simultaneously figured as the "Mother." Poetry, prose, and popular songs invoked and addressed the motherland. This motif even appeared woven in the borders of dhotis, the garment commonly worn by Bengali and brahmin men. In 1910 the English had to order the confiscation of dhotis which flaunted the following Bengali poem in their borders:

> Mother, farewell,
> I shall go to the gallows with a smile,
> The people of India will see this.
> One bomb can kill a man, there are a lakh of bombs in our homes.
> Mother, what can the English do? (quoted in Mahajan 235)

During 1930, in the coastal districts surrounding Midnapur where the Government monopoly over salt manufacture excited popular protest, India was often represented as a mother. "A nationalist song," Tanika Sarkar writes, "compared the salt-earth to the mother's breasts from which no one had the right to take the child away" (80). Nationalist pamphlets contained illustrations of "Mother India in chains and tatters with white men dragging off her rich attire and jewels across the seas" (T. Sarkar 82). The use of the India-as-mother simile implicitly gendered India's nationalist subjects as male. Indian women of that generation accrued status and power as mothers through the birth of sons. India's male sons would liberate her and accord her the respect due her.

MATERIALIZING GENDER

Given the ideological gendering of India in nationalist discourse and, more specifically, in the terrorist movement, the participation of women in the armed struggle takes on a special significance. While terrorist women far exceeded the traditional roles of sisters, daughters, wives, and mothers prescribed for them by South Asian patriarchy, they did not theorize their political work in feminist terms. Rather, they understood their agency in terms of fulfilling a duty and a moral obligation to the nationalist cause. In this regard, perhaps, filial and marital devotion traditionally directed to fathers and husbands was sublimated into a devotion and faith toward the emerging Indian nation. Indeed, the terrorist organization itself was structured hierarchically, mirroring the structure of the South Asian family. It may be because patriarchal social relations were so pervasive, in combination with the terrorists' internalization of British stereotypes of the martial races and the concomitant valorization of the male ksatriya nationalist subject among terrorists, that Dutt's *Chittagong Armoury Raiders Reminiscences* provides scant information on the material practices regarding women in the resistance organization.

Before 1930 few women were admitted to Jugantar, while Anushilan, the other major terrorist organization in the region, prohibited their membership altogether. After 1930, however, women began to participate in all phases of Jugantar's activities, carrying out assassinations and sometimes even leading raids against colonial targets. For example, Preeti Waddadar led a raid on the Pahartali railway club on September 24, 1932. Though she was willing to participate in the raid, she initially expressed reluctance to lead it. Surjya Sen convinced her that her role as a leader would be an inspiration to other potential female recruits (Forbes, "Goddesses or Rebels?" 11). The terrorists defined the raid as a success, since their losses were limited to one fatality with twelve others injured. But Waddadar died in the effort after taking potassium cyanide outside the club. Her suicide, as Forbes notes, has been read a number of ways:

> Her sister claimed she was wounded in the attack and took cyanide to prevent her capture by the British. Others have seen her death as the act of a young revolutionary overzealous to sacrifice herself. She had carried with her a letter to her mother in which she said that she was going to sacrifice her life for "truth and freedom." The urge to become a martyr, a symbol of dedication to the country's freedom, has emerged as a strong element in the decisions made by these young women to participate in dramatic and violent acts. ("Goddesses or Rebels?" 12)

Dutt believed that Preeti, like Waddadar's sister, was wounded and committed suicide to avoid detention by the British. But detailed accounts of her death by other terrorists interpret her suicide as an act of political martyrdom. R. C. Majumdar pieced together this dramatic scene from accounts by Ananta Singh and Ganesh Ghose. After the three-minute raid, one of the fleeing participants ran back to urge Waddadar to hurry and join them. Majumdar describes the scene thusly:

> Handing over her revolver to him, Pritilata said. "All of you escape, do not tarry. Hit the enemy time and again and try to overthrow them; this is my last request. Go with my good wishes to you all, give my respects to 'Masterda'." Pointing above with her finger, she said "That is my destination, the martyrs are calling me". With that she swallowed some potassium cyanide and embraced death. Sewn inside her garment was discovered a picture of Srikrishna. (History of Modern Bengal 280)

Waddadar was the first woman to die in action, and her fellow combatants largely interpreted her death in terms of its symbolic value. "From Preeti's actions," Dutt claims, "people were convinced for the first time that Indian women can do what our men have done. They can give their lives for their country as easily as men can" (44). Majumdar's description of Waddadar's suicide and Dutt's explanation of it suggest that the character of "trust" engendered by the resistance movement implied a strong, symbolic element in which Hindu notions of sacrifice assumed a distinct importance.

Yet because of Dutt's recognition of the power of example for Indian women, it seems odd that she did not engage the question of gender more fully. The Chittagong Armoury Raiders Reminiscences makes little of the special hardships that women must have encountered because of their gender. Dutt does not allude to the prevailing attitudes governing the conduct of single females. Forbes explains how the risk of scandal made it "difficult to arrange meetings between members of the opposite sex" ("Goddesses or Rebels?" 9). Arranging a simple discussion between men and women terrorists could entail complicated maneuvers (9). In fact, few of the women were adequately prepared to use firearms because it was so difficult to arrange secret training sessions for women. Most of the women did complete a course in " 'revolutionary skills' which technically included physical fitness, ju-jitsu, daggers, fencing, motor-driving, and sharpshooting" (9). Forbes speculates that "the reason women were not utilized more frequently or in different ways was more a result of logistical problems in training and supplying weapons to women than due to either the reluctance of males to utilize women or the unwillingness of women to perform violent acts" (9).

In spite of the limitations on their mobility and their right of association, women were assigned many of the same duties as the men in the organization (3). They helped manufacture, smuggle, and hide weapons. They acted as messengers. Women wrote and distributed propaganda. They "absconded," going underground when called to do so and concealing absconding comrades, sometimes providing cover for them by posing as their wives (T. Sarkar 152). They assassinated members of the British ruling elite. Women participated in all stages of action: planning, organizing, and leading raids on the government. They did not, however, assume the top positions of leadership or attempt to transform gender relations within the movement. "They did not even justify their revolutionary actions on grounds of equality in political choice and protest," Tanika Sarkar claims. "They sought to explain their unconventional behavior in terms of a religious sacrifice at a time of exceptional national crisis" (152).

Dutt is also silent about the female combatants' relationships with their natal families. This lacuna in her text is curious given that the Bengali family plays an enormous role in circumscribing a single woman's activities. There are few references to Dutt's own family in her narrative, and indeed the terrorist organization itself emerges as a kind of alternative family. She refers to her elder male and female comrades in kinship terms, calling her closest male comrades "*da*," the abbreviated form of the Bengali "*dada*" (an older brother), and her female comrades "*di*," the abbreviation for "*didi*" (an older sister). Kinship terms in Bengal, as Ronald Inden and Ralph Nicholas remind us, reveal not only kinship roles but also roles defined by sex, generation, and age (71). Dutt's choice of sibling titles is significant inasmuch as the relationship between siblings is one of the most important in Bengal (Inden and Nicholas 5). The love between siblings of opposite sex is the most egalitarian relationship between men and women of the same generation and family (24). Even so, Inden and Nicholas rightly observe:

> Within the family the egalitarian love that siblings have for each other
> is supposed to be subordinated to hierarchical love, based upon the
> differences in their ages. The parental love (*sneha*) that unites elder
> siblings with their juniors and the filial love (*bhakti*) that unites youn-
> ger siblings with their elders is modeled after the hierarchical love
> that parents and children have for each other. (28)

I do not suggest that Dutt decided to call her comrades by the kinship
terms of the patriarchal Indian family simply on account of her gender.
Rather the terrorists as a whole group employed them to refer to one
another. Their usage of these kinship terms relies on the cultural definition of *atmiya-svajana*, used to demarcate "one's own people." "One's
own people" does not have a fixed meaning, encompassing as it does
both filiative and affiliative ties. "Under appropriate circumstances" it
can mean anyone (Inden and Nicholas 3). For example, atmiya-svajana
can be blood relatives, "persons related by marriage, by living together in
the same house, neighborhood, or village, by being members of the
same school class, by working together in the same office, by taking
instruction from the same guru, by going on pilgrimage together," and
so forth (3).

Leonard Gordon describes the organization of the terrorists into basic units of action known as "*dals*" (142). Dals were grouped around a
single dada and often bore his name (142). "In addition to his primary
function as a political leader," Gordon comments, "the *dada* seems to
hold something of the neoparental authority which the older brother
would exercise in a Bengali family" (142). His authority partly derived
from his age, since the dada was older than his followers. Gordon also
notes that the relationship between the dada and his follower reflected
an important religious concept, the *guru-shishya* relationship, in which
"the disciple is to give complete loyalty, devotion, and respect to [the]
teacher" (142). Surjya Sen, the leader of the Chittagong terrorists, was
known as "Masterda." The guru-shishya relationship was formally recognized in Sen's title and reflected his professional status as a school-
teacher. In this regard, the guru-shishya relationship between follower
and leader may be closely related to two facts: many of the dadas were
schoolteachers, and colleges and secondary schools provided the major recruiting grounds for terrorist combatants. The large number of
schoolteachers involved in the movement might be connected tangen-

tially to the high incidence of unemployment among these classes at that time (Mahajan 224–25).

Thus, though Dutt does not explicitly identify the criteria which determined the status of individual terrorist women within the movement, it seems clear that gender, filial, generational, and educational hierarchies played major roles in conditioning social relations. As a young, female student, the gendered terrorist was subject in several ways to the authority of older, movement males, who were often professional educators.

FROM TERRORISM TO ELECTORAL POLITICS: (RE-)PUBLICATION IN CONTEXT

Chittagong Armoury Raiders Reminiscences was first published in 1945, after Dutt's six-year incarceration as a political prisoner in the Andaman Islands and her conversion to communism during that time. In fact, her conversion to communism, as well as that of her fellow combatants, is one of the recurring themes throughout the book and challenges the ideology of heroic-nationalist individualism which it cannot, however, fully transcend. As the high incidence of communist conversions among the terrorists suggests, Dutt's experiences were paradigmatic of a process of political conscientization among Bengali combatants. In the preface to the first edition, P. C. Joshi, the general secretary of the Communist Party of India from 1935 to 1947, defines Dutt's participation in the Bengali terrorist movement as crucial to her later awakening to communism: "To read her own story is to understand a living phase of our national movement, how was it that in the thirties the vast majority of the terrorist detenus and prisoners became communists. . . . These reminiscences reveal how terrorism was the infant as communism is the mature stage of their revolutionary lives" (v–vi). Yet heroic-nationalist individualism haunts the very structure of Dutt's account of collective action, terrorism, and communist conversion, and is most evident in her failure to articulate a coherent Marxist critique of terrorism as an effective means to gain national liberation even though such critiques were then in circulation.

The absence of a Marxist critique of terrorism and of heroic-nationalist individualism in *Chittagong Armoury Raiders Reminiscences* might be linked to Dutt's twofold political agenda at the time of the text's first publication: to secure the release of her incarcerated comrades and to run as the communist candidate in the forthcoming provincial elections, an intention declared in Joshi's preface to the first edition of her text. The book is dedicated to her incarcerated "dadas and comrades," accompanied by a statement voicing "confidence that the people [f]or whom they suffered and fought [w]ill help us to get them out." The explicit mission of the book, according to Dutt, is to bring attention to the plight of political prisoners and to galvanize people into demanding their release. This political mission informs the entire book and is reiterated in individual chapters, particularly the ones on those comrades in detention; these chapters end by spelling out the effects of incarceration on their health and with a plea for their release. While this mission is an explicitly stated one and reaffirmed throughout the text, Dutt's electoral campaign is only mentioned once in the preface. Joshi concludes his preface with the following proclamation: "In every Chittagong home Kalpana Dutt is called 'Amar Meye',—our daughter. This daughter of Chittagong will seek, once again, the verdict of her parents, the people of Chittagong, as the communist candidate in the coming provincial elections" (vi). His electoral proclamation is coded in the rhetoric of atmiya-svajana, universalizing the family unit at the regional level for the purposes of political representation. The Chittagong armory raid was conducted with its status as symbolic capital in mind, to inspire Indians with the confidence that they could defeat the British. Years later, as a candidate for the provincial elections, Dutt could draw on this symbolic capital and its creation of a pantheon of heroic figures at the regional level to acquire support for her electoral campaign.

Indeed, Dutt's electoral campaign informs *Chittagong Armoury Raiders Reminiscences* in a number of ways. Though she frequently refers to her conversion to communism, she fails to acknowledge any of the critiques of terrorism developed by various Marxist theoreticians which might have demythologized the terrorists and ultimately have cost her votes. To avoid what Gramsci terms a "passive revolution" in which a new political formation achieves power without changing the fundamental structure of social relations, an insurgency movement should ideally be organized on two fronts, the military and the social (Rubenstein 29).[11] On the military front, the rebel army "uses irregular tactics, including hit and run attacks, 'expropriations' of arms and money, and selective assassinations, to tie down the regime's forces and hamper its recruitment efforts" (29). On the social front, the leadership should simultaneously set up institutions of "dual power," which are democratically representative, consisting of committees linked to a central political organization (30). The constitution of the committees would be subject to the needs and requirements of the people and, most importantly, be determined by them. Such committees could be organized around issues like health care, agriculture, and education, hence establishing a civil infrastructure which would make the transition to democracy much smoother. In this regard, the organizing endeavors of the Farabundo Marti Front for National Liberation, during El Salvador's Civil War, and the Unified National Leadership of the Uprising in the Occupied Territories, during the first Intifada, have been exemplary.[12] The Chittagong terrorists, however, never moved beyond the military front and into the social front. Their failure to organize alternative structures of civil society constitutes their major weakness, one that Dutt does not acknowledge in her book.

Marxist criticisms of terrorism, which Dutt could have drawn on in her account of the terrorist movement and in her analysis of the limitations of heroic-nationalist individualism, were circulating internationally and in India during the mid twenties and thirties. The July 1925 issue of the *Masses* includes a manifesto by the Young Communist International (YCI) addressed to "The Bengal Revolutionary Organisation of Youth." Though no such organization by this name existed in Bengal, the article was probably produced in pamphlet form and smuggled into India (Adhikari 463). It is reproduced in its entirety in the *Documents of the History of the Communist Party of India*. The manifesto recognizes the "heroic efforts" of the terrorists, but gently reminds them that they have been ineffective, unable "to obtain any considerable concessions," locating this ineffectiveness in the terrorists' failure to understand that workers and peasants—rather than the intelligentsia—are the true agents of change (473). The YCI urges the terrorists "to set to work to organise and rally [these classes] on the basis of a revolutionary programme which would meet their economic and political needs" (Adhikari 476). Such a program, the YCI believes, could be determined by the study of actual conditions for these classes. In addition to incorrectly identifying the intellectual as the revolutionary subject, the terrorist movement, according to the YCI, relied solely on the use of political violence directed at specific colonial officials as a strategy for national liberation. While acknowledging the revolutionary's "moral right to remove the executioners and the garrotters of the people," the YCI points out the limitations of terrorism in no uncertain terms:

> (1) a terrorist act directed against an individual does not remove the whole system: in place of the one who has been removed the British imperialism will appoint another; one official merely takes the place of another, but the system of oppression remains intact; (2) terror demands a tremendous expenditure of effort and diverts attention from the fundamental tasks of rallying, organising and revolutionarily educating the masses. (Adhikari 479)

According to the YCI, terrorism, as figured in the brave but finally individualistic acts of a few elite Bengalis, is incapable of mounting a frontal assault on the colonial system, which would require mobilizing a diverse spectrum of people to effect national liberation and the complete transformation of social relations. Such criticism, of course, fundamentally challenges the ideology of heroic-nationalist individualism by positing the nationalist subject as a collective one who is *not* necessarily a member of the bourgeoisie and whose class allegiances are with subaltern groups, namely peasants and workers. In spite of her avowed communist beliefs and her insistence on the centrality of communist ideology for revolutionary change, Dutt does not incorporate such criticisms of the Bengali terrorist movement into her text.

Her electoral campaign is also evident in Dutt's failure to mention another important aspect of Jugantar's plan to take over Chittagong. The original plan divided the terrorists into four groups, each of which would attack different targets: the Police Armoury, the Railway Armoury, the Telegraph and Telephone Exchange, and the European Club. While the first three are obvious military targets, Dutt neglects to refer to the group's decision to attack a civilian target. The fourth group, under the leadership of Naresh Roy and Triguna Sen, had been instructed to attack the club and kill European civilians to avenge the Jallianwalla Bagh massacre (R. C. Majumdar, *History of Modern Bengal* 264). Several factors help explain the terrorists' plan to attack a civilian target. Innocent Indian children, women, and men had been massacred at the Jallianwalla Bagh, and the murders of British civilians would have established a terrible reciprocity between colonizer and colonized. Furthermore, British civilians had been complicit in the Jallianwalla Bagh massacre, because they had taken up a collection for Dyer, amounting to over £26,000 (no small sum in those days), to show their appreciation and support for the general in the face of the official reprimand (Cockburn 310). The club, moreover, itself represented a site of humiliation and racial inferiorization for Indians, who were excluded from its premises as members, but allowed entry as servants. As Forster's *A Passage to India* shows, clubs like the European Club were racist sanctuaries for Europeans from Indians, and, during civil unrest, refuges. But by 1930, six years after the publication of Forster's novel, the Europeans in Chittagong no longer regarded their club as a reliable sanctuary; instead, during times of native unrest, they sought safety in boats anchored off shore. Because the club was empty on their arrival, the terrorists did not succeed in their macabre mission. Dutt's decision to exclude this information, we might speculate, could be linked to her campaign for office and the necessity of establishing herself as an agent of peace and stability, whose electoral credibility depended on distancing herself from the violence and bloodshed of a civilian massacre.

Dutt's lament over the passing of what she calls "Chittagong's golden age," in which the terrorists were able to carry out their revolt, is similarly significant (25). Chittagong's people, she feels, have fallen under the rule of *goondas*, or thugs. She mentions the degenerate state of Chittagong at least six times, as in these passages:

The spirit of Surjya Sen is still alive in Chittagong. But it has to fight an uphill battle against corrupt elements in our society who have grown strong and powerful profiteers, war contractors, those who trade in destitute women on mass scale. Those of us who worked with him are filled with shame that Surjya Sen's Chittagong should be reduced to its present plight. (16)

Chittagong homes used to buzz with tales of heroism—those very homes today have become dens of cowardice and iniquity today Chittagong is under goondashahi today women in Chittagong sell themselves to lustful soldiers and greedy contractors. (24)

The devastating changes that have taken place in the life of Chittagong in these years cannot be understood without seeing them. There is widespread despondency, rules of social behaviour have been flouted, women from all sections are leading a life of shame. (43)

While Dutt draws on a male "heroic" past to mobilize voters in her electoral campaign, she simultaneously genders the "degenerate state of Chittagong" as female. The urgency of her political campaign derives from the rhetorical link of a moral fall with the sexual traffic in women. Women, specifically prostitutes, become a trope for the degraded condition of the region still under colonial rule. Dutt's election offers them the chance to fight a new battle, the battle against corruption which will "restore Chittagong to its former greatness" (43). The Communist Party will build a "bridge between the glorious past of Chittagong and the heroic future across the decline of the present" (57). And Kalpana Dutt, as the party candidate, will be the chief architect of this project.

Not only was the publication of the first edition of *Chittagong Armoury Raiders Reminiscences* imbricated in electoral politics, but so too was its republication in 1979. Like the earlier edition, the second was published by the People's Publishing House, which also published the *Documents of the History of the Communist Party in India*. A publisher's note to the second edition explains the republication of the text, emphasizing the role that the terrorist combatants played in the national liberation struggle:

> On 1930 entire India was rocked at the daring exploits of Surjya Sen and his comrades initiated by what is called Chittagong Armoury Raid. In the history of India's war of independence—the Youth Revolt of Chittagong is a glorious chapter written in the words of gold. They not only raided armoury and attacked the European club but also they faced the armed force of the mightiest imperialist power in direct confrontation, gave a fight which taught British imperialism a lesson.
>
> The People's Publishing House paid its humble tribute to the valiant heroes in bringing out a book containing their portraits from the pen of one of the legendary figures, Kalpana Dutt. On the eve of the 50th Anniversary of the memorable event we are bringing out the second edition with a new preface from the authoress.

The publisher's note and its emphasis on commemorating the "valiant heroes" of the "glorious chapter" of the "Youth Revolt of Chittagong," as well as on the martial aspects of the Bengali terrorist movement, promulgate the ideology of heroic-nationalist individualism fifty years after the event. Indeed, by reissuing an anniversary edition of Dutt's book, People's Publishing House insists that the Chittagong armoury raid was a seminal event in the Indian national liberation struggle, whose significance should be extended into the present.

This second edition appeared in 1979, the same year that the Janata Party started to dissolve with the resignation of the Socialist leaders Raj Narain and George Fernandes from Morarji Desai's cabinet. The Janata Party had delivered Indira Gandhi a resounding electoral defeat in 1977, as a result of her authoritarian actions from 1975 to 1977 during the "Emergency"—more popularly known as "Indira Raj" for Gandhi's censorship of the press, her suspension of the constitution, the large-scale imprisonment of members of the political opposition, and the intensification of counterinsurgency tactics against guerrilla movements. As in other Third World countries, one-party rule had been the order of the day for most of the post-independence period of the Indian political scene. Moreover, the Congress Party, which dominated Indian politics during this period, was itself dominated by the Nehru-Gandhi dynasty, which dated to the late nineteenth century and the participation of its patriarch, Motilal Nehru, in proto-nationalist politics. "Indian politics," Ved Mehta notes, "since Independence has been bedevilled by the relationships of father and daughter, mother and son, father and son, father-in-law and son-in-law, and husband and wife" (17). In 1979 Indira Gandhi's relatively low profile and the impending dissolution of the Janata Party coalition created the discursive space in which new narratives of national origin could appear.[13] "In the Congress history," Dutt writes in the preface to the second edition, "the revolutionaries were mentioned as 'terrorists' [and] it [is] only now we find that these revolutionaries are recognised as freedom-fighters along with their Congress counterparts" (xiii). Since most of the terrorists converted to communism sometime before India's independence in 1947, their addition to the mythology of national origin, through the republication of Chittagong Armoury Raiders Reminiscences, advanced the credibility of contemporary Indian communists.

The ideology of heroic-nationalist individualism that underwrites Chittagong Armoury Raiders Reminiscences is crucially marshaled in the service of electoral politics, through its initial publication and its commemorative reissue, at two distinct historical junctures, during the colonial period and as part of the post-independence phase of Indian politics. The publication contexts of the book provide a lens through which to interpret its textual absences and its construction of heroic-nationalist individualism. By contextualizing and rereading Dutt's account of the Chittagong Armoury Raid through the categories of collective action and mass empowerment, the limitations of nationalist terrorism and the ideology of heroic-nationalist individualism are made visible.

BRIDGING DISCURSIVE PARTITIONS

I have attempted to situate a discussion of heroic-nationalist individualism and the Bengali terrorist movement within the context of organizational politics—the theories, tactics, structure, and gender ideology—which underwrote the Chittagong Armoury Raid. The attention to women's location within organized armed struggle movements, in particular, has been overlooked within many accounts of Indian women in general and Indian nationalism in particular.[14] For example, many studies mention the assassination of District Magistrate C. G. B. Stevens of Comilla, described by Marjorie Cashmore in *Plain Tales From the Raj*. Noting that Stevens "was greatly loved by all the people of his district," who considered him their "*ma-bap* [mother-father]," Cashmore muses:

> [Stevens] loved India, he was devoted to India and like so many other men he worked long hours for India, and yet he met his end at the hands of two girls in saris. They came along to his bungalow and told his servant that they wanted to see the judge-*sahib*, as they had a petition to present to him. The judge came out on to the verandah and directly he got close to the girls with his hand out to receive the petition one of the girls pulled a pistol from her sari and killed him. (quoted in Allen 202)

Given that there were other Englishmen, contemptuous of Indians, who might have been considered more suitable targets by the terrorists, Cashmore asks why Stevens was marked for assassination. Many accounts refer to this incident, giving the bare details of the assassination and noting the relative youth of the assassins, Santi Ghosh, sixteen, and Suniti Choudhury, fifteen. None of the historical accounts, however, raises Cashmore's question. The failure to inquire behind the rationale to assassinate Stevens implicitly transforms the assassination into an arbitrary event, instead of considering it as a consciously planned action with its own logic which was governed by the exigencies of the Bengali terrorist movement.

Yet Jugantar's choice of Stevens as a victim was anything but arbitrary, as is clear from an interview about Bengali terrorists with Bibhuti Basu, who spent several months in prison because he was near the assassination. Basu stressed that Stevens was acknowledged by the terrorists to be a "very good man." But since the British authorities had murdered one of their comrades in detention at Midnapur District Jail, the terrorists conceptualized this assassination as a way of avenging his death. Because their dead comrade had a wife and small child, the group chose a British man in a similar situation, to draw, in Basu's words, "a parallel" between both murders.[15] As in the terrorists' plan to attack the European Club during the Chittagong armory raid, this assassination established a terrible reciprocity between the families of the colonizer and the colonized. The decision to assign the assassination to female terrorists—we might speculate—helped displace sympathy from the adult male magistrate to the two young girls. In addition, while male terrorists convicted of assassination were generally sentenced to death by hanging, women terrorists were given the more lenient sentence of life imprisonment on account of their gender and, quite often, their youth. Ghosh and Choudhury were sentenced to life imprisonment instead of death. Quite possibly, the movement considered the differential gender and generational consequences of terrorist action when delegating tasks to its members.

Jugantar's decision to assassinate Stevens does not get explained in the pages of nationalist histories or studies of Indian women. The absence of this sort of explanation in Indian nationalist histories bespeaks the necessity of acknowledging that those engaged in nationalist struggles are "thinkers as well as actors" and "that liberation movements have their own intellectual and political histories" (Lyons, "Writing in Trouble" 10). As part of a general corpus of writing on nationalism by nationalists, Dutt's *Chittagong Armoury Raiders Reminiscences* belongs to a body of texts generally neglected by Western scholars working on the problematic of nationalism. As Laura E. Lyons notes, much of the "traditional work on nationalism has focused on illuminating the historical and material conditions that gave rise both to nationalist ideology and to conceptions of the nation-state in the period of the enlightenment. This work remains largely metacritical; that is, it takes as its object of investigation other theories of nationalism" (10). The neglect of such materials suggests that Western scholars have not taken seriously practitioners of nationalism as theoreticians in their own right; as Lyons eloquently argues, "the 'theoretical partition' between writing *about* nationalism and writing *by* nationalists has erected blockades across our intellectual hinterlands which now must be dismantled" (10; emphasis in original). In the South Asian context, the project of dismantling such a partition would entail, as the interview with Bibhuti Basu indicates, both the reading of writing by nationalists and the supplementing of these accounts with oral histories of nationalists.

The necessity of listening to nationalist accounts is even more imperative given that the voices risk being lost to history with advancing age. The deaths of Kalpana Dutt on February 8, 1995, at the age of eighty-one and of Bibhuti Basu on November 13, 1999, at the age of eighty-four suggest the urgency of this particular historiographical mission. In the final analysis, oral histories become an important source for filling in the theoretical gaps and untangling the contradictions that inhere in existing narrative accounts of the Bengali terrorist movement and its ideology of heroic-nationalist individualism.

HEROIC-COLONIAL INDIVIDUALISM: RAJ NOSTALGIA AND THE RECUPERATION OF COLONIAL HISTORY

The European cemeteries of the Indian sub-continent and the rest of South Asia stand apart from the rest, for they enshrine a human history that is often glorious, often tragic and nearly always romantic. . . . The links that bind Britain and the sub-continent together are now nearly four hundred years old. They are older than the Raj and their significance will outlast it. The meeting between Europe and India has a permanent meaning for the world and the form which it took during a crucial time was enshrined in the British Raj. Its cemeteries are . . . a living part of the story. —Sir John Lawrence

All the [English] graves are in very bad condition—weed-choked, and stripped of whatever marble and railings could be removed. It is strange how, once graves are broken and overgrown in this way, then the people in them are truly dead. —Ruth Prawer Jhabvala

COLONIAL REGIMES OF KNOWLEDGE

Indian and Irish feminist and anticolonial movements get mystified and obliterated in contemporary nostalgia-for-Empire discourses. I am concerned with delineating the cultural apparatuses through which colonial historiography and, in particular, the ideology of heroic-colonial individualism continue to circulate. Colonial regimes of knowledge, I argued in chapter 1, rely on various rhetorical strategies to distance themselves from the systemic brutality of colonial power. These rhetorical strategies construct a reductive dichotomy of colonial officials in which some are deemed "bad" and others "good." For the bad officials, the ideology of rogue-colonial individualism displaces colonial violence—as manifest in surveillance, policing, and clashes between natives and the military— into less threatening narratives which single out and pathologize some individual British officials for acts of extreme brutality. For the good officials, the ideology of heroic-colonial individualism valorizes their acts of extreme heroism by making Indians responsible for the violent effects of colonial policy. This chapter first analyzes the rhetorical mechanisms by which colonial officials present themselves as heroic subjects coping with the difficulties of serving the Empire in three (neo-)colonial texts (*Plain Tales from the Raj* 1975, *Souvenir Chowkidar* 1986, and *Heat and Dust* 1975) and then considers the ideological effects of these nostalgic narratives in the context of the emergence of a Raj revival in the mid-seventies.

An investigation into these texts suggests that British history and literature cannot be easily periodized. One must consider the geographical, economic, ideological, and military aspects of British colonialism. The British seizure of territories in the subcontinent, for example, provided both the excuse and the means for extracting raw materials and capital from India to advance industrialization in Britain. The subcontinent became a captive market for surplus commodities and functioned, though to a lesser extent than other sites of settler colonialism, as the dumping ground for surplus British labor. As B. W. E. Alford notes, colonialism was ideologically underwritten by a "sense of duty born of a feeling of superiority, and a widely shared belief that upper-class Englishmen were destined to civilize large areas of the world in their own image" (101). Such notions were articulated in concepts like the "civilizing mission" and the "white man's burden" and enforced by the military, which was used to quell native unrest. It is colonial formations that exhibit these characteristics, which Masao Miyoshi calls "formal" or "administrative" colonialism. By the beginning of the First World War this form of colonialism governed 85 percent of the land surface of the world (731–32). According to Miyoshi, the period between 1945 and 1970 marks "the disappearance of administrative colonization from most regions of the world" and its substitution by transnational corporatism (727–28).[1] Indeed, most British colonies achieved independence during the quarter-century between the end of the Second World War and 1970, with some notable exceptions (Egypt in 1936, Belize in 1981, Brunei in 1984). The decolonization of the subcontinent in 1947 was rapidly followed, for example, by independence for Ceylon and Burma (1948), Sudan (1956), Ghana (1957), Nigeria and Somalia (1960), Kuwait and

Sierra Leone (1961), Jamaica, Uganda, Trinidad, and Tobago (1962), Borneo, Kenya, and Zanzibar (1963), Malawi, Malta, and Zambia (1965), and Aden (1967).

In spite of this massive decolonization, however, the period from 1970 to 2000 cannot be accurately described as "postcolonial." As Anne McClintock has argued, a too careless use of the term "postcolonialism" risks "obscuring the continuities and discontinuities of colonial and imperial power" (294). McClintock urges that various forms of global domination be distinguished, including colonization, internal colonization, deep settler colonization, and neocolonialism (295–96). The problem of "naming" the period of British history from 1975—when *Plain Tales from the Raj* and *Heat and Dust* were first published—to 1997 is magnified by the simultaneous existence of multiple repressive configurations in a decaying capitalist formation. These configurations range from direct continuing military occupation of the North of Ireland, a deep settler colony, and control of the Falkland Islands, to the brutal policing of black and poor white Britons, who are often described, somewhat problematically, as forming an "internal colony" within Britain itself.[2] Such a periodization would also have to account for the peculiar status of Hong Kong and other British dependencies such as Gibraltar.[3] The emergence of the Raj revival in the mid-seventies and early eighties must be understood in the context of Britain's economic decline relative to other Western economies, increasing tensions in the North of Ireland, domestic unrest against the institutionalized repression of black people, and the increased jingoism of white Britons stoked and ignited by the Falklands War.

Raj revival narratives, such as *Plain Tales from the Raj* and the newsletters of the British Association for Cemeteries in South Asia, are written either by ex-colonial officials and their wives who served the Empire in the period leading up to decolonization and the partition of the subcontinent in 1947, or by their descendants. This accounts for the persistence in these recent representations of British colonialism of certain narrative patterns, such as the reliance on nostalgia, the family romance, and the construction of the heroic British male subject. Even though these texts emerged three decades after Indian and Pakistani independence, the events narrated and attitudes articulated within their pages are "colonial" and permeated by the ideologies of English imperial superiority toward South Asians prevalent in the early twentieth century. In other words, these texts are not "postcolonial," because they have not worked their way out of the colonial nostalgia and the ideology of heroic-colonial individualism whose rhetoric I define in this chapter. They provide the dominant colonial narrative of British-Indian relations refuted by Margaret Cousins's and Kalpana Dutt's writings, analyzed in chapters 2 and 3. The circulation of these Raj nostalgia narratives in the seventies and eighties raises real questions about the persistence of nationalist cultural paradigms in the face of the transnationalization which has begun to dominate contemporary discussions of postcolonial studies.

I treat diverse genres in this chapter, examining a short story ("Wressley of the Foreign Office"), a popular history (Plain Tales from the Raj), a newsletter (Souvenir Chowkidar), and a novel (Heat and Dust); my selection of texts has been conditioned by their being materially linked in a discursive network that includes intertextual references among the works, as well as connections among their authors within the culture industry. These narratives have propagated and generated their own textual dynasties; inseminated by earlier texts and supported by the British Association for Cemeteries in South Asia, an organization with research facilities and publication capabilities, Raj nostalgia narratives beget and breed more tomes for the colonial archives. In one sense, my purpose is to expose the discursive modalities of colonial power that disavow the violence of their operations through the ideology of heroic-colonial individualism and the construction of literal genealogies. Colonial regimes of knowledge, as manifest in Raj revival narratives, are marked by four main features. First, in contrast to the attempts to pathologize extreme cases of colonial violence through rogue-colonial individualism, as in the case of General Dyer, the textual construction of the heroic colonial male subject relies upon the tropological function of synecdoche, whereby the individual male becomes paradigmatic of the whole colonial collectivity. Second, the authority of colonial rule is legitimated through recourse to a genealogical narrative that traces the bloodlines of colonial officials back several generations; such a narrative authenticates colonial officials by presenting them as having an ancestral claim to the subcontinent, thereby rendering natural and organic their ties to South Asia. Third, Raj nostalgia narratives construe Indian nationalism in the terms elucidated by Ranajit Guha, as either a "learning process" for elite Indian personalities or as a "law and order problem" of communalism ("Some

Aspects of the Historiography of Colonial India" 38). Lastly, many of these narratives emphasize the difficulty of "surviving" the physical challenges of the Indian environment and foreground the recurring topos of the British graveyard in India. The cemetery is central to the construction of "Anglo-Indian" family trees as a legitimizing strategy that both authorizes the descendants of colonial officials to pontificate about South Asia and to retain some sense of justified ownership over the land; the little plots in which their ancestors are buried constitute for them a valid claim to territory.

The task of this chapter is to exhume the putrefying corpses of colonial nostalgia and the ideology of heroic-colonial individualism as embodied in the rhetorical practices I have outlined above. My own method is to show how Raj nostalgia narratives systematically foreclose certain kinds of historical knowledge which I re-place in my readings of these diverse texts. The reiteration of a nostalgic narrative of colonialism that dramatizes the physical vulnerability of Britons, I argue at the end of this chapter, discloses British apprehensions about immigrants of color and the continuing colonial crisis posed by the conflict in Northern Ireland.

PRODUCING COLONIAL KNOWLEDGE

In "Wressley of the Foreign Office," a short story in *Plain Tales from the Hills* (1899), Rudyard Kipling considers the production of knowledge in the colonial context and devises a template for the narrative threads that will constitute Raj nostalgia narratives in the late twentieth century. He offers an interpretation of the production of colonial knowledge as gendered and grounded in a traditional romantic narrative. Colonial knowledge is obsessively fascinated with genealogy, conceived narrowly in genetic terms, which can only be tested and certified by official documentation. Although knowledge produced in a colonial context can be harnessed to the expansionist project of the state, Kipling obscures the political investments of the colonial intellectual enterprise by locating its originary moment in romantic yearning. "Wressley of the Foreign Office" provides a good paradigm for later Raj nostalgia texts because it demonstrates the ways in which idealist romantic narratives function to abstract nostalgia texts from history and the enterprise of colonial documentation.

In this tale, the narrator imputes to Wressley, an exemplary worker in the Foreign Office, an extraordinary knowledge of the central Princely states:

> When Wressley lifted up his voice, and spoke about such-and-such succession to such-and-such a throne, the Foreign Office were silent, and Heads of Departments repeated the last two or three words of Wressley's sentences, and tacked "yes, yes," on to them, and knew that they were assisting the Empire to grapple with serious political contingencies. (298)

"All men knew Wressley's name and office—it was in Thacker and Spink's Directory," the narrator declares, "but who he was personally, or what he did, or what his special merits were, not fifty men knew or cared" (299). Notwithstanding this claim, the narrator then proceeds to recount an anecdote about Wressley's private life. "Upon a day, between office and office," the narrator says, "great trouble came to Wressley— overwhelmed him, knocked him down, and left him gasping as though he had been a little schoolboy" (299). What terrible force strikes and overcomes him? Wressley becomes enamored with Tillie Venner, "a frivolous, golden-haired girl who used to tear about Simla Mall on a high, rough Waler, with a blue velvet jockey-cap crammed over her eyes" (300). He is "immensely struck with Miss Venner's intelligence," a mistaken assessment in the narrator's view. In love with Miss Venner for a month, Wressley lets his work suffer. At the same time, however, he conceives of "the work of his life," his *Native Rule in Central India*, which he plans on presenting to his beloved as "a gift fit for an Empress" (300–301).

Wressley takes a year of absence from his job, and with Miss Venner's blessing and a load of documents, descends from the cool comfort of Simla and heads to the burning plains of central India to write his book.[4] For 230 days and nights, Wressley labors on his text:

> He caught his Rajahs, analysed his Rajahs, and traced them up into the mists of Time and beyond, with their queens and their concubines. He dated and cross-dated, pedigreed and triple-pedigreed, compared, noted, connoted, wove, strung, sorted, selected, inferred, calendared and counter-calendared for ten hours a day. And, because this sudden and new light of Love was upon him, he turned those dry bones of history and dirty records of misdeeds into things to weep or to laugh over as he pleased. (301)

After the work's completion, "blushing and stammering," Wressley presents his magnum opus to Miss Venner, who reads some of it and says, "Oh, your book? It's all about those howwid Wajahs. I didn't understand it" (302).

Miss Venner has by this time decided to forgo Mr. Wressley's seventeen hundred rupees a month for the equestrian skills of one Captain Kerrington. Wressley takes her review of his work to heart, and buries all but one copy of the Book. Shortly before Wressley's retirement, the narrator comes across this single extant copy on Wressley's shelves. Reading several pages of it over the narrator's shoulder, Wressley remarks: "Now, how in the world did I come to write such damned good stuff as that?" (303). He gives the narrator the copy, cryptically saying, "Take it and keep it. Write one of your penny-farthing yarns about its birth. Perhaps—perhaps—the whole business may have been ordained to that end" (303).

Wressley's conception of *Native Rule in Central India* partially arises from his "peculiar notions as to the wooing of girls," his belief that "the best work of a man's career should be laid reverently at their feet" (300). From the start, Wressley's project is a chivalric one; he is a colonial knight-scholar, whose deed is to journey to the wasteland, the desert plains of India, and undergo a type of trial by fire, composing his work in the scorching heat. His lady-love Miss Venner, toes tingling with anticipation, waits for his return from the quest with evidence of his adventures and affection.

While Wressley's quaint views of women and courtship derive from a textual tradition of chivalry, his views on Indian royalty are tied to the textual tradition of colonial documentation. The documents that accompany Wressley on his journey are the raw material he uses for his work. Though he writes the book in central India, the place where the Rajahs of his book reside, Wressley's location does not significantly aid his research. He fails to use important source material available to him by virtue of his proximity to the Rajahs. For example, Wressley seeks to establish the lineage of Indian royal houses; given that birth records were not kept in any systematic fashion at that time, Wressley's presence in central India allows him to interview local people for their knowledge of births (both in and out of wedlock) and adoptions among the Rajahs. Instead of relying on interviews or local records, however, Wressley uses as his primary sources the official documents that he has brought from Simla.

Wressley makes the journey to refuel his poetic fervor. The narrator explains that Wressley "began his book in the land he was writing of," speculating: "Too much official correspondence had made him a frigid work man, and he must have guessed that he needed the white light of local colour on his palette" (301). The setting in which he composes his book becomes, along with Miss Venner, another source of inspiration. The location furnishes a poetic background for Wressley's writing, but does not advance his analysis in any meaningful way.

Given the cosmetic function of setting in the production of the book and its primary focus on official documents, the absence of native voices in *Native Rule in Central India* comes as no surprise. Rather than interview Indians, Wressley apprehends them through textual representations. The narrator does not explicitly say whether the authors of these representations are British or Indian, but since Wressley must cart the documents from Simla—the Himalayan summer capital of British India after 1827—they would seem to be official British ones, necessary for the everyday duties of colonial governance.

The title of the work, including as it does the word "native," together with the narrator's description of Wressley's interpretation of "his Rajahs," indicates the narrowness of the colonial perspective. In the narrator's description of the work the "native" in the title is narrowly defined as "rajahs," Hindu male royalty. Wressley's understanding of "rule" is restricted to the rajahs' governance and disregards other structures of authority that operated in the subcontinent, such as the joint family, *panchayats* (village councils), *zamindars* (landlords), and religious leaders. Wressley's title ignores "paramountcy," that peculiar arrangement between the British crown and the princes, in which the crown agreed "to protect the rulers and their dynasties from external aggression or internal revolt," provided that they acknowledged the crown's right "to conduct their foreign relations, regulate disputed successions, conduct minority administration, intervene in their internal affairs in case of gross misrule, and lease territories to receive financial subventions in return for military protection" (Stree Shakti Sanghatana 1). In Wressley's mistaken construction of his subject matter, the governance of princely states functions independently of British rule. Wressley's romantic explanation for the origins of his work enables him to remove it from the realm of power and history. If he personally intends to dazzle Miss

Venner with his intellectual prowess, he can pretend that his scholarship is politically disinterested. His work can inhabit the same Platonic realm as his love, existing to no end, other than its own.

However, the subject matter of Wressley's book, the genealogy of Indian princes, was hardly timeless, but of immediate importance to colonial authorities in the culture more widely. In 1848 Governor General Dalhousie vigorously began to implement the "Doctrine of Lapse," enacted by the Court of Directors of the East India Company in 1834. This doctrine decreed that if Indian princes did not have any biological sons, then their states would "lapse" to the Paramount Power, a position which the British government claimed for itself after the fall of the Mughal Empire (K. Datta 760). The doctrine also refused to recognize adopted sons as legitimate heirs to their adoptive fathers' thrones, unless the adoptions had been conducted with the prior consent of the suzerain authority of the British (760). Previously, the company had granted to adoptive sons a status similar to that of first-born biological sons in Britain (Wolpert, *New History of India* 227). Dalhousie used the Doctrine of Lapse to justify the annexation of Satara (1848), Jaipur and Sambalpur (1849), Baghat (1850), Udaipur (1852), Nagpur (1853), and Jhansi (1854) (K. Datta 761).

The Doctrine of Lapse was also used to appropriate pensioners' titles and their pensions, which had been "awarded as compensation for lands long since seized" (*New History of India* 228). The former Peshwa of Poona is the best-known of these deposed rulers. Because he had no "natural heir" at the time of his death, his pension of £80,000 "lapsed" to the company, instead of going to his adopted son, Nana Sahib (228). Nana Sahib later gained notoriety for his part in the Sepoy Mutiny of 1857. He was held accountable for the brutal massacre of British women and children—to whom he had promised safe passage—at "Cawnpore" (Kanpur).

As a result of the rebellion of 1857, the British Parliament passed the Government of India Act in 1858, which transferred all the East India Company's "rights" over India to the crown. The British government even identified the Doctrine of Lapse as one of the causes of the rebellion. In one of her first proclamations to the "Princes, Chiefs and Peoples" of India, Queen Victoria rescinded the Doctrine of Lapse. The crown then attempted to woo the Indian princes, who, according to Stanley Wolpert, were now promised that "all treaties and engagements made with them would be scrupulously maintained." This retrograde policy, which would leave more than 560 enclaves of autocratic princely rule dispersed throughout India during the ensuing ninety years of crown rule, reflected British fears that further annexations might only pro-voke another mutiny. Hereafter, the princes were faithfully assured that they might adopt any heir they wished as long as he vowed loyalty to the crown, whose queen became "empress of India" in 1877. (*New History of India* 240)

Had Wressley's *Native Rule in Central India* been an actual colonial document as opposed to a fictional narrative, it would have been ex-tremely useful for administrative purposes. In this regard, if Kipling's story had been set before the Doctrine of Lapse was rescinded, then an adequate version of Wressley's book could have played a major role in the imperial expansion of the company, by identifying royal adopted sons so that their lands could be seized legally. If it had been set after Queen Victoria's repudiation of the doctrine, Wressley's research, again if adequately executed, could have provided data on the Indian princes, genealogy, and land annexation, which the crown could use in repairing its ties with the princes. But the narrator does not date the story.

Wressley's book is not a colonial document, however. Rather, be-cause *Native Rule in Central India* is a fictional text described in a short story, Wressley's work is twice removed from reality. Instead of using the book to advance both the colonial project and his career within Kipling's fictional world, Wressley denies the book a readership during his profes-sional tenure. But Wressley's construction of native rule as a simple matter of succession among the Rajahs is disseminated to a more gen-eral audience through the agency of Kipling and the short story itself. Through the short story, Kipling offers an interpretation of the produc-tion of colonial knowledge which can be stated in the following tenets: natives can only be apprehended through colonial representations of them already available in official documents; knowledge of natives can be excavated through genealogical research; since the colonial state's archives provide the raw materials of colonial scholarship, whose au-thors are after all colonial officials, the products of intellectual labor can be expropriated potentially for expansionist purposes; the production of colonial knowledge is gendered insofar as it is generated by colonial males and its creation often causes the male colonial scholar to endure physical hardship; and finally, while colonial women can be the recipients of this knowledge, as evidenced by Miss Venner's reaction to Wressley's magnum opus, they will not necessarily recognize its value.[5] By casting a text that might, if real, have been a tool of colonial domination into Wressley's personal narrative, a history of "things to weep or to laugh over as he pleased" with its conceptual origins in the physical fancies of romantic desire, Kipling obscures the political investments of the production of colonial knowledge.

SURVIVORS OF THE RAJ, "ANGLO-INDIAN" NATIONALISM, AND COLONIAL GENEALOGIES

"Wressley of the Foreign Office" comes from Kipling's collection of stories Plain Tales from the Hills; many of the stories in this collection first appeared in the Civil and Military Gazette, a major English-language journal in northwestern India during Kipling's time (Norton xv).[6] In 1974 Charles Allen, the great-grandson of the founder of the Civil and Military Gazette who had first hired Kipling to work on his journal, produced a radio series for the BBC Radio 4 called Plain Tales from the Raj. This series consisted of tape-recorded interviews with over sixty women and men who had served the British empire in the twentieth century. Allen later fashioned sections of the interviews into a written volume of the same name, published in 1975. Both the ancestral connections between Kipling and Allen's family and the intertextual links between their works situate these texts within a discursive network of Raj nostalgia and knowledge production about the Empire. Indeed, as Philip Mason, one of Allen's interviewees, comments, "The answer to why I went to India is Kipling. . . . When I was a small boy I had an absolute passion for Kipling and read everything I could get hold of. Something in those stories appealed to me enormously and gave me a romantic desire to go to this country" (36). Several of the features of colonial knowledge-production that characterize Kipling are echoed throughout Allen's text, notably Kipling's tendency to conceal the interests of the colonial state. Like "Wressley of the Foreign Office," Plain Tales from the Raj stresses the difficulties of "surviving" the physical landscape of India and emphasizes the genealogical motif introduced by Kipling. Yet while Kipling's Plain Tales from the Hills often criticizes the traits of individual "Anglo-Indians,"[7] such as Miss Venner's frivolousness and Wressley's romantic naïveté, Allen's *Plain Tales from the Raj*, nearly a century later, celebrates them by propagating the ideology of heroic-colonial individualism, which is discursively manifest in the tropological operations of synecdoche.

On one level, the universalization of the individual British male subject as representative of the colonial collectivity is enacted through the visual epistemology offered by the text's cover. The subtitle of Allen's text is "Images of British India in the twentieth century." Immediately below this subtitle is a photograph of a seated British couple separated by a large skull, with the skins of two Bengal tigers flanking either side, the skins of two deer lying in front of them, with another row of eight smaller skulls in front of these. Two Indians stand behind the couple, against a background of four more tiger skins. The book describes this picture as "a sportsman and his trophies" (10). If we interrogate the politics of representation established by the cover photograph and description, several assumptions about the British, Indians, and India become apparent. The description of the photograph divides the camera's subject into two categories, the "sportsman" and "his trophies," thus making the British male the center of the photograph. Everyone and everything else in the picture—the British woman, Indian men, and dead animals—belong to him. As "trophies," they are the legitimate prizes of the civilized white man's conquest, whether it is the sexual conquest of the woman, the national conquest of India, or the conquest of nature. The photograph visually enacts colonial relations between the British and Indians. By placing the Indian men and the tiger skins behind the British couple, it gives native people a special status close to that of the animal kingdom. While the British woman is one of her husband's many "trophies," she nonetheless also shares in his power and privilege over Indians.

At the same time, however, we can read the photograph in such a way as to undermine the assumption of British male bravery. One of the Indian males, standing behind the British woman, holds a gun, serving as a discreet reminder that the Indians were the ones who faced the most danger during tiger hunts. They acted as the "beaters" who roused the tigers from cover, while the British men, who took credit for the kill, more often than not were perched safely in *machans*, or shooting platforms.

On another level, Allen generalizes the experiences of his interviewees, viewing them monolithically. In the book's acknowledgments, Allen

PLAIN TALES
FROM THE RAJ
Images of British India
in the twentieth century

Edited by Charles Allen
Introduction by Philip Mason

identifies his subjects as "survivors of the British Raj" (11). The word "survivors" is freely interchanged with the names of the interviewees throughout these early pages. When he does not modify the word "survivors" with the phrase "of the British Raj," Allen capitalizes it. The end result is that the word "Survivors" becomes elevated to the status of a proper noun. Despite their differences of age, class, gender, and race, the interviewees are collapsed under this word. This oversimplification is a metaphor for the whole book, which constructs a generic biography out of the varied experiences of colonial officials and their wives. Moreover, it becomes rapidly apparent that "survival" means the ability to withstand the mortal dangers of India—a sinister topos, a graveyard where, to quote one interviewee, "you could be ill one day and dead the next" (127). Throughout these pages, interviewees reiterate a litany of deadly diseases to which many have succumbed: cholera, dysentery, influenza, malaria, and smallpox. Death also results from attacks by rabid dogs, snakes, tigers, and scorpions. These references to death bear out B. J. Moore-Gilbert's observation that "from the beginning of its contacts with Britain, India came to be regarded with some justice as the 'white man's grave' " (35). The photograph of the "sportsman and his trophies" on the cover of the book, against a background of death, underscores the survival theme. By virtue of their survival, the British couple in the photograph seem to have proven the Darwinian dictum of survival of the fittest, and thus established their fitness to rule. Yet if we read against the grain of the book, the photograph simultaneously challenges the "survival" theme running throughout Plain Tales from the Raj. The dead figures in the photograph are not those of the British couple, but of the tigers and deer killed through their agency. In the figures of the Indian servants and the dead animals, the cover photograph unwittingly reveals the hidden violence of the civilizing mission glorified in Allen's work.

Categorizing his work as an "oral history," Allen claims that it differs from traditional scholarly histories in being "one man's impressionist mosaic of the general image which this material has left him with after long familiarity" (12). Beyond crediting Michael Mason's The Long March of Everyman as a "pioneer" of "oral history," Allen does not reflect on the conventions or ideological dimensions of this particular genre. As colonial officials and their wives, Allen's mostly middle-class interviewees present what Ranajit Guha calls a "colonialist elitist" narration of the period covering the British decolonization of India and the rise of the Indian nationalist movement. This type of historiography, according to Guha, credits the development of Indian national consciousness to "British colonial rulers, administrators, policies, institutions and culture" ("Some Aspects of the Historiography of Colonial India" 37). To the extent that the British government did not commission or authorize its writing, Plain Tales from the Raj is not an officially sanctioned history.

Allen's categorization of his work as an "oral history" gives it a populist ring and makes it accessible to a nonacademic audience. The text's hegemonic perspective on British imperialism, together with its intellectual accessibility and dissemination to a broad audience, allow *Plain Tales from the Raj* to assist official British accounts of colonialism as a civilizing mission.

Allen crafted *Plain Tales from the Raj* by piecing together excerpts of the interviews he conducted with "Anglo-Indians" in the United Kingdom. In other words, each interview does not stand as a discrete whole and is instead "juxtaposed and related" to other excerpts on the same topic (12). In not always identifying the speaker of particular quotations, Allen strategically chooses to blur material distinctions among the interviewees. He explains his decision in the following manner: "Widely separated by age, occupation, rank, geography and personal character, these Survivors all share the experience of British India in the twentieth century. In this sense they are representatives of their age. Accordingly, I have not always identified quotations where commonly expressed attitudes or experiences are given" (12). Allen stresses that what binds the interviewees is their common experience of British India in the twentieth century. Allen's methodology relies on what Homi Bhabha describes as "the progressive metaphor of social cohesion—*the many as one*" (294; emphasis in original). The class differences among the interviewees, differences that were concretized in the class-segregated colonial society, become subsumed in an act of "imagination" that binds the interviewees into a cohesive "political community," that is, in Benedict Anderson's words, "imagined as both inherently limited and sovereign" (15). In arranging the contents topically, Allen desegregates British society: the elite Indian Civil Service and officer classes mingle with the missionaries and Anglo-Indians who existed "on the margins of social distance" (Ballhatchet 96). Allen's stylistic erasure of difference helps create a deep, horizontal comradeship among the interviewees, giving expression to "Anglo-Indian" nationalism.

Allen not only weaves the varied experiences of his interviewees into one seamless narrative of "Anglo-Indian" nationalism, but also conceives his audience as culturally homogeneous. "The 'locality' of national culture," Bhabha reminds us, "is neither unified nor unitary in relation to itself, nor must it be seen simply as 'other' in relation to what is outside or beyond it" (4). Immigrants from former colonies and still existent ones, such as India and Northern Ireland, are also part of the BBC's audience, occupying the in-between spaces, the fissures and ruptures in horizontal comradeship that both Anderson and Bhabha theorize.[8]

The characteristics of the "Anglo-Indian" national consciousness hinted at in Allen are fully elaborated in B. J. Moore-Gilbert's thoughtful study *Kipling and "Orientalism."* Moore-Gilbert traces the emergence of "a political discourse constituting one element of a distinctively Anglo-Indian 'Orientalism,' which is in tension with its metropolitan counterpart" (8). He points to the proliferation of publications for "Anglo-Indians" from the 1830s to the 1850s as seminal in the evolution of a distinct "Anglo-Indian" culture (8). One aspect of this culture was the existence of an "Anglo-Indian" patois incomprehensible to metropolitan residents. By Kipling's time, this patois had sufficiently matured to require its own dictionaries. *"Hobson-Jobson": A Glossary of Anglo-Indian Colloquial Words and Kindred Terms,* an eight-hundred-page work, appeared in 1886 and G. C. Whitworth's *Anglo-Indian Dictionary* was published almost simultaneously (Moore-Gilbert 8). The term "Anglo-Indian" itself marks a distinction between British metropolitan society and British colonial society, by simultaneously declaring a racial identification with white Anglo-Saxons and a geographical identification with India.[9] "Anglo-Indians," Moore-Gilbert claims, "were almost as much amused as irritated by the metropolitan vision of India" (10). In the examples he cites to prove his argument, most of the "Anglo-Indians" object to the exaggerated exoticism of metropolitan representations of India which are often factually wrong in "Indian details"; for instance, one drama reviewer sneers at a play in which lions appear in "asses' skins" (11). These examples ring with the implicit conviction that "Anglo-India" holds a monopoly on the understanding of the "real India," which is unavailable to metropolitan writers.

Allen's interviewees express similar sentiments, but instead of condemning metropolitan writers for having a distorted understanding of India, they challenge one another's versions of India as less authentic than their own. According to several of the women interviewees, the "real India" resides in the villages (111), the *mofussil,* or the upcountry (177), and in the plains during the hot season (123). The false versions of India, not surprisingly, are the cities, the military cantonments, and the hill stations. Though the women interviewees do not explicitly say so, these latter locations host a significant population of "Anglo-Indians."

The "real India," then, can be found in places largely uncorrupted by a significant British presence.[10] In constructing the "real India" in this way, some of the interviewees echo a common desire among anthropologists of finding a pristine community uncontaminated by contact with the West (Pratt 43–44). This desire rests on an essentialist conception of native culture as simple and unchanging, untouched by any historical processes. The utopian elements in this desire, the wish for a lost innocence, resonate with Christian symbolism. Paradoxically, contact with the West constitutes a fall from Edenic innocence even as it introduces "primitive" societies to the "civilizing" influence of Christianity.

The belief that the "real India" exists in the relative absence of individual "Anglo-Indians" ignores the political economy of colonialism, an economy that Supriya Nair explains as follows:

> While the process of colonization effectively underdeveloped the entire (Indian) nation and restructured the relationship between the metropole and the colony into Raymond Williams's model of 'city and country,' the villages within the colonies, located as they were at the base of the economic pyramid, declined even further as a result of British policies of ruinous taxation, unequal distribution of land, and the forcible growth of export crops. Though the decisions were made in the metropolis, the economic and political impact rippled into the core of every village through the system of domination the British had established.

The invisible power of British colonialism extended over the entire subcontinent in altered production and distribution networks; regardless of the size of its "Anglo-Indian" population, no area was free to be an authentically "real India." Furthermore, those interviewees who managed to experience what they claim as the "real India" seem blind to the fact of their presence among the natives and the ways that it might alter the behavior of Indians in their company. The "real India," for them, is a transparent reality, immediately available for their understanding and consumption. A conceptual corollary to the "real India" is the notion of "real Anglo-Indians," inasmuch as those who lay claim to the "real India" consider themselves the "real Anglo-Indians," or at least more authentic than some of their official counterparts.

In spite of self-identified differences, such as the one above, and other contradictions among the interviewees, Allen arranges these excerpts into a composite to follow "the general experience of the great majority of its contributors" (12). This arrangement suggests one grand biography of a colonial official, whose life is charted from early infancy in India—with mention of years spent in England acquiring an education—to his return to India as a colonial official with vast responsibilities at a young age, and concludes with his hasty departure with the coming of Indian independence. A chapter entitled "The Tomb of his Ancestors," which establishes the interviewees' genealogy, tracing their ancestors' involvement with India, embellishes the basic plot, and adds further credence to the biography motif.

Allen understands genealogy in strictly filial terms, with ties between people inherited on the basis of biology and "natural forms of authority" (Said, *The World, the Text and the Critic* 20–21). "Few who went into one or another of the Indian services could fail to claim an 'Anglo-Indian' ancestor," he declares, "It was a fact of Empire" (34). The genealogical theme is developed in two major ways: Allen emphasizes that many of his interviewees have ancestors whose colonial service extends back to the eighteenth century; and he stresses that the progeny of these early colonial officials often intermarried and begot more administrators and soldiers for the Raj, creating family units that were microcosms of the colonial state. Just as the colonial state relied on different branches for its maintenance, so too did different branches of the same family specialize in the areas necessary to maintain the colonial state:

In many families a connection with India had been established with Clive and reinforced many times over thereafter. The Rivetts joined forces with the Carnacs to become one of the best-known families of 'Anglo-India'. The Maynes 'flocked into India' from 1761 onwards, leaving 'two graves in Darjeeling, two in Allahabad, one in Saharashtra [sic], one in Meerut, one in Bangalore, one in Achola and another in Lucknow. The first Ogilvies landed four years later in 1765. When Vere Ogilvie married Christopher Birdwood, the 'boy next door'—and the son of the Commander-in-Chief—their offspring became in due course 'the sixth and seventh generation of children who had started their lives in India'. Some families specialized. When Rosamund Napier married Henry Lawrence in 1914 it was an alliance between two great families of soldiers and administrators. When John Cotton entered the Political Service in 1934 he was the sixth generation in an unbroken male line to serve the East India Company prior to 1858 and the Indian Civil Service thereafter. (34)

By establishing the lineage of his interviewees back over multiple generations and centuries, Allen legitimates the colonial presence, because the colonial domination of the subcontinent is presented as a birthright of colonial officials from elite families. In some cases, according to Allen, colonial officials inherited from their fathers the devotion and respect of the local Indians: "A privileged few followed their fathers, so that 'a young man coming out before the First World War, being the son of a man who'd been in the ICS before him, was greeted in the station that he went to by people who'd known him as a baby, and they would give that man utter and complete loyalty, because he was the son of his father' " (39). The successful functioning of the colonial state, then, is based on the affinity between the colonial official and the natives which is determined genetically by his colonial lineage. Significantly, it is the graves of their colonial ancestors in India, as the litany of graveyard locations above testifies, that authenticate the genealogical origins of colonial officials.

Indeed, *Plain Tales from the Raj* is a deeply personal narrative for Allen, whose grandparents Joan and Geoffrey Allen number among his interviewees. On his paternal grandfather's side, his ancestors' involvement with India, as the Notes on Contributors explain, dates back to 1799 (221). And his paternal grandmother Joan Allen, née Henry, counts among her ancestors the (in)famous John Nicholson, who responded to the rebellion of 1857 in the following manner:

> The idea of simply hanging the perpetrators of such atrocities [against the English] is maddening. . . . As regards torturing . . . if it be right otherwise, I do not think we should refrain from it, because it is a native custom. We are told in the Bible that stripes should be meted out according to faults, and if hanging is sufficient punishment for such wretches, it is too severe for ordinary mutineers. If I had them in my power to-day, and knew that I were to die to-morrow I would inflict the most excruciating tortures I could think of on them with a perfectly easy conscience. (quoted in Dangerfield 232)

The violence underwriting this articulation of counter-insurgency, which is just one example in a multitude of possible others, is never explicitly acknowledged in *Plain Tales from the Raj*. What the Notes on Contributors and the recitation of the exalted colonial genealogies in "The Tomb of His Ancestors" fail to reveal are the brutal operations of colonialism, rhetorical and material, when confronted with Indian challenges to its authority.

NARRATING INDIAN NATIONALISM

The ideology of heroic-colonial individualism has a particularly limited grasp of Indian nationalism, as evidenced by Allen's treatment of the topic in a scant two chapters of his text. His narrative of Indian nationalism has five main features. First, since all of the interviewees are either British or "Anglo-Indian," Indians are always already apprehended through the racialized representations of them by colonial officials. Second, different strands of the nationalist movement are collapsed under the dominant narrative of Gandhian nonviolent noncooperation, even when the events in the text reference the activities of the Bengali terrorist movement. Third, Allen foregrounds the role of elite Indian personalities who are given the British characteristics of being, according to the logic of his work, honorable and well mannered. Fourth, the large numbers of non-elite Indians whose mobilization made independence possible are dismissed as a "law and order" problem of communalism which exceeds the limits placed on it by its elite leadership. Lastly, Allen's narration of communalism represents the intervention of British officials and their wives as necessary, thus explicitly rendering them as heroic subjects and implicitly rendering the Indian elite as incompetent leaders.

Allen never remarks upon the British racial arrogance toward natives which permeates the entire book. The narrative voice fails to distinguish itself from the voices of the interviewees. In fact, Allen often embeds unattributed fragments of quotations within larger sentences. For example, one paragraph in the chapter on "Indians" reads:

The psychology of the two races was often described as complementary rather than matching: 'The Indian was pliant and would say "yes" to everything whether he was going to do it or not, whereas the British were more obstinate, more obdurate people and they wouldn't undertake a thing unless they could see it through.' But if the British were 'a bit Olympian or perhaps a little squirearchical, this was complemented by the attitude of the Indians towards us. They expected the Europeans to be rather superior, encouraging us to behave in that way.' Sycophancy was not something the British enjoyed. 'There was certainly a lot of sucking-up to the British,' states Ian Stephens. 'All sorts of tricks which one had to be wary about. But the wariness itself was a danger because it mightn't be what you thought. What was being misconstrued might really be genuine affection. A genuine desire for normal, human contact.' (194)

Here an opinion on the differences between "Anglo-Indians" and Indians has been granted the status of a scientific truism. By not attributing two of the three quotations discoursing on the "psychology of the two races," Allen implies that these attitudes were so pervasive as to share a universal authorship. The fragments of quotations in his sentences and his own explanatory comments, such as the one on the British distaste for sycophancy, indicate Allen's acceptance of the opinions expressed. Indeed, the narrative voice attempts neither to judge or disclaim any of the more outlandish opinions of the interviewees nor set itself apart from the interviewees in any fashion. That this view paints Indians as unreliable sycophants, the diametrical opposite of the stern and dependable British, should not be lost on the discerning reader. This passage illustrates what Edwin and Shirley Ardener define, in the field of ethnography, as a "bounding problem," in which a dominant group "defines the bounds of society" and speaks for the "muted" marginalized groups within it (23). In *Plain Tales from the Raj*, Indian perspectives are always mediated through the observations of the interviewees. So we are told, by an unattributed "Anglo-Indian" source, that Indians expected and encouraged Europeans to behave in a superior manner. While this passage normalizes the racial superiority of the British by presenting it as the product of the dialectical relationship between colonized and colonizer, the perspectives of one half of the dialectic, the Indians, are missing.

In general, Allen's narration of the nationalist movement endeavors to expunge the violence of colonial rule and to shift responsibility for it to Indian agents who, consequently, become pathologized even further. For example, the chapter "Quit India" opens with a long meditation from Marjorie Cashmore, the wife of a Lutheran missionary, on the assassination of the district magistrate C. G. B. Stevens, which I discussed in the previous chapter. Finding incomprehensible the assassination of such a "greatly loved" official, who was the "*ma-bap*," or mother and father, of the local Indians, Cashmore turns to an Indian friend in the Congress Party for an explanation, stating:

> Here you have devoted servants of India, giving their lives, sacrificing everything in order to serve your people. You have others who come out from England and don't understand India. They've only come out for a few years and they abuse the Indians. I can understand you wanting that type of person out of the country, but this person is serving you, doing more than anybody else for your people and yet you kill him. (202)

The Indian friend laughs and tells her, "Don't you understand? The judge and those like him are hindrances to our getting Home Rule. The other man we needn't bother about because he gives us a cause for kicking out the British" (202).[11] Cashmore's description of the district magistrate's devotion, dedication, service, and sacrifice serves to represent his assassination as irrational and senseless. Allen's inclusion of the unnamed Congress member's levity in response to her tale further characterizes Indians unflatteringly, constituting them as insensitive and callous.

There are two remarkable points about the inclusion of this assassination in Allen's *Plain Tales from the Raj*. Santi Ghosh and Suniti Choudhury, the assassins, belonged to Jugantar, one of two terrorist groups in Bengal, which participated in the armed struggle against colonial rule. Though the terrorists enjoy a high standing in the popular memory of north Indians, their participation in the independence struggle has been by and large marginalized by the dominant narrative of the nationalist movement as a struggle based on the principles of *ahimsa* (nonviolence) and noncooperation. The first noteworthy point in the anecdote is Cashmore's reliance on a member of the mainstream nationalist movement, the Congress Party, for an explanation of the event. Cashmore makes this Congress member, and the Congress Party to which he belongs, metonyms for the entire nationalist movement, which comprised diverse groups. The Congress Party member's answer, however, in no way approximates Jugantar's reasons behind the assassination.

Allen's decision to open this chapter with this anecdote is similarly significant, because it borrows from Cashmore's rhetorical move. The chapter takes its name from what K. M. Panikkar defines as the third phase of the noncooperation movement, the "Quit India" movement of 1942 (205).[12] Mahatma Gandhi suggested this campaign because he was convinced, in his words, that "the time had come for the British and the Indians to be reconciled to complete separation from each other" (quoted in Wolpert, *New History of India* 335). The All-India Congress Committee adopted the "Quit India" resolution on August 8, 1942. In the early hours of the next day, British authorities retaliated by detaining 148 Congress leaders, including Gandhi, Jawaharlal Nehru, Maulana Azad, and others (Mahajan 480). Deprived of its bourgeois leadership, the movement took on the characteristics of a popular revolt as people participated in a multitude of ways: hartals, or strikes, spread across the subcontinent in factories, schools, and colleges. In some locations, angered by lathi-charges, people retaliated by attacking police stations, post offices, and railway stations.[13] Communication was disrupted as they cut telegraph and telephone wires and destroyed railway lines. They set fire to railway carriages and government buildings and also attacked military vehicles. In parts of Uttar Pradesh, Bihar, Orissa, West Bengal, Maharashtra, Andhra, and Madras, Indians gained temporary control and set up parallel governments. "For the first time since the great revolt of 1857," Jawaharlal Nehru declared, "vast numbers of people rose to challenge by force (but a force without arms) the fabric of British rule in India" (quoted in Mahajan 480).

The British government responded by arresting and imprisoning more people, assaulting them, and imposing heavy "collective" fines on Hindus. The government even machine-gunned crowds from the air at Patna, Bhagalpur, Monghyr, Nadia, and Talchar (Mahajan 481). By the end of 1942 the authorities had arrested some sixty thousand Congress supporters; official accounts attribute more than a thousand deaths and three thousand serious injuries to the "riots" from this period (Wolpert, *New History of India* 335). Nehru places the actual death toll at four to ten thousand (Mahajan 481). By beginning the chapter on the "Quit India" movement with an event from the Bengali terrorist movement eleven years before it, and by not sketching out the very different contexts that inform the two movements, Allen has conflated the history of Bengali terrorists with the narrative of the mainstream nationalist Congress party; as a result, the violence of the colonial state, actualized in its use of lethal air power against protestors, has been shifted to individual Bengali terrorists.

The opening anecdote on the assassination of the district magistrate is never integrated into the rest of the chapter. The remainder of the chapter vacillates between descriptions of communal riots and reflections on the personal characters of Muhammad Ali Jinnah and Jawaharlal Nehru. Allen's representation of Indians in a book about British "survivors of the Raj" creates a pantheon of Indian nationalist heroes drawn from the upper classes. In "On Some Aspects of the Historiography of Colonial India," Guha describes some characteristics of colonialist elitist historiography and its tendency to define Indian nationalism as a "function of stimulus and response," in which the Indian elite "respond to the institutions, opportunities, resources, etc. generated by colonialism" (37–38). According to Guha, colonialist elitist historiography imputes the desire for material advancement as the primary motivation driving individual Indian nationalist leaders and, as a result, emphasizes the collaborationist elements in the independence movement over all else ("Some Aspects of the Historiography of Colonial India" 38). Allen's interviewees foreground the role of the Indian elite in the nationalist movement, naming Sarojini Naidu, Jawaharlal Nehru, and Muhammad Ali Jinnah as key figures in the movement. The collaborationist elements, alluded to by Guha, most clearly emerge in what seems to be a common ruling-class consciousness among both the Indian elite and the colonial officials which is concretized in various social settings. While lower-class Indians were machine-gunned from helicopters, some of their upper-class leaders were having tea with the spouses of colonial officials. For instance, Anne Symington, the wife of an ICS officer, speaks of attending tea parties at Sarojini Naidu's: "I met everybody that was anybody in the political world there and they used to say, 'Is it all right to speak in front of Anne?' and she'd say, 'Oh yes, perfectly all right' " (207).

While the reference to Sarojini Naidu underscores the social interaction between colonials and the native elite, the anecdotes about Nehru and Jinnah focus on their characters, judging them on their social manners. Raymond Vernede describes coming to a "gentleman's agreement" with Nehru, receiving Nehru's verbal assurance that he would not participate in politics while on parole to see his ill wife (208). The "gentleman's agreement" illustrates that Nehru and Vernede share a common understanding of class, based on chivalry and honor, where one's word carries all the weight of a binding legal document. Nehru's familiarity with the British version of these concepts is not surprising, given his educational background. Like many of the British officials in India who were produced by English public schools, Nehru received his education in England at Harrow and Trinity College, Cambridge (Nehru 18). Allen legitimizes certain Indian nationalist leaders of the mainstream Congress Party by granting them characteristics that have been closely identified with the British throughout *Plain Tales from the Raj*. In the only other reference to Nehru, Allen contrasts him with Jinnah:

> The contrast between Jinnah and Nehru was marked. Olaf Caroe, who knew both of them well, found both arrogant, but Nehru's arrogance was 'shot through with charm, which Jinnah's certainly wasn't. He was very arrogant and very immovable and he is certainly not one of my heroes.' It was said at Viceregal Lodge that Jinnah was always five minutes late, whereas Mahatma Gandhi was always five minutes early. (209)

By focusing on these details of Jinnah's and Nehru's personalities, Allen gives the impression that his history is a behind-the-scenes-glimpse of the Indian nationalist movement. While reading his work, we must remember that his history does not include the ideas and theories that motivated specific segments of the leadership. Nor does it name or discuss the pivotal events in the period which sometimes brought these theories into crisis.[14]

Guha identifies another aspect of colonialist elitist historiography as its failure to theorize the "contribution made by the people *on their own . . . independently of the elite*" ("Some Aspects of the Historiography of Colonial India" 39; emphasis in original). In Allen's "Quit India" chapter, the mass articulation of this kind of nationalism is represented "negatively" as "a law and order problem" of communalism (39). Allen has lengthy and vivid descriptions of the communal riots that broke out during Mohurram in "Benares" (Varanasi) in 1939 and in Calcutta during 1946. These passages are interspersed with comments such as the one by Penderel Moon, a district magistrate, who says: "There was no answer to [communal rioting], you couldn't prevent it, but you might if you were sufficiently prompt and on the spot at the time, prevent it assuming a very serious form" (204).[15] These sections represent Indians as large, impersonal crowds, made up of individuals pathologically prone to violence and fanaticism. While both Muslims and Hindus were largely responsible for killing over one million people during partition riots, the mutual resentment between the two groups was deliberately nurtured by the British. The colonial policy of establishing separate electorates for Hindus and Muslims, combined with assembly intrigues and official patronage of one group over another, helped drive cleavages between the two groups.[16] And once the riots had started, British official response was quite often inadequate, doing little to minimize casualties. Writing on British responses to the rioting that commenced in August 1946, Sumit Sarkar notes:

> The British, who as late as June 1946 had been making plans to bring five army divisions to India in the context of a possible Congress movement, made no such move while presiding over this awesome human tragedy. In Calcutta in August, in sharp contrast to November 1945 or February 1946, the army was called out only after 24 hours, though the Governor was reminded of his First World War experiences in course of his early morning tour of the city on the 17th. Two other examples, both taken from British sources, may suffice to indicate the extent of official passivity—if not deliberate connivance. Wavell commented on November 9, 1946 in the context of Bihar Muslim requests to use aerial bombardment to stop the riots: "Machinegunning from the air is not a weapon one would willingly use, though the Muslims point out, rather embarrassingly, that we did not hesitate to use it in 1942." In March 1947, the two main bazaars of Amritsar were destroyed, while "not a shot was fired by the police." (*Critique of Colonial India* 134)

Allen's uncritical presentation of the interviewees' comments on communal riots erases British accountability for them.

The disavowal of historical responsibility for the deaths is compounded by the interviewees' self-representation as the saviors of Indians. Allen highlights the heroism of some Britons who either faced menacing crowds in the service of duty or intervened at personal risk to save Indians from certain death. For instance, Mary Wood, the wife of a captain in the army, tells of saving her "poor little sweeper" from the rest of her household servants (211). That the Indian leadership is conspicuously absent in these accounts of communal violence insinuates that they are incapable of containing their followers and politically too incompetent to rule the newly emergent nation. If Indian nationalism has any real heroes, according to *Plain Tales from the Raj*, it is the British who fearlessly confronted homicidal mobs and rescued hapless Indians from certain death. The brutality of colonial rule is displaced on to subaltern natives who are pathologized for communal violence, in the process exculpating the British from any responsibility for either the origins of the riots or their continuance.

As Guha reminds us, elitist historiography is not without its uses since it enables "us to understand the ideological character of historiography itself" ("Some Aspects of the Historiography of Colonial India" 38–39). While Allen's *Plain Tales from the Raj* provides concrete examples of the rhetorical operations of the ideology of heroic-colonial individualism, it does not fulfill the other potential uses of such a work as outlined by Guha. Elitist historiography, according to Guha, can furnish valuable information on "the structure of the colonial state, the operation of its various organs in certain historical circumstances, the nature of the alignment of classes which sustained it . . . the contradictions between the [colonial and national] elites and the complexities of their mutual oppositions and coalitions; of the role of some of the more important British and Indian personalities and elite organizations" ("Some Aspects of the Historiography of Colonial India" 38–39).[17] As we have seen through the course of this reading of the Indian nationalist movement, Allen trivializes many of these topics by focusing on the social mannerisms of individual nationalist leaders at the expense of elaborating on their participation in the pivotal events of the period, the underlying theories that determined their actions, and their interactions with subaltern classes. Rather than the serious historical analysis promised by his "oral history," *Plain Tales from the Raj* offers what more closely approximates nostalgic snapshots in a retired colonial official's photo album, discursively depicting the "images" in the subtitle of Allen's book.

TOMBS, TOMES, AND THE PRODUCTION OF COLONIAL ARCHIVES

In an interview with Pat Barr, another writer of the Raj revival, Charles Allen explains his motivations for writing on "Anglo-India." He reveals:

"I felt increasingly strongly that good decent people (like my own father who was in the political service) were being vilified simply for being part of an historical process over which they had no control" (Llewellyn-Jones, *Souvenir Chowkidar* 39). Allen's *Plain Tales from the Raj* proved quite popular: over 200,000 copies of the first edition were sold worldwide, resulting in the publication of a second Indian edition in 1992. In the preface to the second edition, Allen reflects on the critiques of colonialism that surfaced in the decades following the Second World War; while it was "necessary" to condemn colonialism, particularly for newly emergent nations, in his view, all too often individual colonial officials became "scapegoats, to be vilified as racist oppressors or, in Britain, to be mocked as figures of fun" (11). *Plain Tales from the Raj*, Allen boasts, helped to alter some of these "simplistic" perceptions, "not by glorifying or mythologizing the Raj but by allowing voices that had been silent to speak up for themselves" (11). His book, in his words, "humanised" an institution and revealed it as a multifaceted endeavor constituted by both "damaging" and "beneficial" aspects; consequently, "the Raj ceased to be politics and became history, no more and no less a fit subject to be chronicled than the Roman occupation of Britain or the Mughal occupation of Northern India" (11). Barr notes that Allen "feels justly proud" since his work helped, in his own assessment, "to blow the old colonial stereotypes out of the window" (Llewellyn-Jones, *Souvenir Chowkidar* 39). Indeed, flush with the success of his Raj chronicle, Allen went on to complete a trilogy, *Tales of Empire*, which included the volumes *Tales from the Dark Continent* and *Tales from the South China Seas*, thus rendering for African and Pacific Island historiography the service he had already contributed to South Asian historiography.

Much of the recent scholarship on the Raj, heralded by Allen's *Plain Tales from the Raj*, has emerged under the aegis of the British Association for Cemeteries in South Asia (BACSA), an organization to which Allen belongs, and which was formed in October 1976, a year after the publication of *Plain Tales from the Raj*. Along with Allen, some other writers of the Raj revival such as Pat Barr (*The Memsahibs* and *The Dust in the Balance*), M. M. Kaye (*The Far Pavilions*), and Alan Ross (*Blindfold Games*) belong to this curious society. Barr's interview with Allen quoted above appears in a special issue of the BACSA newsletter, *Chowkidar*, published semi-annually. This issue—entitled *Souvenir Chowkidar*—which celebrates the tenth anniversary of BACSA, features a history of the organization, an outline of its goals, a detailed update on its work, photographs, and poems by its members.

The idea of BACSA germinated with Theon Wilkinson, who discovered "the appalling condition of many of the European cemeteries" while "retracing the steps of three generations of the family" on a trip to India in 1972 to celebrate his son's twenty-first birthday (*Souvenir Chowkidar* 1). Wilkinson outlined a plan to interested parties focused upon "the State, the Churches, the British High Commission, the local community" and consisting of the following proposals:

> a) to preserve a few of the historically important cemeteries in South Asia's heritage; b) to turn decaying and 'abandoned' cemeteries in cities to social uses; c) to record all sources of information on cemeteries and inscriptions for historical and genealogical purposes, and—*most importantly* d) to publish a book to draw attention to the urgent need for action. (1; emphasis in original)

To accomplish the fourth task, Wilkinson published *Two Monsoons* two and a half years after the initial proposal. The advance publicity leaflets distributed for the book contained "an invitation to join in forming a loose association of 'Friends' to do something about the cemeteries in South Asia" (1). One of the earliest responses to Wilkinson's call to action came from Major General G. M. Dyer (whose nickname we are told is "Moti"), the president of the Indian Army Association and the chairman of the Indian Cavalry Officers Association.[18] The two men hatched "strategy" over glasses of whiskey, turning Dyer's kitchen table into a "BACSA battle map" (2). Under their leadership, the shape of BACSA emerged: BACSA would rally diverse legions "from all corners of the world" under an "identity of interest" (2). This "identity of interest" was BACSA's stated threefold mission: "advancing education in the history of all places in South Asia associated with European residence," "conducting research into the history of such places and publishing results," and "preserving European cemeteries" in South Asia (44).

Wilkinson's narration of BACSA's origins is itself a battle plan. This plan evokes what Patrick Brantlinger defines as a narrow conception of "imperialism": "an officially sanctioned policy of direct military seizure and government of one nation or territory by another" (7). Instead of directly seizing territory, however, BACSA has been expansionist in its claim on cemeteries and its recruitment during its first decade. Between

1977 and 1986 its membership increased from 269 to over a thousand, its overseas membership from 27 to 130. BACSA's members span the globe; they can be found in all the continents except for Antarctica and South America. They reside in Thailand, Zimbabwe, Canada, Italy, Bahrain, Australia, and South Africa, to name a few places. But as its member Michael Stokes notes, the rapid growth in membership may come to pose a threat to its "clubbability," which is "the strength of BACSA" (80). In this regard, Wilkinson's inclusion of Dyer's nickname in the publication is probably meant to enhance the "horizontal comradeship" of the society, reminiscent of military brotherhood. Indeed, BACSA has even established a local outpost in India itself, in the form of the Association for the Preservation of Historical Cemeteries in India (APHCI), whose primary goal has been the restoration of the South Park Street Cemetery in Calcutta. Several affiliated organizations abroad also aid BACSA: five such organizations exist in Australia, with one in Bangladesh and one in India. The creation of APHCI, and BACSA's affiliation with these other organizations, guarantees that the sun never sets on the work of BACSA. Even so, Michael Stokes exhorts BACSA members to "establish viable replicas of APHCI in half a dozen or so of the principal cities of India, Pakistan and Bangladesh" (79).

In the first pages of *Souvenir Chowkidar*, Wilkinson lays out his strategy for preserving European cemeteries, a strategy entailing the careful selection of specific projects such as "repairing 200 feet of wall, restoring a particular tomb or installing a water supply" (3). Though BACSA ranks projects on the basis of "historical and architectural importance," project selection is based primarily on the availability of local contacts "willing to carry out the work on a stage-by-stage basis, oversee the expenditure and carry on reasonable maintenance afterwards" (3). The recruitment of local contacts, Wilkinson warns, necessitates "patience and great sensitivity in enabling the local community to identify themselves with the work and see it in terms of their heritage" (3). "Army commanders, businessmen, academics, and journalists" make effective local contacts (3). According to Wilkinson, their work can be abetted in Britain by appealing for funds to different sectors of BACSA for projects of interest to specific professions. For example, army officers can be recruited to fund projects in the North-West Frontier, and tea-planters for work in Assam. Moreover, Wilkinson suggests that touring BACSA members visit these sites and report on the progress of work, taking photographs as evidence.

Wilkinson's strategy is a shrewd one. In choosing small, practical projects, he shows that he understands how activism grows from its successes. Progress can easily be assessed by visible changes; the photographs of touring BACSA members are crucial, enabling other members to see that their efforts have made a difference. Furthermore, Wilkinson recognizes that a cash influx from BACSA is not enough to guarantee the restoration of European cemeteries. The long-term goal requires a local network in place that will maintain the restored cemeteries. Wilkinson suggests that local Indian contacts can be convinced of their "identity of interest" with their former rulers. He sees middle- and upper-class Indians as better suited to act as local contacts. It is not surprising that these classes should include church leaders, army commanders, and professors: British missionaries left an indelible mark on the subcontinent; the structure of the army was inherited from the colonial administration; and India's university system was first coordinated nationwide in 1854 under Macaulay (Panikkar 246). Given their historical links with the British Empire, these groups might be predisposed to see the preservation of European cemeteries as part of "their own heritage" (Llewellyn-Jones, *Souvenir Chowkidar* 3). Academic professions and journalism have the added advantage of being highly charged ideologically. Because they shape the opinions and attitudes of others, academics and journalists can prove useful in convincing other groups of the necessity for cemetery preservation by offering "free advertising" of BACSA's efforts.

Wilkinson's strategy of recruiting local Indian contacts to administer the restoration and maintenance of European cemeteries echoes the older colonial policy of cultivating a class of natives who would administer the Indian empire. But while Macaulay envisioned a class of natives who would be "interpreters" between the British and the Indians, specifying that they be "Indian in blood and colour, but English in taste, in opinions, in morals, and in intellect," Wilkinson is not so bold (quoted in Wolpert, *New History of India* 215). For him it is enough that these local contacts faithfully serve the dead, guarding the European graves against the encroachment of vandals and natural decay.

The function of the local contact is emblematized in the cover and title of BACSA's newsletter, *Chowkidar*. After rejecting suggestions such as "Grave News" and "Among the Tombs" as possible titles, Rosie Llewellyn-Jones, the editor of the newsletter, settled on *Chowkidar*. A chowkidar is a night watchman, a visible presence to deter would-be vandals and criminals. Llewellyn-Jones explains that she "recalled the old habit of India's watchmen, who would patrol the urban streets, crying out the hours and guarding the sleeping town" (Llewellyn-Jones, *Souvenir Chowkidar* 56). She found the chowkidar a fitting symbol for BACSA, because its aim "was to patrol the Asian cemeteries, report back where something was wrong and to provide the means to put it right. It was also to 'cry out the hours' thus opening peoples' eyes and ears to the urgent needs of the cemeteries at that time" (56). The pictorial representation of the chowkidar, on the cover of the newsletter, is from a nineteenth-century East India Company painting. Rosemarie Wilkinson "drew in the background of tombs so it was quite clear what he was watching" (56).

In India a chowkidar is usually hired privately either by individual landowners or by an entire locality. He makes his nightly rounds through the neighborhood, periodically tapping a bamboo lathi against the ground and blowing a whistle. In the event of an actual attack or robbery, the chowkidar's effectiveness depends on assistance from others in the neighborhood. Alone and armed solely with his lathi, he does not present a very formidable obstacle to criminals. Also, whereas a chowkidar typically protects the living, BACSA's emblem has him guarding the dead. What does BACSA's chowkidar guard against? The various threats to European cemeteries are: "decay from age," the overgrowth of "natural vegetation," "vandals," and "trespassers" (13). Beyond his ostensible function, however, the figure of the native chowkidar who stands vigilant over the departed colonial master's grave is a collective colonial fantasy about the relationship between the rulers and their subjects. The chowkidar is sentimentalized as the loyal servant who continues to serve his just master, long after the master's departure and the demise of British rule in the subcontinent.

This sentimentalized representation of the loyal native contrasts sharply with the reality of his situation presented, ironically enough, in the very pages of the *Souvenir Chowkidar*. Zoë Yalland describes the conditions at the Kacheri Cemetery in Kanpur, over her yearly visits to the site which began in 1970. "For many decades the dead slept undisturbed," Yalland writes, "thanks to a tribe of brown monkeys that took up residence and became guardians of the cemetery" (7). But by 1970, when the monkeys had been "netted and sent off for medical research," the desecration of the dead began in earnest.

In connection with her research on British families in Kanpur, Yalland searched for the tomb of John Maxwell. She was successful, finding the tomb "topped with a massive slab of marble in excellent condition" (7). Four years later, Yalland reports the marble's mysterious disappearance:

> After much searching and questioning it was discovered in the chowkidar's quarters, being used to scrub clothes upon, and broken in two. . . . On my yearly visits to Kanpur it became distressing to see the condition of the cemetery: the boundary wall broken, trees fallen, a paan shop at the western end attracting undesirable customers who entered the cemetery for calls of nature or to gamble. The chowkidar himself, on no salary, grazed his buffaloes and goats, chaining them to tomb pillars and drying cakes of dung on the tomb stones. (7–8)

In this vignette the chowkidar does not prove as loyal as the simian guardians of the cemetery. He is blamed for the deterioration of the cemetery. Instead of guarding the repose of the dead and the sanctuary of the graveyard, the chowkidar engages in the very acts he is supposed to deter, stealing outright the marble tombstone. To add insult to injury, he converts the ornamental tombstone into a household appliance, using it as a washing slab. But why does he find it necessary to do so? Yalland casually informs us that the chowkidar does not earn a salary. In lieu of a salary, it would seem that the chowkidar is eking out a meager subsistence by using the resources at hand. As it is, grazing grounds are scarce in the arid climate of Kanpur. By grazing his livestock on the cemetery grounds, the chowkidar saves on animal feed.[19] Similarly, he can sell the dry dung cakes that he does not himself use for fuel, at a small profit. Yalland is not concerned with the pitiful economic condition of the chowkidar, however. The chowkidar is summarily replaced with another "caretaker" and we never learn his fate (8). In her attitude toward poverty Yalland is typical of BACSA members; as another member remarks rather self-righteously, "poverty does not excuse the failure to prevent destruction and desecration" (13). Of course, Yalland's indignation at the tomb's desecration is particularly ironic if we recall that many Indian tombs and architectural wonders, such as the Taj Mahal and the Lal Kila, were systematically plundered by the British, as evidenced by these monuments' chipped marble walls from which precious stones have been crudely chiseled out and looted.[20]

In BACSA we have the theme of India as the "white man's grave" literalized; India for this group is the "necropolis." BACSA's member James Stevens Curl describes a necropolis as a

> city of the dead, with all the character of the town. Here are no problems of change of use, or alterations through tawdry changes of fashion: the inhabitants never move, and the streets are mercifully bereft of bustle. The architecture of death is in some respects, the purest of all architecture, because it is concerned with form and expression, and with the housing of coffins, sarcophagi, or urns. Its only enemies are time, vandals, and the envious. (38)

This quotation dramatically illustrates BACSA's phobia toward change. For Curl the necropolis offers the ultimate aesthetic and historical experience. It is a fossil, untouched by either the living individuals who shaped its "coffins," "sarcophagi," and "urns" or the history of the dead who inhabit them. The necropolis, as Curl would have it, exists outside history in the realm of pure aesthetic forms.

The construction of India as a necropolis seems even more bizarre when we reflect on the funerary customs of most inhabitants of the subcontinent. While many Mughal emperors erected elaborate mausoleums for themselves and their wives, their funerary habits were quite different from those of ordinary people. Indian Muslims bury their dead in areas designated for this purpose and rarely mark graves with the identity of the deceased. The majority of India's other religious communities—Hindus, Sikhs, and Jains—dispose of their dead through cremation, generally scattering the ashes in one of India's rivers.[21] Parsis offer the bodies of their dead to the natural elements, by placing them in towers. The only other funerary relic resembling a tombstone in India is the sati stone, which commemorates a woman who has committed sati. But in this case the sati stone functions as a shrine, for the act of sati transforms the woman into a minor deity. The necropolis as an aesthetic construct is not native to India.

For all Curl's protestations, and however much BACSA members might choose to ignore history, BACSA is embarked on a battle against time itself. With every passing day, the physical elements take their toll on the tombstones. Michael Stokes sounds this somber reminder to other members in the closing pages of the *Souvenir Chowkidar*: "As each year passes, as the state of abandoned cemeteries deteriorates, as pressure for building land increases and as the jungles advance, our task becomes ever more difficult. Time is not on our side: after another ten years much of what is still recordable will have gone" (78).

BACSA's other mission—to research the history of European residences and publish the results—also militates against the effects of time by providing a written record of a rapidly vanishing past. The society has accumulated and organized an impressive archive of materials. BACSA maintains files on "nearly every cemetery in India" and has collections of photographs, diaries, letters, journals, "books, post-cards, menus, dance-cards, cook's chitties, dolls, badges, medals, coins, stamps, silver trophies and paintings" (66). Though the organization's files are not open to the public, nor to BACSA members "in the normal way," members can petition the Executive Committee for permission to produce a "Records publication" (65). In other words, BACSA is able to provide the raw material for its members' publications. Its constitution empowers it "to print, publish, translate, sell, lend and distribute books" in furtherance of its general aims (44).

In 1981 BACSA decided to launch its own series of publications by its members. The first book of the series, *And Then Garhwal*, by Audrey Baylis, chronicles the story of an ICS officer who lived some hundred years ago. Wilkinson describes the book as "based on diaries, letters and family photographs" (63). The foreword of this first book contains the following prescription for the series: "Each book will be by a BACSA member, and about some particular person or family, incident or campaign, district or town involving Europeans in Asia" (45). The favorite genre of the series appears to be the family history. By the time *Souvenir Chowkidar* appeared in 1987, BACSA had published eight books, including four family histories: Audrey Baylis's *And Then Garhwal* (1981); Sir Rodney Pasley's *Send Malcolm* (1982); William Trousdale's edited journals of a father and son, *The Gordon Creeds in Afghanistan* (1984); and Evelyn Desiree Battye's *The Fighting Ten* (1984). BACSA publishes two books a year on assigned topics. The topic for 1984 was families on the Northwest Frontier in the nineteenth century, that for the following year the Indian police (46). Reflecting on the success of BACSA's publication mission, Theon Wilkinson notes:

Each book has tended to break into new ground and brought a fresh crop of members with different experiences in different parts of South Asia. BACSA is enriched by this diversity and with eight books now published since 1981 can positively assert that both the original objectives have been achieved: to disseminate knowledge on the social history of Europeans in South Asia; and to raise funds to preserve and record their monuments. (46)

Tombs generate tomes whose publication proceeds are directed toward identifying and preserving even more tombs; colonial ideology is thus revived through the discursive resurrection of its deceased officials.

FROM THE GRAVEYARD TO THE HOLY LAND

The discursive network linking Kipling, Allen, and BACSA extends to Ruth Prawer Jhabvala and her novel *Heat and Dust* (1995) as well. BACSA provided background photographs of old cemeteries for a documentary on Jhabvala.[22] In addition to writing novels, Jhabvala often collaborates with Ismail Merchant and James Ivory on their film productions; the team produced a film version of *Heat and Dust* in 1982, which credits Allen's *Plain Tales from the Raj* as one of its sources for dialogue. Jhabvala's novel participates in the reproduction of heroic-colonial individualism by treating the motifs of graves, genealogy, and knowledge production thematized by Allen and BACSA.

In this novel Jhabvala juxtaposes two narratives: one of a young Englishwoman who comes to India to research a family scandal, the other of her grandfather's first wife, Olivia, who left him for a Nawab. Jhabvala alternates the narrator's first-person diary entries set in the present with sections that describe Olivia's life in the 1920s. These latter sections are written in the third person. Like Charles Allen and the members of BACSA, the narrator attempts to recuperate her family history by fashioning Olivia's story from old letters and transcripts of tape-recorded interviews. In this respect the narrator's methodology is similar to Allen's, whose *Plain Tales from the Raj* is based on transcripts of interviews, and that of the BACSA authors, whose publications often germinate from archival correspondence.

Most of the narrator's story and all of Olivia's are set in the hot season, when temperatures in north India average around 115 degrees

Fahrenheit. The title refers to the setting and the heat plays a major part in the novel: Jhabvala pathologizes the heat, blaming it for Olivia's temperamental mood swings. Olivia's husband Douglas repeatedly invokes the heat to explain her emotions; after they quarrel, he excuses her behavior, telling her: "the climate is making you irritable. That's only natural, it happens to all of us. And of course it's much worse for you having to stay home all day with nothing to do" (40). Indeed, Olivia's attraction to the Nawab seems connected to the summer months. By stubbornly refusing to follow the colonial tradition of spending the hot season in a hill station, Olivia leaves herself vulnerable to the Nawab's charms. The name of the fictional city Satipur, where Olivia chooses to pass the summer months, is an ironic commentary on her relationship with Douglas: "Sati" means "good wife," whose loyalty is demonstrated by her willingness to die on her husband's funeral pyre.

Since all the other Englishwomen have retreated to Simla, Olivia and Douglas have few social engagements to occupy them. They find themselves spending Sunday evenings strolling through the English cemetery. Olivia calls "these Sunday excursions their visiting rounds" (105). Olivia is taken with the inscription on an Englishman's tomb, and comes to think of the deceased young lieutenant E. A. Edwards as a "particular friend" (105). For Olivia, the dead have replaced the living as companions. The cemetery is a necropolis and a haven, whose inhabitants are familiar to her.

The inscriptions on the tombs emphasize the family relationships among the deceased and provide evidence of their colonial genealogies. Edwards's tomb, for example, describes him "as a soldier ever ready where Duty called him, a dutiful son, a kind and indulgent Father but most conspicuous in the endearing character of Husband" (105). This inscription foregrounds his family identity, establishing him in a historical context that spans three generations of a particular family. Edwards's family has strong ties with India: five of his brothers have died in battle with him during the Sepoy Mutiny of 1857. Like Edwards, Olivia's husband Douglas, an ICS officer, can trace his family history in India. He tells her of "other young men, his own ancestors, lying in graveyards in other parts of India" (154). Graveyards are the living record of colonial family history.

Olivia has no experience of India and no relatives buried there. For this reason, she is on the border of "Anglo-Indian" society, where one gains entrance and acceptance based on the length and extent of one's family history in India. Because Olivia has no past ties to India, she projects future ones for herself through childbearing. The grave that exerts the most "powerful effect" on her is the "newest grave" in the cemetery, "that of the Saunders' baby, and the Italian angel was the newest, brightest monument" (25). Olivia transforms this grave, and the cemetery in general, into a fertility shrine, making it the equivalent of the Indian Baba Firdaus's shrine, where Indian women pray for the birth of a child: "She had brought a few flowers for the Saunders' baby. She knelt to place them at the feet of the Italian angel. When she got up, her face was radiant; she took Douglas' arm and whispered into his ear 'I made a wish. . . You know, the way they do at Baba Firdaus' shrine on the Husband's Wedding Day' " (106–7). While at the grave on another visit, she fantasizes about a child and the difference it could make in her life: "if she had a baby—a strapping blond blue-eyed boy—everything would be all right. She would be at peace and also at one with Douglas and think about everything the same way he did" (107). By producing an idealized Anglo male heir, Olivia will be able to belong to the "Anglo-Indian" community in Satipur.

Unfortunately for Olivia, the Indian shrine of Baba Firdaus, where she has sexual relations with the Nawab, proves more potent than the Saunders baby's grave. Pregnant at last, but uncertain of her child's paternity, she resorts to an abortion. Ironically it is Dr. Saunders, the father of the dead baby in the graveyard, who discovers Olivia's pregnancy and illicit abortion when he treats her for her "miscarriage." Olivia flees from the hospital and seeks refuge with the Nawab. She lives out her life in a small unspecified hill station, in a house provided by the Nawab, who visits her several times a year.

The parallel story of the narrator repeats Olivia's in some respects. The narrator has intercourse with an Indian man in the same shrine many years later. Baba Firdaus proves again to be a potent force, and the narrator finds herself pregnant. Here the two narratives diverge. While the narrator briefly considers abortion, she decides against it, opting instead to have her baby. She goes to the same hill station where Olivia once lived to have her baby.

The narrator greatly identifies with the subject of her research. The Merchant-Ivory film version of *Heat and Dust* makes the narrator's identification with Olivia even stronger. Another character in the film, Chid, accuses her of thinking of herself as Olivia's reincarnation. In deciding to have a child of mixed ancestry, the narrator takes the course of motherhood rejected by Olivia. She can have a biracial child, an act that Olivia found impossible in the censorious climate of colonial India. The narrator's quest into her family history in India ends with her establishing biological ties to the country. She finds an alternative metaphor for India besides that of the graveyard. She is "tired of the materialism of the West" (95). She explains her reasons for coming to India as a "hope of finding a simpler and more natural way of life," thus constructing India as a preindustrial society less complicated than its metropolitan counterpart (95). In this regard, her decision to live in a relatively underpopulated hill station and to become a mother can be read as an attempt to establish a "more natural way of life." The narrator's figuration of India into what William Empson termed "a version of pastoral," like the necropolis of BACSA, also attempts to turn back time.

As for Olivia, though she "had always been strongly affected by graveyards," by the end of the novel they no longer exert such a forceful pull on her. In fact, she "specifically requested cremation" for herself (174). The narrator speculates that Olivia's ashes have been scattered over the mountains. In death, Olivia repudiates the graves of her countrymen. By not transforming the landscape of India with a monument of her own, Olivia affiliates herself with the majority of Indians whose ashes, after death, become part of India's rivers and soils. We can read Olivia's cremation as a repudiation of the "Anglo-Indian" fascination with cemeteries and as an expression of Jhabvala's attempt to break out of the binary logic of colonialism that insisted on an absolute social separation between Europeans and Indians. But inasmuch as Jhabvala positions the colonial encounter within a sexual narrative, a trope pioneered by E. M. Forster's *A Passage to India* and developed in Paul Scott's *The Raj Quartet*, the novel fails to offer a substantial critique of British colonialism. In other words, Jhabvala does not use either the narrator's or Olivia's sexual encounter to alter significantly the relationships between Indians and the English. Olivia's dalliance results in an abortion. The narrator's retreat to the Himalayas to await the birth of her child, in the hopes of establishing a "a simpler and more natural way of life," participates in the contemporary clichéd formulation of India as the land where Westerners go to discover their spiritual selves.

RAJ NOSTALGIA AND (NEO-)COLONIAL CONTEXTS

Before considering the ideological effects of Raj nostalgia narratives and heroic-colonial individualism, it may be helpful to untangle the economic and political intricacies that knit together British economic decline, deep settler colonization in Northern Ireland, and the rise of what some members of the Centre for Contemporary Cultural Studies in Birmingham call "state authoritarianism" within Britain's contiguous borders (CCCS 16). For it is these factors that both inform and constitute the aporias of colonial and neocolonial narratives and herald the emergence of a full scale Raj revival in the mid-seventies and eighties.

Britain's loss of geopolitical power—its fall from premier imperial nation to marginal global player on the international stage—can primarily be attributed to its economic decline in the era inaugurated by the end of the Second World War.[23] The period between 1950 and 1973, often described as "the long boom" for Western economies, was propelled in part by postwar reconstruction programs that provided an initial push toward economic recovery, the transfer of technology and commercial capital from the United States to other industrialized countries, the demand for higher levels of public expenditure, high expectations of growth which helped sustain a culture of investment, and a flexible labor force which accommodated structural changes in agriculture and industry (Alford 247–48).[24] In most of the European countries, moreover, economic growth was accompanied by the establishment of extensive state welfare programs. In Britain, public expenditure rose from 26 percent of GDP in 1937 to 37.5 percent in 1951, to 42.9 percent in 1973 (Alford 248).

Yet Britain's economic growth during the long boom—as measured by GDP, balance of payments, and manufacturing productivity—lagged behind other industrialized countries such as France, Germany, Japan, and the United States.[25] Several factors contributed to Britain's lackluster economic performance during the long boom: pressure on the currency, a deficit in the balance of payments, inflation, and industrial inefficiency. To combat economic decline, the government resorted to an assault on the rights of workers, notably their right to strike (and to call wildcat strikes in particular), through such legislation as the Industrial Relations Act of 1971 and the Employment Act of 1981. The world recession of 1974 further exacerbated economic problems as productivity declined, the currency sank to record lows, and the number of unemployed exceeded one million. In 1976 the Labour government under James Callaghan applied to the International Monetary Fund (IMF) for a large loan to "save the pound." As a condition of granting the largest loan it had bestowed in its history, the IMF sought guarantees that Britain would curb its deficit spending, leading to reductions in planned expenditures on education, food subsidies, housing, roads, overseas aid, and defense (Arnstein 427). These measures, in addition to steps taken earlier in 1975 to check inflation by controlling wages, helped improve the balance of payments and stabilize the exchange value of the pound for several years.

The government's attempts to limit wage increases to 5 percent in 1979, however, precipitated numerous strikes from many sectors of the workforce, including truck drivers, water workers, ambulance drivers, hospital staff, and even gravediggers. Consequently, Liberals and Scottish Nationalists backed a parliamentary motion of no confidence against the government brought by the Conservatives. The Labour government failed to muster the requisite number of votes necessary to defeat the motion, paving the way for a general election. Margaret Thatcher, who had served as the secretary of state for education and science under Edward Heath's administration, led the Conservative Party to power. As Walter Arnstein remarks, upon assuming office Thatcher prosecuted an explicit agenda of privatization. Her first priority

> was to provide incentives for private industry by reducing all income tax rates on individual wages (the highest marginal rate was reduced from 83 to 60 percent and later to 40 percent) and on corporations (for which the highest rate dropped from 52 to 35 percent). At the same time, inheritance taxes were reduced, and the movement of funds in and out of the country was freed from state regulation for the first time since before World War II. Inflation was to be kept under control by "monetarism," the use of government powers to curb the amount of money pumped into the economy. The growth of expenses on social services, education, and housing subsidies was to be restricted, and families who rented council houses . . . were to be encouraged to buy them. In the course of five years, the number of people working for government, national and local, was scheduled to decline by 15 percent. (433)

Over the next decade, Thatcher's administration denationalized many of the industries—such as seaport facilities, cross-channel ferries, the British Oil Corporation, Jaguar automobiles, British Airways, British Gas, and British Telecom—which had been public corporations under successive Labour governments since 1945 (Arnstein 440–41). Between 1973 and 1987 the proportion of the population employed in industry was reduced by approximately 12 percentage points (Alford 315). "The government's monetarist strategy," as Louis Kushnick explains, was "predicated on cutting non-repressive state expenditure, relying on market forces to facilitate profitable economic activity—in Britain and outside—and cheapening labour within Britain by cutting the social wage and weakening or destroying working-class organisations" (188).

By the mid-eighties, the government's policies, along with the microprocessor revolution and the global consolidation of capital into transnational corporations, had resulted in a 10 percent unemployment rate, which translated into roughly three million people out of work.[26] A structural shift in the British economy toward permanent high levels of unemployment, widespread dissatisfaction among workers, and the decline in the industrial sector are symptomatic of a crisis in the British capitalist formation. Yet even as the government made massive cuts in public expenditure, it reallocated resources between other state programs and substantially increased spending on defense and law enforcement (Bridges 178). A significant amount of these resources was funneled to the security apparatuses in Northern Ireland, one of the most resilient sites of British deep-settler colonialism stretching back to the twelfth century, in response to legitimate political demands made by the nationalist minority.[27]

In Ireland, British eight centuries of colonial rule gave rise to state-sanctioned discrimination, through both ideological and repressive state apparatuses, against natives, principally Catholics in the earlier period and republicans in the later period. This discrimination was embodied in legislation such as the Statutes of Kilkenny (1366), the Penal Laws (1695–1829), the Special Powers Act (1922–72), and the Prevention of Terrorism Act (1974 and 1976).[28] While the current "troubles" in Northern Ireland have their genesis in this long history of deep-settler colonization, particularly by Scottish and English settlers in the seventeenth century, they may be traced more immediately to the British decision to partition the island in 1921 along sectarian lines and the ensuing civil war between those who supported and those who opposed this compromise.[29]

The six counties of Northern Ireland were carved out of the historic province of Ulster to guarantee a loyalist Protestant majority; Catholic nationalists, who constituted between one third and two fifths of the population in the North, became a minority. In addition to being the target of large-scale pogroms waged by loyalists, a third of whom were armed in the early years following partition, the Catholic nationalist minority was subject to systemic discrimination. As Mike Tomlinson notes, this discrimination was underwritten by the British government, which agreed, under the Social Services Agreement Act of 1949, to pay the expenses of maintaining the British welfare state in the North that could not be met by local taxes, an arrangement which has come to be known as the "subvention":

> In theory, social services (including housing, health, education, social security benefits) were to be provided at the same standards as in Britain. In practice, however, this "parity" amounted to a financial convention to underwrite the "Orange state", not a political practice to ensure that universal standards prevailed. Discriminatory policies and practices designed to marginalise the Irish nationalist minority became defining characteristics of the state, most notably in the areas of economic development, housing and public sector employment. With the agreement of the Catholic Church, which at the time was hostile to state-based social provision, the education system was similarly institutionally divided on a religious basis and differentially funded. (9)

By 1968 the nationalist minority had realized that their civil rights could not be acquired within the parameters of the existing state of Northern Ireland. Consciously emulating the African American civil rights movement, civil rights organizations took to the streets in a series of marches to demand fair allocation of housing, laws to prohibit discrimination in local government, an end to gerrymandering, repeal of the Special Powers Act, and the disbanding of the "B" Specials (Evans and Pollock 131). After a number of attacks against the nationalist minority by the Royal Ulster Constabulary (RUC) and the "B" Specials, in 1969 the British government deployed its troops to Belfast and Derry to protect Catholics. Initially welcomed by Catholics as a defense against loyalist violence, the army soon became an occupation force in its own right and aligned itself with the Protestants (Farrelly and Ridgeway 31).

Three months after the massacre of thirteen peaceful protesters in 1972 by British paratroopers during a civil rights march in Derry in what has become known as "Bloody Sunday," the British government suspended the Northern Ireland Parliament at Stormont and imposed direct rule from Westminster. Since the early seventies, the British government has sought to crush the republican movement with methods which have even earned them the censure of the European Commission of Human Rights in Strasbourg: namely, the internment of a significant portion of the population, the use of torture to extract confessions from suspected IRA members in no-jury courts, the manipulation of Protestant paramilitary death squads to terrorize the nationalist community, the use of Special Air Service (SAS) units to carry out intelligence operations and assassinations, and the deployment of troops against civilians. Furthermore, the security policies of "criminalisation, Ulsterisation, and restoration of police primacy," introduced in 1976, ended the special category status for prisoners convicted of "terrorist" offenses and inspired fierce opposition among IRA prisoners that would lead to the hunger strikes of 1980 and 1981 (Newsinger 55).

Such operations—surveillance, policing, and detention—have required the British state to commit significant amounts of labor and capital to its security enterprises. By 1972, for instance, British repressive state apparatuses in Northern Ireland consisted of a myriad of forces including 16,867 regular British soldiers; the Ulster Defence Regiment (UDR), 8,728 strong; 12,000 police officers (the RUC and SAS); MI5 (the internal security apparatus) and MI6 (the external security apparatus); Ulster Special Branch detectives; and an assortment of local detectives, agents, and informers (Wichert 145). As Mike Tomlinson points out, the "conflict has become an integral part of the economy of the North and is responsible for employing, directly and indirectly, as much as one quarter of the full-time work force" (8). The cost of maintaining the troops in Northern Ireland, RUC, UDR, and the judicial system—excluding the subvention and the millions of pounds paid out as compensation for IRA bombings—amounts to £1,200 million annually (Evans and Pollock 172). Northern Ireland, like South Africa during the final years of apartheid and the present-day occupied territories of Palestine, demonstrates that the last refuge of deep-settler colonization may very well be the police state.

While security procedures in the six counties were modeled on Brigadier Frank Kitson's prescriptions for what are quaintly known as "low intensity operations," patterned on counter-insurgency methods developed in British colonial campaigns after 1945, these methods were marshaled during the seventies and eighties against black and poor Britons living within mainland Britain. The erosion in living standards and employment opportunities, coupled with both the reluctance of the police to protect blacks from racist attacks and their eagerness to target blacks as criminals, solidified tensions between the police and Afro-Caribbean and South Asian communities.[30] According to Paul Gilroy, the movement from full employment to structural unemployment has heralded fundamental changes in the way surplus labor power is now perceived as a surplus population which requires new forms of state control ("You Can't Fool the Youths" 214). Gilroy highlights the importance of community in the state's strategies of coping with what Gramsci termed an "organic crisis."[31] The state utilizes

> new mechanisms of social control and surveillance which, recognising the strength of communities, attempt to penetrate them in new strategies for containment—"control is shifted from the criminal act to the crime-inducing situation, from the pathological case to the pathogenic surroundings, in such a way that each [black] citizen becomes, as it were, an a priori suspect or a potential criminal." ("You Can't Fool the Youths" 214)

What has shifted, in other words, is the state's willingness to substitute forms of direct state intervention, often embodied in the use of force against civilians, for more indirect forms of social control (Centre for Contemporary Cultural Studies 17).

The government's "new strategies for containment," however, have drawn on older forms of state repression developed in the laboratories of Northern Ireland. The policing methods of the RUC, the surveillance and intelligence-gathering techniques of security forces, and the British army's weaponry and patrolling style inform the two dominant strands of policing in contemporary Britain: fire-brigade policing and community policing. Fire-brigade policing is primarily reactive and heavy-handed, consisting of automobile patrols that are backed by a central mobile reserve unit which can be deployed rapidly. This method of policing has resulted in the creation of Special Patrol Groups (SPGs) in major cities, which act as riot-control units. Robert Mark, appointed commissioner of police for London in 1972, was particularly taken by the techniques used by the RUC and "had his 200-strong SPG trained in 'snatch-squad methods' (to arrest ringleaders), 'flying wedges' (to break up crowds) and random stop-and-search and roadblock techniques, 'based on the army's experience in Ulster' " (Bunyan 165). In addition, counter-insurgency equipment employed in Northern Ireland, such as CS gas, water cannons, and the often-lethal plastic bullets, were sanctioned for use by the police in British cities (Bunyan 169). The second method of policing, the more benign-sounding but no less pernicious "community policing," also uses information-gathering and retrieval systems developed in the six counties to place black communities under surveillance. Tony Bunyan elucidates:

> Harnessing technological advances and drawing on the experience in Northern Ireland, computerised record-keeping systems were developed capable of embracing the whole population. The most obvious example was the extension of the Police National Computer to hold the records not just of 'criminals', but of all car-owners and vehicle licence holders, covering over half the adults in the country. The government-appointed Lindop Committee on Data Protection reported that the Special Branch (and via it the other security agencies) had access to this computer through a 'flagging' system that could bring its attention to any misdemeanour committed by someone of 'interest'. (162)

As even an ex-superintendent acknowledges: "Many will . . . find a parallel with the Northern Ireland tragedy, particularly when they examine the aspirations and the difficulties encountered by Ulster Catholics and our own Black West Indian population. The friction between these people and their police forces is not just a co-incidence, and must surely give food for thought" (quoted in Gilroy, "Police and Thieves" 171).[32]

Members of the Centre for Contemporary Cultural Studies in Birmingham have characterized the British state in this period as an incipient form of "state authoritarianism" which corresponds neither "to the normal liberal-democratic state form, nor to fully exceptional forms like Fascism" (17). They argue that while the state has failed to reconfigure democracy on a new basis, democracy has not been completely eliminated and continues to exist in residual forms (17). State authoritarianism is constituted by three main features: the state defines legitimate political activity on the part of its citizens and residents much more restrictively, thus allowing it to criminalize certain kinds of protest; it intensifies its control over the lives of those living within its purview; and the state curtails the "formal" liberties of its subjects unequally, according to its racialization and pathologization of certain groups (17). In Britain, state authoritarianism has been based on the economic disenfranchisement of blacks who are targeted as criminals, for engaging in extra-parliamentary protests, by both preventive and reactive measures materialized in community and fire-brigade policing.

Many Afro-Caribbean and Asian immigrants arrived in Britain after 1948 in response to the increased demand for unskilled labor in the early period of postwar reconstruction. These descendants of ex-slaves and previously indentured servants, from Commonwealth countries and former colonies, found themselves excluded from decent housing and entertainment venues under the restrictions of the color bar. As in the colonies where a divide-and-rule policy was often implemented to exacerbate cultural and political differences among natives and discourage them from organizing against colonial authority, so too British capital sought to divide immigrant labor by ethnicity and national or colonial origin. In general, Afro-Caribbean immigrants were absorbed into the service sector to work in the transport, health, and hotel industries, Asian immigrants into the industrial sector to work in foundries, factories, and textile mills (Sivanandan 113).

While these early immigrants tended to engage in what A. Sivanandan calls forms of "settler politics" focused on electoral politics within existing party frameworks, their progeny have become more militant in response to successive legislation aimed at limiting the immigration of people of color and the state's assaults on black civil liberties as well. The Commonwealth Immigrants Bill of 1962, regulating the entry and settlement of black immigrants, and the Kenyan Asian Act of 1968, barring free entry to Britons of Asian origin from Kenya, anticipated the Immigration Act of 1971, which effectively halted black immigration by differentiating between "patrial" and "non-patrial" populations. Only patrials, defined as those with a parent or grandparent who had been born or adopted in the United Kingdom, had a right of abode under the act. Non-patrials, in contrast, were permitted entry under highly circumscribed conditions, with the length, location, and nature of their entry regulated. "Their residence, deportation, repatriation and acquisition of citizenship," Sivanandan explains, "were subject to Home Office discretion" (Sivanandan 131). The act also allowed constables and immigration officers to arrest without warrant anyone who had entered or was suspected to have entered the country illegally or exceeded the permissible length of her or his visit. As Sivanandan points out: "Since all blacks were, on the face of them, non-patrials, this meant that all blacks were illegal immigrants unless proved otherwise" (131). Moreover, the retrospective nature of this legislation in effect rendered suspect all black citizens regardless of the duration of their tenure in Britain.

By the mid-seventies, bans and entry certificates, arrests on the basis of the notorious "Sus" laws, degrading vaginal searches of black female immigrants at Heathrow, deportations, and detentions had taxed the patience of black immigrants, who became more militant in their attempts to protect their communities from police brutality and racist attacks.[33] The ubiquitous presence at black political events of the police, often in large numbers and in heavily armed units such as the paramilitary SPGs, insured that Afro-Caribbean and Asian immigrants would respond to police provocation. Such was the case at the Notting Hill Carnival of 1976, when black youth responded with bricks, bottles, and fire to sixteen hundred police officers patrolling the festival (Sivanandan 137). Resentment against such police operations as Swamp 81—conceived ostensibly to combat "muggings" and street crime—in Brixton in April 1981, in which one thousand people were stopped and interrogated in the first four days, sparked arson attacks by youths against buildings where blacks had been discriminated against and police vehicles (CARF Collective 224). As one black youth remarked, these actions were "not against the white community" but "against the police. They have treated us like dirt. Now they know it's not that easy" (225). In July of the same year, similar uprisings erupted in Southall, Liverpool, and Manchester. With over thirty towns and cities ablaze, the government moved to contain unrest through counter-insurgency strategies: it authorized the establishment of army camps to hold convicted rioters; the police were to be equipped with armored vehicles; and CS gas, rubber bullets, and water cannons would be issued to chief constables (228).

Just as the uprisings of 1981 shook the confidence of white Britons in the state's ability to maintain "law and order" domestically, so the Falkland Islands conflict in May 1982 provided a site to displace those anxieties into jingoism and support for an anachronistic, imperial war effort.

The Falkland Islands, a British South Atlantic dependency and a remnant of deep-settler colonization dating back to the late seventeenth century, were invaded by Argentinian forces in April. Prime Minister Margaret Thatcher then ordered British troops to recapture the islands. In spite of being outnumbered by the Argentinians, the British forces were successful in their mission. Righteously packaged to the public as a war to liberate Falkland Islanders from foreign rule and to uphold international law, the war boosted support for the Conservatives and enabled them to win the elections of 1983 with the largest share of parliamentary seats that any party had gained since the end of the Second World War (Arnstein 438–39).

By 1990, when the prime minister resigned as leader of the Conservative Party to assume a seat in the House of Lords as Baroness Thatcher, British living standards, which had been among the highest in Western Europe in 1950, had declined to among the lowest (Glynn and Booth 188). Britain's economic decline, the continuing colonization and militarization of Northern Ireland, and British immigration policy form the context for the Raj nostalgia phenomenon.

The material links between Charles Allen, BACSA, and Ruth Prawer Jhabvala and their works connect them within a discursive network that has resurrected and revivified colonial ideology. During the seventies and eighties, a reanimated colonial ideology was replayed as cinematic spectacle in movies like *Gandhi*, *A Passage to India*, *The Far Pavilions*, and the Granada Television production of *The Jewel in the Crown*. While I have analyzed the rhetorical mechanisms of the textual embodiments of Raj nostalgia and heroic-colonial individualism throughout this chapter, I turn now to a consideration of the ideological effects of this phenomenon, which are fourfold. First, as we have seen from *Plain Tales from the Raj*, Raj nostalgia presents a nondialectical narrative of colonial history, in which the stories of the colonized and their struggles against oppression are either marginalized or not represented at all. These accounts present conservative distortions of history. Salman Rushdie identifies the largest distortion as "the view [which underlies many of these works] that the British and Indians actually understood each other jolly well, and that the end of the Empire was a sort of gentleman's agreement between old pals at the club" (*Imaginary Homelands* 101).

Second, Raj nostalgia helps to displace interest in contemporary India by offering exotic representations of the colonial past in its stead.

These exotic representations of the subcontinent contrast sharply with the grotesque images of India circulated through satellite news. Arjun Appadurai and Carol Breckenridge elaborate this second point in a piece published in *Inscriptions* (having been rejected for the Op-Ed page of the *New York Times*): "India today comes across as a country of assassinated leaders, frenzied Sikhs, a grotesque film industry, an incompetent and callous industrial sector and endangered brides. What sane American, if asked to choose between colonialism with a human face and its apparent aftermath, would not want Indians to want the world they have lost?" (7) BACSA's indifference to the plight of the Kacheri Cemetery's chowkidar is an extreme case in point.

Third, the Raj revival falsely constitutes Britain as monolithically Anglo. In England, where the legacy of the Empire is a racially mixed population, the cultural apparatus of Raj revivalism excludes black immigrants from the imagined community of the nation (Sharpe, "Scenes of an Encounter" 1). Neocolonial ideology derives from what Abdul Jan-Mohamed has called the manichean allegory of multiple, polarized categories such as subject and object, good and evil, white and black, and it also equates political status with racial difference. People of color become naturalized as oppressed and subservient. Both Rushdie and Sharpe point to how conservative politicians, notably Margaret Thatcher, have harnessed colonial nostalgia in the service of militarism against people of color in the Third World. In the aftermath of the Falklands War, Thatcher triumphantly declared: "We have learned something about ourselves, a lesson which we desperately need to learn. When we started out, there were the waverers and the fainthearts . . . The people who thought we could no longer do the great things which we once did . . . that we could never again be what we were. There were those who would not admit it . . . but—in their hearts of hearts—they too had their secret fears that it was true: that Britain was no longer the nation that had built an Empire and ruled a quarter of the world. Well, they were wrong" (quoted in Rushdie, *Imaginary Homelands* 131). As Rushdie rightly observes, Thatcher's use of the word "we" is "an act of racial exclusion" that refers solely to white Britons. The cultural apparatus of Raj revivalism similarly excludes immigrants from the imagined community of the British nation, by denying them a history.

Finally, the circulation of narratives of Raj nostalgia helps to mystify and deflect criticism from Britain's far more intransigent eight-hundred-year colonization of Ireland. BACSA's initial ventures in the publication of colonial family histories in 1981 coincided with both the Royal Wedding and the Irish hunger strikes. The royal nuptials initiated Charles's much-publicized search for an eligible, aristocratic virgin and hence articulated a national preoccupation with purity, bloodlines, and the perpetuation of familial dynasties. At the same time that the prince was hunting for a suitably chaste consort, members of the IRA and Irish National Liberation Army were going on a hunger strike to protest the British government's criminalization policy toward political prisoners. In fact, the government worried about the potential for negative publicity that would accrue from juxtaposing images of the royal extravaganza against those of the emaciated republican prisoners, even as it launched unprecedented security measures to guard the royal coterie against the rumored threat of attacks from the IRA (Lyons, "Writing in Trouble" 280).

Ireland does surface occasionally in some Raj narratives, where it occupies an uneasy position as both a colonized territory, manifest as the site of colonial graveyards, and a producer of colonial military and administrative personnel. In a detailed article in *Souvenir Chowkidar*, James Stevens Curl traces the history of "European Funerary Architecture in India": "It is no accident that the first burial-grounds in the British Isles were formed by Dissenters . . . or in areas where rationalist ideas were coming to the surface, as in Scotland and Ulster," Curl writes. "Edinburgh and Belfast can both boast fine and spacious eighteenth-century cemeteries, unattached to churches, and adorned with splendid monuments, mausolea and planting" (32). Curl argues that these cemeteries have their conceptual origins in India. He points to the Stephenson family grave in "the tiny Presbyterian churchyard at Kilbridge, Co. Antrim" as evidence that Europeans have imported Indian forms into Ireland and Scotland. The Stephensons, "who had connections with India," chose as their eternal resting place, "a miniature Taj Mahal complete with dome, pointed arches, and pinnacles" (36). Curl reflects:

> It is thus clear that families with involvements in the East India Company not only acquired exotic tombs in the new cemeteries in India, but wished to emulate them at home. Those who had seen monumental mausolea in India were not going to settle for humble stones when they returned to the British Isles. Many elaborate tombs and

monuments in the home country, therefore, were attempts to recreate a grandeur that was not unusual in India, while a growing awareness of the possibilities of cemetery design was suggested by the magnificent necropoleis [sic] of Europeans in the sub-continent. (Llewellyn-Jones, *Souvenir Chowkidar* 36)

According to Curl, Europeans attempted to copy the grandeur of Moghul tombs, singling out the tomb of Humayun in Old Delhi and the Taj Mahal in Agra as exemplary (Llewellyn-Jones, *Souvenir Chowkidar* 33).

Owing to uncertain employment in Ireland and a colonial economy which provided few opportunities for land ownership as it tried to consolidate small agricultural land holdings into larger units for the mass production of livestock, many Irishmen sought employment in the British armed services. In the period from 1770 to 1857, over half the soldiers in the East India Company's "European Regiments" were Irish (Kipling, "Soldiers Three" 174). After 1857 and the transfer of the subcontinent to crown rule, seven of ten numbered battalions were Irish ("Soldiers Three" 174). Yet it is probably not the common Irish soldier, whose income was quite modest, who is referenced in Curl's description of Irish cemeteries, but members of the powerful landed class, the Anglo-Irish Ascendancy, who were the descendants of English colonial settlers. Charles Allen refers to this group in *Plain Tales from the Raj* in his claim that certain groups had a genetic proclivity to rule India:

> If certain families made India their vocation so, too, did certain peoples: 'Anybody with a Celtic streak was immediately more at home in India. They seemed to integrate better than the very conventional English.' Ever since the late eighteenth century, when India proved 'a godsend for the younger sons of the Manse,' Scots and, to a lesser extent, Ulstermen, had dominated the administration, continuing to provide nearly half the ICS well into the twentieth century. (35–36)

Allen's and BACSA's invocation of Ireland simultaneously foregrounds Irish participation in British imperialism, even as it elides the record of that imperialism in Ireland.

The ideology of heroic-colonial individualism—like its Janus-faced twin, rogue-colonial individualism—seeks to sanitize colonial history through its disavowal of the brutality of colonial rule. Heroic-colonial individualism disarticulates colonialism from its constitutive violence by representing colonial officials as heroic figures who serve the Empire at great physical risk to themselves and by displacing the violent effects of colonial policy onto native subjects who are figured as the efficient cause of such violence. As "Survivors" of the Raj, these colonial officials are further legitimated to rule over the subcontinent through the propagation of genealogical narratives which emphasize their ancestry and ties to South Asia. Yet at the time when narratives of Raj nostalgia were reinvigorating colonial ideology by reproducing knowledge of the Empire, those from the former colonies living within Britain, as well as colonial subjects in the North of Ireland, were posing political challenges to different forms of British state violence.

NOTES

Introduction

1   In order to avoid collapsing distinctions between dominance and resistance, I avoid using the term "colonial subject" to describe Indian subjects living under colonial rule. My use of the terms "colonial subject" and "metropolitan-colonial subject" references British colonial officials and their wives; my use of the terms "native subject" and "nationalist subject" refers to South Asians living under British colonialism, who are further distinguished on the basis of class background through such adjectives and nouns as "elite," "elite-subaltern," and "subaltern."

2   For a thorough history of the origins of modern selfhood, see Charles Taylor's *Sources of the Self: The Making of the Modern Identity*. In "Individual, Group, and Democracy," Jean Baechler defines the individual as "the geometric locus of an indefinite number of determinations, which each in turn may be defined along a scale that moves from the greatest generality to the greatest particularity" (17). Baechler links this conception of the individual to questions of agency and notes that the degree to which the individual opts to affiliate with groups or to remain singular is determined by sociohistorical factors such as those of "culture, historical time, political regime, social position, representation, or educational background" (19). While invoking such factors, however, Baechler's meditation on the relationship between the individual, groups, and democracy is curiously ahistorical.

3   Cousins was not the only western feminist participant in the Indian nationalist movement: Annie Besant and Margaret Noble were also active. Because all three women settled in India, they are distinct from other western women who only visited the subcontinent. For further information on women travelers, see Dea Birkett, *Spinsters Abroad: Victorian Lady Explorers*; Nupur Choudhuri and Margaret Strobel, *Western Women and Imperialism: Complicity and Resistance*; Laura Donaldson, *Decolonizing Feminism: Race, Gender, and Empire-Building*; and Inderpal Grewal, *Home and Harem: Nation, Gender, Empire, and the Cultures of Travel*.

4   For a careful reading of "Can the Subaltern Speak?" and its limitations regarding its ability to adumbrate native resistance, see Asha Varadharajan's "Gayatri Chakravorty Spivak: The 'Curious Guardian at the Margin,'" in *Exotic Parodies:*

Subjectivity in Adorno, Said, and Spivak. Varadharajan accuses Spivak of "a conservative misreading and annexation of deconstruction" (90), remarking that "the
prospects for counterhegemonic ideological production seem bleak indeed if the
discovery that the colonized have no history within the context of colonial production is matched by the contention that they cannot know and speak for
themselves" (95). For more laudatory readings of Spivak's essay, see Rey Chow's
"Where Have All the Natives Gone?" and Linda Martín Alcoff's "The Problem of
Speaking for Others," in Judith Roof and Robyn Wiegman, Who Can Speak?
Authority and Critical Identity. For an excellent account of the debates regarding
subalternity, gender, and agency in the South Asian context, see Ania Loomba's
"Challenging Colonialism" in Colonialism/Postcolonialism.

5   Feminist scholarship on questions of agency is diverse and rich. See in particular
the following edited collections: Chandra Talpade Mohanty, Third World Women
and the Politics of Feminism; Amrita Basu and Elizabeth McGrory, The Challenge of
Local Feminisms: Women's Movements in Global Perspectives; Patricia Jeffery and Amrita
Basu, Appropriating Gender: Women's Activism and Politicized Religion in South Asia; and
Judith Kegan Gardner, Provoking Agents: Gender and Agency in Theory and Practice.

6   Sidney Tarrow's Power in Movement: Social Movements and Contentious Politics provides "a broad theoretical framework for understanding the place of social
movements, cycles of contention, and revolutions within the more general category of contentious politics" (3). While his book draws primarily on British,
French, and North American examples of social movements, his analysis can be
used to theorize the "repertoire of collective action" that informs agency in
national liberation struggles.

7   Four notable exceptions to the single-site, discrete-period paradigm of post-
colonial studies are Patrick Brantlinger's Rule of Darkness: British Literature and
Imperialism, 1830–1914, Barbara Harlow's Resistance Literature and Barred: Women,
Writing, and Political Detention, and Edward Said's Culture and Imperialism. All four
texts demonstrate the isomorphic parallels between seemingly distinct colonial
formations.

8   Marcus also recommends several other modes of construction such as to: follow
the people; follow the metaphor; follow the plot, story, or allegory; and follow
the conflict. For literary critics and historians, following the metaphor and tracing the circulation of signs, metaphors, and symbols in discourse and modes of
thought can prove especially useful in revealing the structural integrity and coherence of seemingly contingent social and geopolitical relations. For further
meditations on ethnography and fieldwork relationships more generally, see
George Marcus, "The Uses of Complicity in the Changing Mise-en-Scène of
Anthropological Fieldwork."

9   David Arnold's Police Power and Colonial Rule: Madras, 1859–1947, Kenneth Ballhatchet's Race, Sex and Class under the Raj: Imperial Attitudes and Policies and Their
Critics, 1793–1905, Liz Curtis's The Cause of Ireland: From the United Irishmen to Partition, and Leonard Gordon's Bengal: The Nationalist Movement, 1876–1940 men-

tion the material links between India and Ireland in their scholarship, but these references have been peripheral to other concerns among these scholars and only exist in footnotes and casual observations in their work. S. B. Cook's *Imperial Affinities: Nineteenth Century Analogies and Exchanges between India and Ireland* offers the most extensive treatment of these connections.

Chapter One

1   As their report makes clear, the Hunter Committee apparently did not feel that Dyer's failure to seek medical attention for the wounded warranted censure. The report reads:

> General Dyer's action in not attending to or making provision for the wounded at Jallianwala Bagh has been made the subject of criticism. It has to be remembered, however, that he was acting with a very small force and that after firing ceased he at once withdrew to his quarters at Ram Bagh. On being questioned as to whether he had taken any measures for the relief of the wounded, General Dyer explained that the Hospitals were open and that the medical officers were there. "The wounded only had to apply for help. But they did not do this because they themselves would be in custody for being in the assembly. I was ready to help them if they applied." He added that it never entered his head that the Hospitals were not sufficient for the number of wounded if they cared to come forward. It has not been proved to us that any wounded people were in fact exposed to unnecessary suffering from want of medical treatment. (United Kingdom, Parliament, *Report of the Committee* 31)

2   An obvious example of "rogue-colonial individualism" occurs in the figure of Governor Eyre, who employed all sorts of draconian measures to repress the Jamaica Rebellion of 1865. He is preceded by a number of other officials, such as those eighteenth-century freebooters Robert Clive and Warren Hastings in India, who had to be reined in and reformed by the colonial state in order for it to claim that it was operating according to the colonial "rule of law."

 For the British who wanted to feel that their Empire was more virtuous than any other empires, there was the case of King Leopold's Congo represented in Joseph Conrad's *Heart of Darkness*. Indeed, Mr. Kurtz functions much like a "rogue-colonial individualist" in that novel. And compared to the saintly Scotsman David Livingston, Henry Morton Stanley was near "rogue" status in the British press as the brash North American who used too much violence and gunplay in his forays into the "dark continent."

3   The status of "crimes against humanity," such as massacres, in international law has long been a vexed one, particularly prior to World War II. The Statute of the International Court of Justice identifies five major sources for prosecuting "crimes against humanity": treaties (namely, the First Hague Convention of 1907 and the never-ratified Treaty of Sèvres); judicial decisions which specify certain

acts or omissions can constitute a crime against humanity as in the Corfu Channel Case; customs which are "defined as a general practice that is accepted as law" (Matas 95); the teachings of the "most highly qualified publicists" (Matas 96); and general principles of law recognized by "civilized" nations (Matas 94). The latter three categories are especially fluid and open to much interpretation. For example, what exactly qualifies as custom? Which intellectuals and writers qualify as publicists? And which countries qualify as "civilized" ones? For further reading on the status of massacres in international law, see Vahakn N. Dadrian, "Genocide as a Problem of National and International Law: The World War I Armenian Case and Its Contemporary Legal Ramifications"; Linda Malone, "The Kahan Report, Ariel Sharon and the Sabra-Shatilla Massacres in Lebanon: Responsibility Under International Law for Massacres of Civilian Populations"; and David Matas, "Prosecuting Crimes against Humanity: The Lessons of World War I."

More recently, the targeting of ethnic groups for mass expulsion and physical repression has been used to justify so-called "humanitarian intervention," which, as Barbara Harlow has argued, has replaced the rhetoric of the "civilizing mission" to authorize aggression by the United States against Third World and developing nations ('Civilizing Mission' 31). Yet the legal case for "humanitarian intervention" is an ambiguous one given the gap between the "rights of states" on the one hand, as specified in article 2 of the United Nations Charter, and the "rights of individuals" on the other, as specified in the Universal Declaration of Human Rights. While the UN Charter prohibits the use of force against sovereign nations not engaged in outside aggression, the Universal Declaration of Human Rights states that "everyone has the right to a standard of living adequate for the health and well being of himself and of his family, including food, clothing, housing and medical care and necessary social services, and the right to security in the event of unemployment, sickness, disability, widowhood, old age, or lack of livelihood in circumstances beyond his control." A fundamental premise of the latter document is that each individual has inalienable rights that cannot be forfeited because of a government's misconduct. Indeed, one could argue that recent bombing campaigns by the United States in Iraq, Somalia, Afghanistan, and Yugoslavia are a form of collective punishment which violate the fundamental rights of life, health, education, food, and an adequate standard of living, of those individuals living within these states, guaranteed by the Universal Declaration of Human Rights, the International Covenant of Economic, Social and Cultural Rights, and other international treaties.

4   At least one member of the Commons, Brigadier General Surtees, invoked the necessity of maintaining British prestige in his defense of Dyer. During the debate on Dyer, he declared:

> I will ask hon. Members to consider carefully the effect of this Debate, not only in India, but among the civilised and uncivilised peoples among whom we rule. There are vast areas in Africa and the Pacific, where the sole British

representative is the one white man. It is up to him to keep the native race more or less in order, to look after administration, to see to justice, and, as far as possible, to stamp out violence and vice. In the most favourable circumstances this official is allowed a small armed native guard, but in the case of any serious upheaval, he and his police would be scattered like chaff, but for one thing. That one thing is British prestige. Once you destroy that British prestige, then the Empire will collapse like a house of cards, and with it all that trade which feeds, clothes, and gives employment to our people. (United Kingdom, *Parliamentary Debates* 1775)

5 Jawaharlal Nehru found such aspects of Dyer's character troubling. In *An Autobiography*, he describes sharing a train compartment with Dyer and his horror at hearing Dyer speak of his conduct at Amritsar. Nehru recounts an episode from 1919:

> Towards the end of that year I travelled from Amritsar to Delhi by the night train. The compartment I entered was almost full and all the berths, except one upper one, were occupied by sleeping passengers. I took the vacant upper berth. In the morning I discovered that all my fellow-passengers were military officers. They conversed with each other in loud voices which I could not help overhearing. One of them was holding forth in an aggressive and triumphant tone and soon I discovered that he was Dyer, the hero of Jallianwala Bagh, and he was describing his Amritsar experiences. He pointed out how he had the whole town at his mercy and he had felt like reducing the rebellious city to a heap of ashes, but he took pity on it and refrained. He was evidently coming back from Lahore after giving his evidence before the Hunter Committee of Inquiry. I was greatly shocked to hear his conversation and to observe his callous manner. He descended at Delhi station in pyjamas with bright pink stripes, and a dressing-gown. (43–44)

6 Richard Attenborough's film *Gandhi* includes the scene of the massacre, which was crucial in convincing Mahatma Gandhi that colonialism was based on systemic violence and that the British had to be ousted from India. The renowned Indian director Govind Nihalini shot this scene in the film. Nihalini includes women and children among Dyer's victims, thus showing how colonial violence impacts all native people regardless of gender and age.

7 I have not been able to access the report of the Indian National Congress Committee investigation into the massacre and have had to rely on the lengthy quotations from this document provided in the texts of V.N. Datta, Rupert Furneaux, and Raja Ram.

8 I am grateful to Joginder and Harbans Bhola for communicating this information to me. On a trip to Amritsar in January 2000 Professor Harbans Bhola was kind enough to check into the matter of female fatalities. According to his transcribed notes, based on Secretary S. K. Mukerji's handwritten records, the geographical and religious composition of the casualties is as follows:

BY PLACE OF RESIDENCE

Persons from Amritsar Rural	70
Persons from Amritsar City	294
Persons from Cities of Gurdaspur, Batala and Taran Taran	17
Total	381

BY RELIGION

Hindus	212
Sikhs	90
Muslims	59
Female martyrs	2
Unknown	20
Total	381

9   The Commons voted first on the Spoor resolution, which was defeated by 247 to 37; Carson's resolution failed with 230 negative votes and 129 affirmative ones.

10   Montagu became the first secretary of state for India to visit India during his term in office. His trip coincided with World War I and earned him the criticism of Conservatives like Sir Michael O'Dwyer, who felt that reformist efforts detracted from the war effort and, in particular, the recruitment of native soldiers to fight the British cause. Even Churchill, Montagu's ally in the disciplinary action taken against Dyer, was moved to comment on this trip during the Dyer debate:

> I was astonished by my right hon. Friend's sense of detachment when, in the supreme crisis of the War, he calmly journeyed to India, and remained for many months absorbed and buried in Indian affairs. It was not until I saw what happened in Egypt, and, if you like, what is going on in Ireland to-day, that I appreciated the enormous utility of such service, from the point of view of the national interests of the British Empire, in helping to keep alive that spirit of comradeship, that sense of unity and of progress in co-operation, which must ever ally and bind together the British and Indian peoples. (United Kingdom, *Parliamentary Debates* 1732)

For O'Dwyer's critique of Montagu's trip and the concept of dyarchy, see his memoir *India as I Knew It: 1885–1925*. This memoir also contains an extended defense of Dyer and the decision to impose martial law in Punjab.

11   As Michael Edwardes points out, the franchise was limited to those who owned property. Furthermore, local, regional, and national electorates were determined on a sliding scale, which insured that only the wealthiest would be able to vote for the top tier of government. Those who qualified to vote in the provincial council elections numbered around five million; the electorate for the Central Legislative Assembly numbered nearly one million; and only seventeen thousand met the property qualifications to vote for the Council of State. India's population was then over 300 million (200).

12   For an excellent discussion of how discourses of antisemitism permeated the debate on Home Rule in Ireland, see Paul Canning's British Policy towards Ireland, 1921–1941. Canning argues that the diehard movement, which "had its roots in the conservative reaction to the revolutionary surge sweeping Europe in the wake of the Bolshevik Revolution" of 1917, attributed unrest in India, Palestine, Egypt, and Ireland to communism and an international Jewish conspiracy (17). Indeed, Lord Sydenham, who served as a governor of Madras and later as the secretary of the Committee of Imperial Defence, cast De Valera as a "Spanish Jew" (quoted in Canning 18). In 1921 he warned: "If we are ever to know what Ireland really wants the Terror must be broken up at any cost. It is all very like Russia, and at the back of the IRA is Bolshevism. A Red Army in Ireland could set up a Soviet and proceed to loot in the best Russo-Jewish style" (quoted in Canning 18). Many of these views were aired in the Morning Post; Canning also reveals that Dyer's biographer, Ian Colvin, regularly provided headlines for this publication (19).

13   Alfred Dreyfus was a French Jewish military officer who was unjustly accused and condemned for treason in the late nineteenth century. The "Dreyfus Affair," as it came to be known, resulted in a wave of antisemitism across Europe. As Edward Said notes, it became a "rigorous test" for intellectuals who could either speak in Dreyfus's defense or succumb to nationalist, antisemitic fervor by remaining silent and, hence, acquiescent in his sentence (Representations 8).

14   Stanley Wolpert certainly imputes antisemitic motives to Michael O'Dwyer and his reactions to Montagu. In his novel Massacre at Jallianwala Bagh, Wolpert describes O'Dwyer's response to the news of the disturbances at Amritsar. "It's what comes of having that Jew in Whitehall," O'Dwyer tells his commissioner Arthur Kitchen (124). He continues by sneering: "He's Gandhi's friend. . . . Isn't that what he told the Commons when I barred the dirty little terrorist fakir from my province? Didn't that Levantine lecher stand up then and say, 'I am proud to consider Mr. Gandhi one of my friends?'. . . The niggers and the Jews, Arthur—they're birds of a feather!" (124)

15   In The Life of General Dyer, Ian Colvin, Dyer's biographer and apologist, exposes Churchill's selective adherence to the concept of minimum force by describing his role as home secretary in the "battle of Sidney Street" in 1911:

> two desperadoes, who had taken refuge in a house in the East End of London, fired promiscuously with Mauser pistols, first at the police who tried to arrest them, and then at any one who came along the street. From the ample Press accounts . . . we gather that Mr Churchill arrived about 11.30 A.M. and took charge of operations. He had as his General Staff the Assistant Commissioner of Metropolitan Police, the Commissioner of City Police, and Mr Blackwell of the Home Office. His forces consisted of from 1000 to 1500 police partly armed with shotguns and revolvers; 90 men with rifles and a machine-gun of the Scots Guards; a section of Horse Artillery with one field gun, and a strong reserve of the London Fire Brigade. There was no reading of the Riot Act. . . . "It is some time," says one admiring account, "since the Home Secretary was

under fire, but his old military capacity had not deserted him. He was full of resourceful suggestions. His first suggestion was that metal shields should be improvised to enable the police to approach the building. Then the astonishing suggestion was made that a cannon should be brought to blow in the front of the building. . . ." The gun, fortunately for everything in the proposed line of fire, arrived too late to be brought into action; but in the meantime there was rapid practice, controlled or uncontrolled, from shot-guns, revolvers, and rifles. In the end the building was set on fire. . . . It is at any rate certain from the reports that the fire engines were not allowed to put out the fire until after the roof had collapsed and the garrison had been burnt to death. (299–300)

16   This section and the following one elaborate on arguments made in an article written with Laura E. Lyons, "Dyer Consequences: The Trope of Amritsar, Ireland, and the Lessons of the 'Minimum' Force Debate."

17   Writing in the last stages of the Mutiny, which he was in the process of suppressing, Sir Hugh Henry Rose wrote to his fellow military officer Sir Colin Campbell about the advisability of instituting a military police force in India on the Irish model. He explained:

> The great thing with these Indians is not to stay at long distances firing; but after they have been cannonaded, to close with them. They cannot stand. By forcing the Pass of Mundinpur I have taken the whole line of the enemy's defences in rear, and an extraordinary panic has seized them. I hope I am not over-sanguine, but I think that matters as far as we have gone look well. All in our rear is really police work; and all I want is a reserve to occupy the country I take, and prevent my flanks and rear being turned as I advance. *A military police, organised on the Irish Constabular system, is what is needed here, and in India generally.* (quoted in Burne 108; emphasis mine)

18   Bill Rolston first made this compelling argument in the context of the historical links between Ireland and North America. See his article "The Training Ground: Ireland, Conquest and Decolonisation."

19   Dyer was actually gazetted to the Second Battalion of the Queen's Royal West Surrey Regiment. However, since this battalion was already in India, he was sent to Ireland to serve with the First before joining the Second (Colvin 11).

20   Ironically, accounts of Dyer's conduct at Amritsar would become part of the syllabi at some of the military-educational apparatuses. A Staff College training manual from the 1960s, for example, points out that "the lessons to be drawn from this account are as applicable today as they were half a century ago" (quoted in Mockaitis 24). Amritsar provided a negative example, of what to avoid, when the military was called upon to assist civil authorities.

21   The tendency to pathologize Dyer's actions is not unique to Wolpert; Rupert Furneaux's journalistic account *Massacre at Amritsar* also examines the moral implications of Dyer's actions in the context of his background as a British subject. Like Wolpert, Furneaux wrestles with the temptation to identify the

massacre as somehow foreign and wholly alien to the British experience. He muses:

> It is natural that we should wish to find some reasonable explanation for Dyer's conduct which it seems impossible to justify. He was a British officer, a Colonel, an acting Brigadier, who, on his own showing, callously and in cold blood shot down an unarmed and unresisting crowd of natives, directing his fire to where the crowd was thickest, picking off those trying to escape . . . . If the act had been done by a German, a Russian or an Afrikander, we would not bother to seek an explanation. We would probably condemn a man of another race out of hand. Therein lies the danger that we may try too hard to find an excuse for Dyer; because our national pride demands it, we may delude ourselves, we need to realize. (176)

Even as he disavows the rhetorical strategy of those earlier narratives that sought to distinguish between Dyer's actions and British behavior, Furneaux seems fixated on the relationship between the two. This presents him with something of a predicament as he is committed to resolving the question of Dyer's culpability in order to assign individual moral responsibility for the carnage at Amritsar.

As Furneaux points out, the Amritsar disturbances were referred to by Dyer's critics as a "riot," by his partisans as a "rebellion." The naming of the disturbances played a crucial role in assigning responsibility and blame for the bloodshed. If the disturbances were deemed a local riot, then Dyer was guilty of committing a massacre. But if they signaled a rebellion, then he was credited with anticipating and suppressing a second mutiny. After painstakingly sifting through the documentary evidence surrounding Dyer's actions at the Jallianwala Bagh, Furneaux asks: "Was Dyer's act a ghastly mistake, or an appalling error of judgment, or was it sheer bloody massacre, an atrocity in the full meaning of the word, a crime against humanity, which we should condemn without question?" (176). That Furneaux's book bears the title *Massacre at Amritsar* suggests that it ultimately finds Dyer guilty of a terrible atrocity.

Furneaux seems to understand that the question of Dyer's culpability is crucially tied to his national identity as a British colonial. But to find Dyer guilty of a massacre would be to impugn British civilization itself. Furneaux creatively resolves this dilemma by both admitting to Dyer's guilt and absolving him of responsibility for his actions. Dyer's conduct at Amritsar, Furneaux proposes, has its origins in the medical condition which finally led to his demise in 1927:

> Arterial sclerosis has a retrograde effect, and it may have been creeping up on [Dyer] in 1919. If that was so, his judgment, at times of extreme mental stress, may have been so impaired as to diminish his responsibility. He seems to have been prone to outbursts of indignation, such as when he imposed his crawling order and when he had the boys who were suspected only of the assault on

Miss Sherwood flogged. Those acts alone suggest that Dyer was victim of some mental disorder, for they are otherwise beyond belief. (177)

"That is the kindest excuse we can find for Dyer," Furneaux concludes, a "naturally kind and humane man" (177–78). In the final analysis, Furneaux disassociates Dyer's use of force from the British colonial project by pathologizing it.

22   Some of the most interesting narratives of Dyer continue to circulate in contemporary Indi-pop, a fusion of traditional South Asian musical styles such as bhangra and classical ragas with funk, soul, and hip hop, among others. Several groups such as Crew Creative and P.D.M. have paid tribute to Udham Singh, the legendary trade unionist who was executed on July 31, 1940, for assassinating Sir Michael O'Dwyer at Caxton Hall in London, at the end of a joint meeting of the East India Association and Royal Central Asian Society. According to popular lore among diasporic South Asians, Singh's assassination of O'Dwyer was a deadly case of mistaken identity: Singh's real intentions were to shoot General Dyer, whom he had confused with O'Dwyer. According to Rupert Furneaux, however, the evidence supports the contention that Singh's target had been O'Dwyer all along. Before he was overpowered, Singh also managed to wound Lord Zetland (the secretary of state for India), Lord Lamington (a former governor of Bombay), and Sir Louis Dane (a former lieutenant governor of Punjab) (Furneaux 168).

As revealed at his trial, Singh was sixteen years old and living in Punjab during the Amritsar massacre; Dyer's actions made him loathe British colonialism. In the transcripts of his trial, which were only recently released by Scotland Yard and are available at the Udham Singh Centre in Birmingham, Singh anticipates Guha's argument about the failure of the British bourgeoisie to actualize its universalist project, by noting that "machine guns on the streets of India mow down thousands of poor women and children wherever your so called flag of democracy and Christianity flies" (misc.activism.progressive [newsgroup], 22 July 1997). That Singh attacked other civilian officials in Caxton Hall, in addition to assassinating O'Dwyer, to avenge the Jallianwala Bagh massacre indicates that he understood the connections between civil and military authorities.

Chapter Two

1   I would like to thank Jane Marcus for generously sharing her copy of *We Two Together* with me. Cousins's texts, published in India and now out of print, are difficult to locate in the United States. *The Awakening of Asian Womanhood* can be ordered through interlibrary loan from the Texas Woman's University Library. *Indian Womanhood Today* is available at the University of Texas (Dallas) Library. A short collection of WIA and AIWC documents, published under the misleading title *Mrs. Margaret Cousins and Her Work in India*, is at the University of Illinois (Urbana-Champaign) Library.

2   Conversations with Rachel Jennings on the relationship between identity poli-

tics, solidarity, and feminist criticism have helped clarify, for me, what is at stake in feminist debates on identity. See Jennings's "The Fight Against Union Carbide: Reclaiming the Strategy of Transnational Solidarity" (unpublished manuscript).

3 One of the most thoughtful treatments of this question is Judith Roof's and Robyn Wiegman's edited collection *Who Can Speak? Authority and Critical Identity*. For a cogent analysis of the politics of representing others, see in particular Linda Martín Alcoff's article "The Problem of Speaking for Others."

4 For a lucid analysis of the charge of "westernization" often leveled against Third World feminists, see Uma Narayan's "Contesting Cultures: 'Westernization,' Respect for Cultures, and Third World Feminists," in her *Dislocating Cultures*. Narayan insightfully argues that such charges, when emanating from Third World contexts, often fail to account for the ways in which feminists have been shaped by the specificity of their experiences and the ways in which "their feminist analyses are results of political organizing and political mobilization, initiated and sustained" from within those sites (13).

As a result of the partition of the island and the intensification of the anti-colonial struggle against British occupation in the North in the last several decades, the debate on the relationship between feminism and nationalism is an ongoing one in Ireland. For a brief sketch of the different strands of the women's movement in Northern Ireland, see Margaret Kelly's "Women in the North" in *Is Ireland a Third World Country?*, edited by the Centre for Research and Documentation. For a more detailed discussion of the role of women in the Republican movement and debates within Women Against Imperialism on the question of Northern Ireland, see Margaretta D'Arcy's remarkable *Tell Them Everything*. Laura E. Lyons's "Feminist Articulations of the Nation: The 'Dirty' Women of Armagh and the Discourse of Mother Ireland" offers an insightful reading of D'Arcy's text. For an analysis of feminism and the role of women in Sinn Fein, see Laura E. Lyons, " 'At the End of the Day': An Interview with Mairead Keane, National Head of Sinn Fein Women's Department." Finally, a special issue of *Feminist Review* 50 (summer 1995) is devoted to exploring the relationship between feminism and nationalism.

6 For a detailed assessment of the links between the American and Irish suffrage movements, see Mona Hearn's " 'The Tune of the Stars and Stripes': The American Influence on the Irish Suffrage Movement."

7 For an insightful reading of Countess Markievicz's prison letters, see David Lloyd's "Nationalisms against the State: Towards a Critique of the Anti-Nationalist Prejudice."

8 Formed in 1914, Cumann na mBan established the following goals in its first meeting:

> 1. To advance the cause of Irish liberty. 2. To organize Irish women in furtherance of this object. 3. To assist in arming and equipping a body of Irishmen for the defence of Ireland. 4. To start a fund to be called the Defense of Ireland Fund. (quoted in McKillen 57)

Though each branch of Cumann na mBan was affiliated with a volunteer company or battalion in its region from which it took military orders, the organization considered itself independent. For more information on Cumann na mBan, see Beth McKillen's "Irish Feminism and Nationalist Separatism, 1914–1923." In this article McKillen also argues that the IWFL and Cumann na mBan dissipated valuable energy in petty bickering with one another, which "hindered the development of an effective feminist movement in Ireland prior to 1916" (59).

9   "Apple-pie beds" are beds that have been, in American English, "short sheeted."

10   Alternatively, given the whole range of sexual practices between revulsion at sexual intimacy and revulsion at reproductive sex, Cousins's allusion to the "artistic" might also be read as a code for nonreproductive sexuality, specifically oral gratification or nongenitally focused sexuality.

11   Natterstad and Levenson do not indicate whether the letters' focus on Francis Sheehy-Skeffington, Hanna's husband, rather than on League members is representative of the letters appearing in the Evening Telegraph. Francis Sheehy-Skeffington might have become strongly associated in the public eye with women's suffrage through the weekly Irish Citizen, the IWFL's print organ, which he founded with James Cousins. I am speculating here, as the time between the launching of the Irish Citizen in May 1912 and Asquith's visit in July of the same year seems to be a short period for a journal to become established and identified with specific individuals.

12   For an excellent analysis of Sylvia and Christabel Pankhurst, in particular, and their contradictory class and colonial politics in relation to one another, see Inderpal Grewal's chapter "Empire and the Movement for Women's Suffrage in Britain" in her Home and Harem: Nation, Gender, Empire, and the Cultures of Travel.

13   Accounts of their sentencing also vary. Sheehy-Skeffington says that Leigh was sentenced to three years of penal servitude, and Evans to one year of hard labor (Owens and Sheehy-Skeffington 23). But Leah Levenson and Jerry H. Natterstad, Sheehy-Skeffington's biographers, write that the English women were sentenced to five years' penal servitude (41).

14   For a thorough discussion of hunger strikes in contemporary Ireland, see Laura Lyons's chapter " 'Standing on the Threshold of Another Trembling World': Writing the 1981 Hunger Strike in the Past, Present and Future Tense" in her "Writing in Trouble: Protest and the Cultural Politics of Irish Nationalism." For an account of the H-Block hunger strike, see Sinn Fein's video "The H Block Hunger Strike." I should note that this video never mentions the suffragettes' hunger strikes in the history it presents of this particular political tactic.

15   Hanna Sheehy-Skeffington does not mention Margaret Cousins even once in her "Reminiscences of an Irish Suffragette," though she gives credit to James Cousins for having founded the Irish Citizen with her husband Francis (Owens and Sheehy-Skeffington 13). This omission may be due to Cousins's having left Ireland in June 1913, during the critical period leading up to the Easter Rising of 1916. Nonetheless, Sheehy-Skeffington's failure to mention Cousins is surprising, given that the two were close friends and continued to correspond long after

Cousins's departure from Ireland. Leah Levenson and Jerry H. Natterstad quote from their letters in *Hanna Sheehy-Skeffington: Irish Feminist*.

16   Harlow cites Ngugi wa Thiong'o's *Detained: A Writer's Prison Diary*, Indres Naidoo's *Robben Island: Ten Years as a Political Prisoner in South Africa's Most Notorious Penitentiary*, and Molefe Pheto's *And Night Fell: Memoirs of a Political Prisoner in South Africa* among other examples of prison writing.

17   Historically, the Irish prisoner's class status seems to be a factor in her or his treatment in prison. For example, Ann Devlin, the servant of Robert Emmet, was imprisoned in the dungeons of Kilmainham Gaol, while her employer the wealthy Emmet was housed in more spacious chambers above. See Hester Piatt's pamphlet *Ann Devlin: An Outline of Her Story*. Under Margaret Thatcher's "criminalization policy," IRA prisoners were often brutalized and tortured. See the video "The H-Block Hunger Strike," produced by Sinn Fein. See also Margaretta D'Arcy's *Tell Them Everything*. Many of these prisoners come from working-class backgrounds.

18   James Cousins contributed thirty-five chapters of *We Two Together*, compared with Margaret's twenty-four. He inaugurates the text with the chapter "Beginnings," which establishes a conventional temporal sequence for the duography, starting with his birth and working its way to his present self writing. Margaret uses the same temporal organization in her sections. *We Two Together* moves from the past continuously to the present. The bulk of James's contribution, along with the ordering of his chapters, enables him to set the narrative agenda. The difference in Margaret's narrations of the Irish and Indian women's movements partially derives from the difference in James's activities in both lands. James's activities in Ireland were sharply focused on his literary production which brought him into the company of prominent Irish cultural nationalists like AE, George Russell, and W. B. Yeats. At the time of the Revival, James was hailed as "the voice of the North" (quoted in Dumbleton 7). William Dumbleton summarizes Cousins's important contribution to the Irish literary renaissance in this way: "He was instrumental in bringing together in 1902 the Fay brothers, their acting group, and AE to stage a first performance of two plays: Russell's play *Deirdre*, featuring Cousins and Padraic Colum in the cast; and Yeats' *Cathleen ni Houlihan*, starring Maud Gonne in the title role. Thus, with the union of Irish actors and Irish plays, was Irish theater established" (7). In addition to writing drama for the Irish theater, James produced a prolific amount of poetry, some of which took as its theme the suffragette movement. Cousins's Irish literary activities also included editing the *Irish Citizen* with Francis Sheehy-Skeffington. The *Irish Citizen* primarily functioned as the print organ of the IWFL, but in its pages could be found the leading political debates of the age. James's sections of *We Two Together* contain detailed descriptions of these overtly political activities.

In India, however, James's interests turned from Irish cultural politics to Indian aesthetics. As part of the faculty of the Theosophical College at Madanapalle, he immersed himself in the study of Hinduism, metaphysics, and aesthetics, resulting in numerous publications which eventually led him to the international lecture circuit. While undertaking these activities, he would make time to serve as the art advisor to the government of Travancore, a princely state, and to act in his later years as the vice-president of Kalakshetra, an academy of the arts at Adyar. These activities are duly recorded, in elaborate detail, in the duography.

While both Cousinses report their participation in the Irish suffrage movement in highly focused chapters, Margaret's accounts of the Indian women's movement are more diffuse. In these sections, she often mixes political anecdotes with descriptions of vacations and her music recitals, letting us know what concerto she played for which raja. Margaret's accounts of the WIA and the AIWC also contain very little of the organizational detail that characterizes her portrayal of the IWFL. Though Margaret and James wrote separate chapters of their duography, in the process of writing they read one another's work, "discussed it, and made plans for more" (We Two Together 739). The duography progressed, according to Margaret, "systematically and rapidly" (739). That James was more actively involved in politics and the suffrage movement in Ireland than in India helps to explain the narrative discrepancy between Margaret's accounts of the Irish and Indian women's movements. James could supply her with additional details of shared experiences of the Irish suffragette movement, such as his adventures at the IWFL's open-air speeches. But in India, with his energy consumed in scholarly activities, James had little direct participation in the Indian women's movement. The vacations together and joint attendance of concerts, on the other hand, provided shared experiences which help account for the lengthy descriptions of these activities in We Two Together. Commenting on the duography's references to receptions in their honor, Margaret remarks: "We could no more leave out occasional references to cordial receptions and garlands than Isadora Duncan could omit horseless carriages and wild applause from 'My Life' " (740).

19   In 1956 the AIWC honored Cousins by naming after her their extensive collection of texts on women in India and abroad; the Margaret Cousins Memorial Library, at 6 Bhagwan Das Road in New Delhi, continues to be an important resource for feminist archival research. For someone like Cousins who conceived of writing as a method of solidarity and feminist mobilization, the constitution of a feminist archive seems an appropriate tribute.

20   Many of the Westerners who most ardently supported the Indian nationalist cause—such as Annie Besant, Margaret Cousins, and Dorothy Jinarajadasa— were theosophists.

21   For a more detailed description of the resolutions, along with the names of which members proposed specific ones, see Aparna Basu's and Bharati Ray's Women's Struggle: A History of the All India Women's Conference, 1927–1990.

22   This rhetoric is analogous to the dominant strain of the American women's movement in the 1840s and 1850s, which was equally bourgeois and nationalist in orientation.

23   Gandhi's excessive reliance on Hindu mythology alienated many Muslims. Tariq

Ali, for example, says of Gandhi that "his entire political style was that of a Hindu leader. His speeches were full of mystical symbolism deriving from the past of Hinduism and designed to convince his followers that only a social-pacifist solution was possible in India" (20–21). Though the Congress Party was theoretically a secular organization, in practice it based its arguments on Hindu symbolism and mythology. Congress leaders often incorporated Hindu anthems and the worship of Hindu gods into political events (Ali 20). Not surprisingly, this imagery was distasteful to many Muslim nationalists, causing them to withdraw from the movement (Ali 20). Gandhi seemed unconscious of the political implications of his use of Hindu symbolism, as his abhorrence of communalist violence demonstrates. But by 1947 relations between Hindus and Muslims had deteriorated to such an extent that both sides agreed to partition, to which Gandhi himself had registered his extreme opposition. Over a million people were murdered during the communal riots following partition. For an excellent analysis of the events leading up to partition see the first chapter of Tariq Ali's *Can Pakistan Survive? The Death of a State.*

Chapter Three

1   I want to stress that the simile of terrorism-as-crime also occurs in India, but in other contexts. For example, most Indians consider the violence that was perpetrated by Sikh separatists in the name of Khalistan as a form of terrorism which demanded "law-and-order" solutions.

2   Those executed for their part in the Rising were Eamonn Ceannt, Tom Clarke, Cornelius Colbert, James Connolly, Edward Daly, Michael O'Hanrahan, Seán Heuston, Thomas Kent, John MacBride, Seán Mac Diarmada, Thomas MacDonagh, Michael Mallin, Padraic Pearse, William Pearse, and Joseph Plunkett. Countess Markievicz's death sentence was commuted to penal servitude for life on the basis of her gender.

    Sinéad O'Connor's haunting ballad "The Foggy Dew," on the Chieftains' CD "The Long Black Veil" (1995), pays tribute to these executed Republican leaders.

3   Lalor was the great mid-nineteenth-century land reformer who placed the fight against forcible evictions at the center of the Irish national liberation movement. His inclusion among the other twentieth-century Irish nationalists signals an incipient awareness among the Bengali terrorists that the struggle for national liberation would also have to confront the class issue, as the later conversions to communism among their ranks indicate.

    Specific works that the terrorists read included Dan Breen's *My Fight for Irish Freedom* and Pieras Béaslaí's *Michael Collins and the Making of Modern Ireland.*

4   This ordinance allowed the government of Bengal to arrest and detain suspected "terrorists" without trial. It also permitted the government, according to David Laushey, "to try cases involving terrorists before a tribunal without jury and without right of appeal." For more information see Laushey's *Bengal Terrorism and the Marxist Left.*

5   In her chapter "Taking Tarzan Seriously," Marianna Torgovnick charts the ways in which Tarzan solidifies his identity by subjugating African natives and white women in the series of twenty-four Tarzan novels by Edgar Rice Burroughs. Torgovnick argues that the early novels "defamiliarize axiomatic Western norms and raise the possibility of their radical restructuring" by showing how values—such as standards of beauty—are culturally determined. For example, in the first novel of the series, *Tarzan of the Apes*, Tarzan finds his reflection in a pond ugly since he has been conditioned to accept the apes' aesthetics of appearance. "But such radical, relativistic moments are counterbalanced and finally overcome by others," Torgovnick writes, "in which [Tarzan's] self is increasingly defined, in ways that yield security and satisfaction, by comparisons with Others" (*Gone Primitive* 48).

The first novel of the series was published in 1912, while the earliest Tarzan movie appeared in 1917. Approximately fifty Tarzan films have been produced since then. The early novels were appropriately serialized in American men's and boys' magazines (Torgovnick 70). But the novels, comics, and films had an international audience which included Africans, Indians, and Middle Easterners (Torgovnick 263).

6   Though Ghose himself was probably a kayastha, a member of the scribe caste, he clearly identified with the martial aspects of *ksatriyahood*. In the nineteenth century, some *kayasthas* claimed *ksatriya* status (Gordon 327).

7   Mahasweta Devi's short story "Draupadi" rewrites the relationship between *sharam*, nudity, and political protest. In it Draupadi confronts Senanayak with her bleeding, brutalized, naked body. This confrontation, according to Gayatri Spivak, challenges "the man to (en)counter her as unrecorded or misrecorded objective historical monument" (*In Other Worlds* 184). But, as Ramón Saldívar has pointed out to me in conversations, we can very well ask: What happens to Draupadi in the next frame after the story ends? Will Senanayak release her because he now recognizes her as a "powerful 'subject,' " or will he more probably have her killed in the manner of other tribal rebels?

The film *Mirch Masala* offers a better example of effective gendered resistance in its representation of female pickle factory workers who use chili powder as a weapon against a feudal landlord intent on sexually exploiting one of them. This practice was actually used by peasant women against their feudal landlords in the Telangana struggle, as some of the narratives attest in the Stree Shakti Sanghatana's *"We Were Making History": Women and the Telanagana Uprising*.

8   I do not want to dismiss as irrelevant the hundred years or so between the high incidence of *satis* in Bengal during 1815–28 and Das's assassination attempt in 1932. I do not claim that attitudes towards *sati* did not change in this period, because they did. The incidence of *sati* decreased significantly. I do want to suggest, though, that a hundred-year period can be relatively short from an ideological perspective, given that it may cover just several generations of a family, a major transmitter of tradition and culture.

9   The reference to the "ten-headed goddess" in this quotation is probably an error and meant to read "ten-handed goddess."

10   I am grateful to Richard Lariviere for bringing this detail to my attention.

11   For example, during the Anglo-Irish War of 1919–20 Sinn Fein set up courts to administer justice, while the Irish Republican Army engaged in guerrilla tactics.

12   For more information on women's participation in the Palestinian movement, see Philippa Strum's *The Women Are Marching: The Second Sex and the Palestinian Revolution*, Joost R. Hiltermann's *Behind the Intifada*, and Orayb Arej Najjar's *Portraits of Palestinian Women*. The following documentaries also include valuable information: Michal Aviad's *The Women Next Door*, Elizabeth Fernea's *Witness for Peace*, and Erica Marcus's *My Home, My Prison*.

   For information on women's participation in CO-MADRES and the Farabundo Marti Front for National Liberation, see respectively *Hear My Testimony*, by Maria Teresa Tula and Stephen Lynn, and *A Dream Compels Us*, by the New Americas Press.

   In addition, Barbara Harlow's *Barred: Women, Writing, and Political Detention* includes an excellent detailed discussion of women's participation in both the FMLN and PLO among other popular struggles and national liberation movements.

13   For an insightful analysis of how Indira Gandhi functioned as polysemic sign in Indian political discourse, see Gita Rajan's "Subversive-Subaltern Identity: Indira Gandhi as the Speaking Subject."

14   Histories of the nationalist period typically marginalize the participation of women or focus on the participation of a few elite women—such as Sarojini Naidu—from prominent nationalist families. For example, Stanley Wolpert's *A New History of India* mentions only Sarojini Naidu and Kasturbai Gandhi in several sentences in two chapters devoted to the nationalist movement. The editors of *An Advanced History of India* limit their discussion of women's participation to the detail that some women accompanied Gandhi on his famous salt march to Dandi in 1930 (974). (The inclusion of this particular detail seems odd, given that Gandhi had originally prohibited women from marching with him, exhorting them instead to picket toddy shops. In fact, Margaret Cousins took him to task for this decision in the pages of *Stri Dharma*.) As Gayatri Spivak argues in "Subaltern Studies: Deconstructing Historiography," even the Subaltern Studies Group, which is sensitive to the marginalization of subaltern classes, has been remiss in acknowledging women's contributions to Indian independence (*In Other Worlds* 197–221). Tanika Sarkar's *Bengal 1928–1934: The Politics of Protest* is a notable exception to this general tendency. But though her comments are helpful, they are generally drawn from readings of novels written by males who were not part of the terrorist movement, like Rabindranath Tagore. Tagore's novels *Ghare Baire* and *Char Adhyay*, as Sarkar notes, trivialize political women by placing them in conventional bourgeois love narratives; the women do not become politicized out of conviction, but fall victim to charismatic men. Once in the political arena,

the women become, in the words of Tagore's character Atin, "unbalanced, un-natural" (quoted by Sarkar 153).

Texts devoted specifically to recovering the history of Indian terrorist move-ments fleetingly mention, but do not elaborate on, the contributions of women. Apart from their inattention to gender, some of this work is quite fine, par-ticularly Leonard Gordon's *Bengal: The Nationalist Movement, 1897–1940* and D. M. Laushey's *Bengal Terrorism and the Marxist Left*. Unfortunately, Gordon and Laushey restrict their focus to organizations active before 1919. While both Gordon and Laushey have extended discussions of the structure and composition of terrorist groups operative before 1919, they give little of the organizational details of groups after 1928, the period in which the Chittagong terrorists had shifted their strategies from assassinations to larger-scale offensives. (There seems to be a significant amount of literature on the Bengali terrorist revolutionaries written by them. Since they are in Bengali and not available in English translation, I have not been able to draw on them. Readers fluent in Bengali might want to examine Ananta Singh's *Chattagram Yuba Birodh, Keu Bale Biplabi, Keu Bale Dakata,* and *Agnigarva Chattagram;* Sachindranath Guha's *Chattagram Biplaber Banhisikha;* and Preeti Waddedar's *Chattogram Biplaber Bahnisikha.*)

The majority of the historical writings on Indian women that I surveyed fell into a genre characterized by the Stree Shakti Sanghatana in *We Were Making History* as "compensatory history" (19). These histories "locate" "the great women" who have been "left out of male accounts" and place them "alongside the great men of history" and, thus, measure women's participation in social movements by the actions of a relatively small number of elite women (19). In this sense, compensatory history of the nationalist period is the female version of bourgeois nationalist elitist historiography. Kumari Jayawardena's *Feminism and Nationalism in the Third World,* Manmohan Kaur's *Role of Women in the Freedom Movement (1857–1947),* and Jana Matson Everett's *Women and Social Change in India* share this view. Though the Stree Shakti Sanghatana acknowledge "the consci-entizing force of such efforts," they argue that "the critique provided by compen-satory history is obviously not radical enough" (20).

Both Vijay Agnew and Geraldine Forbes have written in some detail on women terrorists. Forbes's article "Goddesses or Rebels? The Women Revolutionaries of Bengal" places the women terrorists within the larger context of the Gandhian nationalist movement, insisting that Gandhi helped provide the "groundwork" "for the entry of women into" terrorist organizations, by making political par-ticipation for women socially acceptable (4). While Forbes carefully delineates the literary and ideological influences that shaped these young women, she does so within the framework of the natal family. The family becomes the primary unit of collectivity for Forbes. As a result, her analysis implicitly devalues the organi-zation's role in motivating and theorizing the activities of terrorist women. Vijay Agnew devotes a chapter of her book, *Elite Women in Indian Politics,* to female terrorists and other women—such as Aruna Asaf Ali and Sucheta Kripalani—who made up the left wing of the Congress Party. But like Forbes, Agnew downplays the influence of terrorist organizations over female members, focusing instead on the women's religious and cultural backgrounds. Both Agnew's and Forbes's work can be considered compensatory history, since their articles profile well-known elite women without examining the material practices, in terms of gender, of the organizations to which the women belonged.

15   Radha Kumar offers a different interpretation of Stevens's assassination in her fine study *The History of Doing: An Illustrated Account of Movements for Women's Rights and Feminism in India, 1800–1990*. According to Kumar, Ghosh and Choudhary decided to kill Stevens for sexually harassing Indian women. She cites Ela Sen, who says of the assassination,

> In the hilltracts no Bengali girl of good family was free from the attention of magistrates, who exploited their position of authority. Therefore two young girls sought to end the degradation by making an example of a certain magistrate. To them it appeared that brutality must be paid back in its own coin, and boldly they walked up to him in his office and shot him dead. They knew they would be immediately arrested but preserved a calm and courageous attitude then, as later when under trial. Their courage did not desert them even when they were transported for life. The whole world was shocked by this "revolting" incident, by what was called the "shameless" conduct of these girls, but none knew what was behind. Even when a member said of another at the Assembly: "Let him go and ask the brave girls of Bengal why they have committed these deeds," it was slurred over and no proper investigations were made. (quoted in Kumar 86–87)

Yet I found no other account that corroborated the charge of sexual harassment. On the contrary, local informants emphasize both Stevens's compassion toward Indians and his fair-mindedness more generally. Kumar's version of the assassination also differs from mine insofar as she maintains that Stevens was the magistrate of Tipper and that Ghosh and Choudhury acted on their own outside of an organized political framework.

Chapter Four

1   For Aijaz Ahmad, however, the period of "high decolonization" roughly corresponds to the years between 1945 and1975, which he further subdivides into two phases (39). Ahmad notes:

> A very large number of sovereign states emerged in Asia and Africa during the first twenty years after the Second World War, mainly under the hegemony of the respective national bourgeoisies and subordinated to regimes of advanced capital. The next decade, 1965–75, was dominated by the wars of national liberation which had a distinctly socialistic trajectory, even though the level of prior economic development and the scale of imperialist devastations preempted the possibility that socialist construction would have a reasonable chance. (30)

Ahmad's *In Theory: Classes, Nations, Literatures* provides one of the most convincing and cogent accounts of the institutionalization of literary studies in the last several decades and their vexed relationship to left politics in the American academy.

2   Following British antiracist activists, I use the term "black" in the British sense as a political signifier for people of Afro-Caribbean and Asian background. Such usage builds alliances between disparate communities by foregrounding their common experiences under British colonialism in the past and repressive policing practices in the present. The Organisation of Women of Asian and African Descent, for example, says of the sign "black": "When we use the term 'Black,' we use it as a political term. It doesn't describe skin colour, it defines our situation here in Britain. We're here as a result of British imperialism, and our continued oppression in Britain is the result of British racism" (quoted in Bryan, Dadzie, and Scafe 24). Elsewhere in the text, I will distinguish South Asian immigrants from Afro-Caribbean ones since racialized discourses have constructed each of these communities differently.

3   Comprising an area of 2.3 square miles, Gibraltar currently houses some 1,800 British troops.

4   The "hills" in Kipling's title furnish the setting for most of the stories in the collection, which offers vignettes of British life in the hill stations. Situated mainly in the Himalayan foothills at altitudes of three to seven thousand feet, hill stations provided an escape from the heat of the plains, enabling the British to "survive" the hot season (Dehejia and Pal 96). "The men on the plains would pack up their wives and children," Mary Ann Lind writes, "and send them to the hills in what eventually became an elaborate annual migration" (11). Hill stations literally transformed the Indian landscape into an English one. With Tudor-style buildings, small Gothic churches, tennis courts, cricket fields, clubs, and race courses, these towns became small English enclaves. Some of the better known hill stations include Mussoorie, Dalhousie, Nainital, and Darjeeling. The most famous one, however, was Simla, the summer capital of the viceroy from 1827, and the partial setting for Wressley's tale. Lind reports that "it took 10,000 men from the surrounding hill villages to carry the provisions for this hot weather haven. Huge trunks packed with gowns, sweets, and books, were all borne on the backs of native men. Before the railroad was built to Simla, the women were carried on palanquins up the steep and tortuous paths" (11). Though Kipling was supportive of British imperialism, considering it, in Edward Said's assessment, "India's best destiny to be ruled by England," he was often critical of British individuals in his fiction (Introduction to *Kim* 23). In *Plain Tales from the Hills*, Kipling developed several stock characters—particularly that of the memsahib— which would come to haunt "Anglo-India."

5   Miss Venner is an example of a "memsahib," which can be loosely translated as "Mrs. Master" or "Lady Sahib" (Lind 1). Originally equated with respect, the term later referred to any European woman in India. Kipling is credited with giving it negative connotations through his series of portraits of Englishwomen

in *Plain Tales from the Hills*. Mrs. Hawksbee, a recurring character in the stories, popularly epitomizes the memsahib as a scheming, manipulative, condescending woman who frittered her summers away in the idle social environment of the hill station. The memsahib also bears the brunt of the blame for the increased separation between Indians and the British after the opening of the Suez Canal in 1869.

Kipling's rendition of the memsahib troubles some of Charles Allen's interviewees. Challenging it, Frances Smyth says:

> British women in India were like British women anywhere else, they were a lot of individuals. But there were certain attitudes which you took up, perhaps, from all the others. Such as, you don't mingle with Indians too much; you remember that you're British; and in the way you treat your servants. The older women would get together with you and say, "You know, you won't do your husband any good, my dear, by going and doing those sort of things," in a disapproving way. And so, if you were a good little wife, you probably thought, "Well, I'd better not." (177)

The recuperation of the Raj has given rise to a subgenre which is encouraging a more charitable view of the memsahib. Chief among these are Pat Barr's studies *The Memsahibs: In Praise of the Women of Victorian India* and *The Dust in the Balance: British Women in India, 1905–1945*, Mary Ann Lind's *The Compassionate Memsahibs: Welfare Activities of British Women in India, 1900–1947*, and Margaret MacMillan's *Women of the Raj*.

6   Kipling's title for his first collection of short stories elicited the following comments from the *Saturday Review*:

> Could there be a much less attractive title than *Plain Tales from the Hills*? Residents in British India and subscribers to the *Civil and Military Gazette* may know what it means, and hasten to get hold of the book accordingly; but to the untraveled inhabitants of London and the United Kingdom generally it would seem almost as hopeful to undertake the perusal of a volume entitled *Straight Talk from Beulah*. (quoted in B. J. Moore-Gilbert 9)

I have not been able to establish whether "Wressley of the Foreign Office" was first published in the *Civil and Military Gazette* or later added to the collection.

7   The word "Anglo-Indian" originally applied to the British in India. In 1900, however, it was officially adopted to describe people of mixed Indian and British ancestry. It continued to be used in both contexts for the next forty years. I use it in quotations to refer to the British in India and without quotations to refer to people of mixed ancestry.

8   I do not want to suggest that the immigrant subgroup is a monolith. Here, Stuart Hall's work on audience responses to mass culture seems applicable. Hall argues that audiences have three potential responses to mass culture: dominant, negotiated, and oppositional. The dominant reading takes the text at face value; the negotiated response accepts the overall system of the text, but may challenge

particular claims; and the oppositional response rejects the capitalist system in the interests of the subordinated class. An ideal audience, from Allen's perspective, would have a dominant response to *Plain Tales from the Raj*. The actual responses of audiences probably vary in the ways that Hall has suggested. See Hall's "Encoding and Decoding in the Television Discourse."

9   In *A Various Universe: A Study of the Journals and Memoirs of British Men and Women in the Indian Subcontinent, 1765–1856*, Ketaki Kushari Dyson describes the changing applications of the linguistic terms "native" and "Indian." Dyson writes:

> One interesting phenomenon is the gradual evolution of the word native from its 'native' meaning to its more unpleasant innuendoes. In the early part of the period (of British rule) the word is neutral and descriptive, but towards the end it can be closely associated with the idea of inferiority, e.g. in the phrase 'an interesting picture of native, savage, and half-civilised life'. At first both *native* and *Indian* are used about Indian things and people, but gradually *Indian* comes to be appropriated to the British in India, while in Miss Eden's comment that the Gurkhas looked 'quite unlike natives' *native* is synonymous with *Indian*. So we get the strange linguistic situation where an Indian means a sahib living in India and the customs of these sahibs are called Indian customs, while the Indians are almost always called natives. 'A gentleman' means a European gentleman, an upper class Indian being called 'a native gentleman' or 'a native of rank'. Similarly, unless qualified, 'a lady' refers to a European lady. (116)

10   This construction of a "real India" is echoed in E. M. Forster's *A Passage to India*. In the early part of the novel, Adela Quested repeatedly announces "that she was desirous of seeing the real India" (26). Adela, however, identifies the "real India" in specific class terms. For her it is constituted by middle- to upper-class Indians, the native equivalents of her own class background, with whom she naively believes she can socialize. Thus, she dismisses the Indians she sees in the streets as inauthentic. She tells Mr. Turton: "I'm tired of seeing picturesque figures pass before me as a frieze. . . . It was a wonderful when we landed, but that superficial glamour soon goes" (27).

11   Both Indian and Irish nationalists referred to independence as "Home Rule."

12   K. M. Panikkar defines the first stage as Gandhi's alliance with the Khalifat leaders, when Congress acquired a mass following between 1920 and 1924. The second stage started with the Dandi march and the salt satyagraha from 1929 to 1932 (205).

13   Lathis are long bamboo canes typically wielded by police forces.

14   For a detailed analysis of Gandhi's and Nehru's theories see Partha Chatterjee's *Nationalist Thought and the Colonial World: A Derivative Discourse?* For an analysis of Gandhi's appropriation of indigenous concepts of gender see Ashis Nandy's *The Intimate Enemy: Loss and Recovery of Self under Colonialism*. For an analysis of Gandhi's mobilization of women in the national movement, see Kumari Jayawardena's *Feminism and Nationalism in the Third World*. For a general summary of

how Gandhi functioned as a polysemous signifier for different groups, see Sumit Sarkar's *"Popular" Movements and "Middle Class" Leadership in Late Colonial India: Perspectives and Problems of a "History from Below.*" For specific case studies of Gandhi as signifier, see Gyan Pandey's "Peasant Revolt and Indian Nationalism: The Peasant Movement in Awadh, 1919–1922" and Shahid Amin's "Gandhi as Mahatma: Gorakhpur District, Eastern UP, 1921–2" in *Selected Subaltern Studies*, ed. Ranajit Guha and Gayatri Chakravorty Spivak.

15   In *A Passage to India*, Aziz's incarceration on charges of assaulting Adela Quested coincides with preparations for Mohurram. The drumbeats of the festival are enough to inspire fear in the British characters, who band together to withstand a potential native attack. Forster alludes to Mohurram riots at several places in the novel. The suggestion that the natives are consumed with communal frenzy, however, is undercut by Forster's representation of the growing politicization of the masses who rally to Aziz's defense. Support for Aziz in the novel is articulated across communal lines and takes on a nationalistic character: Muslim women fast and (Hindu) sweepers go on strike. It is as if Forster resorted to the law-and-order narrative of communal riots because he was unable to imagine a nationalism united across communal differences.

Some of the most perceptive criticism of the novel in recent years attends to the rhetorical operations of gender. Jenny Sharpe's "The Unspeakable Limits of Rape: Colonial Violence and Counter-Insurgency" (in *Allegories of Empire: The Figure of Woman in the Colonial Text*, and widely anthologized) opened up this line of inquiry and remains one of the best readings of the novel. Teresa Hubel's "Liberal Imperialism as a Passage to India," in her meticulously researched *Whose India? The Independence Struggle in British and Indian Fiction and History*, argues that the novel should be read as a meditation on male friendship across the colonial divide. In "E. M. Forster's Queer Nation: Taking the Closet to the Colony in *A Passage to India*," Elaine Freedgood brilliantly engages the homoerotic elements of the novel by showing how the "epistemology of the closet" colludes with the "epistemology of the colony." Freedgood's reading relies, in part, on uncovering the etymologies of specific words in the novel. For example, she remarks on Forster's use of "queer," a term which was used for "homosexual" in the 1920s, to describe the relationship between Aziz and Fielding. Her reading of the novel can be further legitimized by examining the etymologies of other words that Forster uses in the pivotal scenes of the novel. The use of "climax" (which was used for "orgasm" in 1918), "servitor" (a synonym for "intercourse" as early as the sixteenth century), and "intercourse" (which was associated with sexuality by Malthus in the late eighteenth century) in the cave scene and in the colliding boat scene sexualizes the representation of Aziz's and Fielding's relationship and substantiates Freedgood's argument.

16   In *A Critique of Colonial India*, Sumit Sarkar describes how the British government promoted the Muslim League over Congress in the closing years of the Second World War:

League ministries in Assam (August 1942) and NWFP (May 1943) became possible only because most Congress MLAs were in jail. The pro-Congress Muslim premier of Sind was dismissed by the Governor (October 1942) and European MLAs in Bengal propped up the Nazimuddin Ministry from March 1943. (120–21)

17   While Allen represents Indian nationalism in the most superficial terms, his treatment of the structure of the colonial state is not much better. Of a total of 219 pages, one chapter, "The Day's Work," takes up nine and a half. The poverty of information about the workings of Empire annoyed even Paul Scott, the author of *The Raj Quartet*. Scott stated his "exasperation" with the book, commenting in a review of *Plain Tales from the Raj* that appeared in the *London Times*,

> We want to know about the hour-by-hour *bandobast* in the Political Officer's *daftar*. How did he convey his confidential signals to the Viceroy? Who cyphered them? We want to know what the PWD officer did between 9 am and 5 pm; get hold of the exactness of the hourly life of a junior magistrate. We want to know about the reality of the land records, about the cost of a canal or irrigation system, who paid for it and whether it worked. What did a forestry officer *do*? To what extent did the Medical Missionaries fill a gap left by the *raj*? How was a municipality funded? What was the cost of primary education, and who bore it? (14)

Though Scott's *The Raj Quartet* would later be adapted for television by Granada Television in 1984, becoming one of several mass cultural artifacts in Britain and the United States that sentimentally evoke the Raj, Scott's novels criticize the racism and class pretensions of "Anglo-Indian" society. The four volumes of *The Raj Quartet* were published between 1966 and 1975 and were much acclaimed by reviews in major British and American opinion-shaping publications: the *London Times*, *New Yorker*, *Saturday Review*, *Daily Telegraph*, *Christian Science Monitor*, and *New York Times*.

Scott's work is what Raymond Williams terms a "residual" cultural artifact (*Marxism and Literature* 123). While it appears to be counterhegemonic in its presentation of racist officials, the work still draws its terms from the dominant culture. Daphne Manners's rape by a gang of Indian peasants forms the basis for the narrative, relying on the racist representation of native men as rapists of white women. Moreover, as Salman Rushdie points out in his essay "Outside the Whale," Scott exploits other reactionary clichés as well: Merrick, the absolute villain in the volume and the only major character with grammar school origins, turns out to be a sadistic, closeted homosexual.

18   There is some evidence—though not conclusive—that G. M. Dyer may be the son of General R. E. H. Dyer, who carried out the Amritsar massacre of 1919, which I discuss in chapter 1. General Dyer had two sons, Ivon and Geoffrey, both of whom joined the army. Quite possibly the latter is the BACSA member G. M. Dyer.

Wilkinson makes a parenthetical comment, "as it is now known," after the Indian Army Association, indicating that this association is probably an "Anglo-Indian" association instead of an Indian (in the contemporary sense) one. The name of the association underscores Dyson's point (in footnote 9) that the "Anglo-Indians" appropriated the term Indian for their own.

19 And though letting animals graze in the cemetery may be disrespectful to the dead, I must point out that when I lived in I. I. T. Kanpur at about the same time, in 1976, a common means of "cutting the grass" was to allow people to graze their animals in the lawn.

20 I am grateful to Abhijit Basu for this observation.

21 Hindus sometimes bury the corpses of small children, but in unmarked graves.

22 BACSA has garnered a good deal of public attention in diverse media such as film, radio, press, and TV. For example, Prem Kapoor taped interviews with BACSA members, "talking about their family connections," for a film about the British in India based on their tombstones; Sue Farrington touched on BACSA in a radio talk on Pakistan for "Women's Hour and the World Service"; and the journal The Lady published Hazel Craig's article "The Survivors of Two Monsoons" (Llewellyn-Jones, Souvenir Chowkidar 68–69).

23 Economic decline, as B. W. E. Alford cautions, is a conceptually slippery category to define given that it is not based solely on absolute standards but must take into account relative measurements. His explanation is worth quoting at length:

> Whilst absolute changes in economic well-being over time have meaning it does not follow that they are always historically meaningful. In terms of quantifiable income per head, virtually every country in the world has become better off over the past century. The rise in income per head in Britain can be traced from a much earlier period. At the same time, it can be observed that countries that were once among the leaders on these terms have been outpaced by others, by so much that whilst their levels of income have risen they have become poor by the standards of the rich. In this sense, economic decline is a relative concept similar to relative deprivation as a measure of poverty. Likewise, it is meaningful because it defines standards in terms of what has actually been attained. Nations like individuals, it may be claimed, judge their comparative economic standing and performance within a time-frame of expectations. The precise length of time depends on the range of and nature of expectations involved. If, for example, a family moved from middle-class to working-class status over a century, it would generally be agreed that the fortunes of the family had declined, even though it might be shown that the comparable working-class income had risen over the period to a level above that received by the middle-class family at its outset. There is an obvious and strong sense in which the same kind of relative judgement applies to nations. (332–33)

24 Economists generally attribute the end of the long boom to the quadrupling of oil prices almost overnight by the Organisation of Petroleum Exporting Countries (OPEC) in 1973.

25 For instance, the growth rate in GDP for the period 1950 to 1973 was a mere 3 per cent in Britain, compared with 5 per cent in France, 6 per cent in Germany, 9.3 per cent in Japan, and 3.7 per cent in the United States (Glynn and Booth 201).

26 While my narrative of British economic decline focuses on domestic effects of state policy, state policy itself is shaped by global structures of capital in alliance with different national, regional, and geopolitical interests.

27 The formal colonization of Ireland has its origins in Henry II's decision to assert control over it in 1171, based on the authority of a papal bull granting him the territory sixteen years previously by Pope Adrian IV, the only Englishman ever to be named a pope.

28 The Statutes of Kilkenny (1366), aimed at suppressing Irish culture, banned the use of the Irish language, native Brehon law, Irish styles of riding and dress, and entertainment by Irish minstrels (Butler-Cullingford).

    Enacted between 1695 and 1705, the Penal Laws sought to restructure society and ensure the "ascendancy" of Protestants by banning Catholics from voting, serving in the army or navy, assuming elected office, attending the university in Dublin, practicing law, or owning land on more than a short lease (Butler-Cullingford).

    The Special Powers Act, in effect from 1922 to 1972, allowed the state to detain and imprison indefinitely those whom it considered a threat to its security, as well as to enter homes without securing warrants, impound property, suspend habeas corpus, and abolish inquests.

    The Prevention of Terrorism Acts of 1974 and 1976 banned the IRA and gave the police broad powers to hold and deport "suspected terrorists."

29 See Robert Schaeffer's excellent study *Warpaths: The Politics of Partition* for an analysis of the rhetoric of contemporary regional conflicts in Kashmir, Palestine and Israel, and Northern Ireland. Schaeffer argues that conflicts perceived to be long standing and intractable actually have their origins in the last several decades, and in the abject failure of Britain's use of partition to subdue the demands for independence made by anticolonial movements in the former Empire. The lines of partition were drawn by British officials with four objectives in mind: "to protect minorities, to reward wartime allies, to avert civil war, and to curry political support in Britain" (100). For the British, partition was a far more expedient solution to the calls for self-determination than complex, long-term constitutional negotiations which would have entailed a continuing British presence in the colonial territories. Unfortunately, the legacy of partition has been the systemic disenfranchisement of minority populations and ongoing territorial disputes among regional powers. Schaeffer believes that the sectarian nature of partition, more than anything else, has given a "permanent and irreconcilable" appearance to ethnic and religious differences (102). He notes that "the failure of partition" has all too often been used to discredit the concept of self-determination itself (254).

30 "Background: British Racism" provides detailed documentation of the failure of

the police to protect Afro-Caribbeans and South Asians from racist attacks (*Race and Class*, vol. xxii).

31 For an analysis of how the state itself becomes a factor in the reproduction of an organic crisis and Britain's movement toward state authoritarianism, see John Solomos et al., "The Organic Crisis of British Capitalism and Race: The Experience of the Seventies," in Centre for Contemporary Cultural Studies, *The Empire Strikes Back: Race and Racism in 70s Britain*.

32 Paul Gilroy quite emphatically states that the invocations of Northern Ireland in discussions of policing in mainland Britain should not be taken as "evidence" that Northern Ireland functions as a "laboratory" for developing contemporary policing techniques, maintaining that such a theory is too "conspiratorial."

33 The Institute for Race Relations distinguishes between two forms of the Sus law. Sus 1 is a section of the 1824 Vagrancy Act that enables the state to accuse and try individuals based on no other evidence than that of acting suspiciously in the eyes of two police officers. Sus 2 derives from the Immigration Act of 1971 and enables the police to arrest anyone whom they suspect of being an illegal immigrant. While Sus 1 targets Afro-Caribbean males, Sus 2 is used against the Asian population (Kushnick 187–206).

BIBLIOGRAPHY

Abrams, M. H., E. Talbot Donaldson, Hallett Smith, Robert M. Adams, Samuel
Holt Monk, Lawrence Lipking, George H. Ford, and David Daiches, eds. *The
Norton Anthology of English Literature* . Vol. 2. 4th ed. New York: W. W. Norton,
1979.

Adhikari, G. *Documents of the History of the Communist Party of India*. Vol. 2, 1923–1925.
New Delhi: People's, 1974.

Agnew, Vijay. *Elite Women in Indian Politics*. New Delhi: Vikas, 1979.

Ahmad, Aijaz. *In Theory: Classes, Nations, Literatures*. London: Verso, 1992.

Alcoff, Linda Martin. "The Problem of Speaking for Others." *Who Can Speak? Authority
and Critical Identity*, ed. Judith Roof and Robyn Wiegman, 97–119. Urbana: University of Illinois Press, 1995.

Alexander, Jacqui M., and Chandra Talpade Mohanty, eds. *Feminist Genealogies, Colonial
Legacies, Democratic Futures*. New York: Routledge, 1997.

Alford, B. W. E. *Britain in the World Economy since 1880*. London: Longman, 1996.

Ali, Tariq. *Can Pakistan Survive? The Death of a State*. London: Penguin, 1983.

Allen, Charles. *Plain Tales from the Raj*. New York: St. Martin's, 1975; Calcutta: Rupa,
1992.

——. *Tales from the Dark Continent*. New York: St. Martin's, 1979.

——. *Tales from the South China Seas: Images of the British in South-east Asia in the Twentieth
Century*, ed. Charles Allen and Michael Mason. London: Andre Deutsch, 1983.

Althusser, Louis. *Lenin and Philosophy*, trans. Ben Brewster. New York: Monthly
Review, 1971.

Amin, Shahid. "Gandhi as Mahatma: Gorakhpur District, Eastern UP, 1921–2."
Selected Subaltern Studies, ed. Ranajit Guha and Gayatri Chakravorty Spivak, 288–
344. New York: Oxford University Press, 1988.

"Amritsar: By an Englishwoman." *Blackwood's Magazine* 1254 (April 1920): 441–46.

Anderson, Benedict. *Imagined Communities: Reflections on the Origin and Spread of
Nationalism*. London: Thetford, 1983.

Appadurai, Arjun, and Carol Breckenridge. "The Passage of India." *Inscriptions* 1 (Dec.
1985): 6–7.

Ardener, Edwin. "The 'Problem' Revisited." *Perceiving Women*, ed. Shirley Ardener.
London: Malaby, 1975.

Arnold, David. *Police Power and Colonial Rule: Madras, 1859–1947*. Delhi: Oxford University Press, 1986.

Arnstein, Walter. *Britain Yesterday and Today: 1830 to the Present*. Lexington, Mass.: D. C. Heath, 1998.

Ashcroft, Bill, Gareth Griffiths, and Helen Tiffin, eds. *The Post-Colonial Studies Reader*. New York: Routledge, 1995.

Baechler, Jean. "Individual, Group, and Democracy." *Democratic Community*: NOMOS XXXV, ed. John Chapman and Ian Shapiro. New York: New York University Press, 1993.

Bakhtin, M. M. *The Dialogic Imagination*, ed. Michael Holquist and trans. Caryl Emerson and Michael Holquist. Austin: University of Texas Press, 1981.

Bala, Usha. *Indian Women Freedom Fighters, 1857–1947*. New Delhi: Manohar, 1986.

Balandier, G. "The Colonial Situation: A Theoretical Approach (1951)." *Social Change: The Colonial Situation*, ed. Immanuel Wallerstein. New York: John Wiley and Sons, 1966.

Ballhatchet, Kenneth. *Race, Sex and Class under the Raj: Imperial Attitudes and Policies and Their Critics, 1793–1905*. New York: St. Martin's, 1980.

Bardon, Jonathan. *Belfast: An Illustrated History*. Dundonald: Blackstaff, 1982.

Barr, Pat. *The Dust in the Balance: British Women in India, 1905–1945*. London: Hamilton, 1989.

———. *The Memsahibs: In Praise of the Women of Victorian India*. London: Century Hutchinson, 1976.

Basu, Amrita and Elizabeth McGrory. *The Challenge of Local Feminisms: Women's Movements in Global Perspectives*. Boulder: Westview, 1995.

Basu, Aparna, and Bharati Ray. *Women's Struggle: A History of the All India Women's Conference, 1927–1990*. New Delhi: Manohar, 1990.

Basu, Bibhuti. Personal interview with author, 17 May 1991.

Béaslaí, Piaras. *Michael Collins and the Making of a New Ireland*. New York: Harper and Brothers, 1926.

Beverley, John. "The Margin at the Center: On Testimonio (Testimonial Narrative)." *Modern Fiction Studies* 35 (spring 1989): 11–28.

Bhabha, Homi. "DissemiNation: Time, Narrative, and the Margins of the Modern Nation." *Nation and Narration*, ed. Homi Bhabha, 291–322. London: Routledge, 1990.

Birkett, Dea. *Spinsters Abroad: Victorian Lady Explorers*. London: Blackwell, 1989.

Black's Law Dictionary. Abridged 6th ed. St Paul: West, 1991.

Bose, Purnima, and Laura E. Lyons. "Dyer Consequences: The Trope of Amritsar, Ireland, and the Lessons of the 'Minimum' Force Debate." *boundary 2* 26, no. 2 (summer 1999): 199–229.

Bourne, Jenny. "Homelands of the Mind: Jewish Feminism and Identity Politics." *Race and Class* 29 (summer 1987): 1–24.

Brantlinger, Patrick. *Rule of Darkness: British Literature and Imperialism, 1830–1914*. Ithaca: Cornell University Press, 1988.

Brasted, H. V. "Irish Nationalism and the British Empire in the Late Nineteenth Century." *Irish Culture and Nationalism, 1750–1950*, ed. Oliver MacDonagh, W.F. Mandle, and Pauric Travers, 83–103. New York: St. Martin's, 1983.

Breen, Dan. *My Fight for Irish Freedom*. Dublin: Anvil, 1981.

Brennan, Timothy. *Salman Rushdie and the Third World: Myths of the Nation*. New York: St. Martin's, 1989.

Bridges, Lee. "Keeping the Lid On: British Urban Social Policy, 1975–81." *Race and Class* 23 (autumn 1981–winter 1982): 171–85.

Bryan, Beverly, Stella Dadzie, and Suzanne Scafe. "Chain Reactions: Black Women Organising." *Race and Class* 27 (summer 1985): 1–28.

Bunyan, Tony. "The Police against the People." *Race and Class* 23 (autumn 1981–winter 1982): 153–70.

Burchfield, R. W., ed. *A Supplement to the Oxford English Dictionary*. Oxford: Clarendon, 1972.

Burne, Owen. "Article on Lord Strathnairn." *Asiatic Quarterly Review*. Jan. 1886.

Butler-Cullingford, Elizabeth. Unpublished chronology of Irish history. 1989.

Canning, Paul. *British Policy towards Ireland: 1921–1941*. Oxford: Clarendon, 1985.

CARF Collective. "Notes and Documents." *Race and Class* 23 (autumn 1981–winter 1982): 223–44.

Centre for Contemporary Cultural Studies. *The Empire Strikes Back: Race and Racism in 70s Britain*. London: Hutchinson, 1982.

Centre for Research and Documentation. *Is Ireland a Third World Country?* Belfast: Beyond the Pale, 1992.

Chakrabarty, Dipesh. "Postcoloniality and the Artifice of History: Who Speaks for 'Indian' Pasts?" *Contemporary Postcolonial Theory: A Reader*, ed. Padmini Mongia, 223–47. New York: St. Martin's, 1996.

Chakravarti, Uma. "Whatever Happened to the Vedic Dasi? Orientalism, Nationalism and a Script for the Past." *Recasting Women in India: Essays in Colonial History*, ed. Kumkum Sangari and Sudesh Vaid, 27–87. New Delhi: Kali for Women, 1989.

Chatterjee, Partha. "The Nationalist Resolution of the Women's Question." *Recasting Women in India: Essays in Colonial History*, ed. Kumkum Sangari and Sudesh Vaid, 233–53.

——. *Nationalist Thought and the Colonial World: A Derivative Discourse?* London: Zed Books, 1986.

Chattopadhayay, Kamaladevi. *Indian Women's Battle for Freedom*. New Delhi: Abhinav, 1983.

Chaturvedi, Mahendra, and Bhola Nath Tiwari, eds. *A Practical Hindi-English Dictionary*. New Delhi: National Publishing, 1982.

Cherniavsky, Eva. *That Pale Mother Rising: Sentimental Discourses and the Imitation of Motherhood in 19th-Century America*. Bloomington: Indiana University Press, 1995.

Choudhuri, Nupur, and Margaret Strobel. *Western Women and Imperialism: Complicity and Resistance*. Bloomington: Indiana University Press, 1992.

Chow, Rey. "Where Have All the Natives Gone?" *Displacements: Cultural Identities in Question*, ed. Angelika Bammer, 125–51. Bloomington: Indiana University Press.

Chrisman, Laura, and Patrick Williams, eds. *Colonial Discourse and Post-Colonial Theory.* New York: Columbia University Press, 1994.

Clifford, James, and George F. Marcus, eds. *Writing Culture: The Poetics and Politics of Ethnography.* Berkeley: University of California Press, 1986.

Clymer, Kenton J. *Quest for Freedom: The United States and Indian Independence.* New York: Columbia University Press, 1995.

Cockburn, Alexander. *Corruptions of Empire: Life Studies and the Reagan Era.* London: Verso, 1987.

Colvin, Ian. *The Life of General Dyer.* London: Blackwood, 1929.

Cook, S. B. *Imperial Affinities: Nineteenth Century Analogies and Exchanges Between India and Ireland.* New Delhi: Sage, 1993.

Cousins, Margaret. *The Awakening of Asian Womanhood.* Madras: Ganesh, 1922.

———. *Indian Womanhood Today.* Allahabad: Kitabistan, 1941.

———. *We Two Together.* With James Cousins. Madras: Ganesh, 1950.

Crooke, William. *Hobson-Jobson: A Glossary of Colloquial Anglo-Indian Words and Phrases.* 4th ed. Delhi: Munshiram Manoharlal, 1984.

Curtis, Liz. *The Cause of Ireland: From the United Irishmen to Partition.* Belfast: Beyond the Pale, 1994.

Dadrian, Vahakn N. "Genocide as a Problem of National and International Law: The World War I Armenian Case and Its Contemporary Legal Ramifications." *Yale Journal of International Law* 14, no. 2 (summer 1989): 79–157.

Dangerfield, George. *Bengal Mutiny: The Story of the Sepoy Rebellion.* London: Hutchinson, 1933.

D'Arcy, Margaretta. *Tell Them Everything.* London: Pluto, 1981.

Datta, Kalikinkar, R. C. Majumdar, and H. C. Raychaudhuri. *An Advanced History of India.* Delhi: Macmillan, 1978.

Datta, V. N. *Jallianwala Bagh.* Ludhiana: Kurukshetra University Press, 1969.

Dehejia, Vidya, and Pratapaditya Pal. *From Merchants to Emperors: British Artists and India, 1757–1930.* Ithaca: Cornell University Press, 1986.

De Valera, Eamon. *India and Ireland.* New York: Friends of Freedom for India, 1920.

Digby, William. *"Prosperous" British India: A Revelation from Official Records.* New Delhi: Sagar, 1969.

Dine, Janet. "Intention: History and Hancock." *Journal of Criminal Law* 51 (1987): 72–81.

Dirlik, Arif. "The Postcolonial Aura: Third World Criticism in the Age of Global Capitalism." *Critical Inquiry* 20 (winter 1994): 328–56.

Donaldson, Laura E. *Decolonizing Feminisms: Race, Gender, and Empire Building.* Chapel Hill: University of North Carolina Press, 1992.

Dumbleton, William. *James Cousins.* Boston: Twayne, 1980.

Dutt, Kalpana. *Chittagong Armoury Raiders Reminiscences.* New Delhi: People's Publishing, 1945.

Dyson, Ketaki Kushari. *A Various Universe: A Study of the Journals and Memoirs of British Men and Women in the Indian Subcontinent, 1765–1856.* Delhi: Oxford University Press, 1978.

Edwardes, Michael. *British India, 1772–1947*. Calcutta: Rupa, 1993.

Evans, Phil, and Eileen Pollock. *Ireland for Beginners*. New York: Writers and Readers, 1994.

Everett, Jana Matson. *Women and Social Change in India*. New Delhi: Heritage, 1979.

Fanon, Frantz. *The Wretched of the Earth*, trans. Constance Farrington. New York: Grove, 1963.

Farrell, Michael. *Arming the Protestants: The Formation of the Ulster Special Constabulary and the Royal Ulster Constabulary, 1920–1927*. London: Pluto, 1983.

Farrelly, Patrick, and James Ridgeway. "The Belfast Connection." *Village Voice*, 8 Feb. 1994, 29.

Fein, Helen. *Imperial Crime and Punishment: The Massacre at Jallianwala Bagh and British Judgement, 1919–1920*. Honolulu: University of Hawaii Press, 1977.

Forbes, Geraldine H. "Caged Tigers: 'First Wave' Feminists in India." *Women's Studies International Forum* 5 (1982): 525–36.

——. "From Purdah to Politics: The Social Feminism of the All-India Women's Organizations." *Separate Worlds: Studies of Purdah in South Asia*, ed. Gail Minault and Hanna Papanek, 219–44. Delhi: Chanakya, 1982.

——. "Goddesses or Rebels? The Women Revolutionaries of Bengal." *Women, Politics, and Literature in Bengal*, ed. Clinton B. Seely, 3–17. East Lansing: Asian Studies Center, Michigan State University, 1981.

——. "The Ideals of Indian Womanhood: Six Bengali Women during the Independence Movement." *Bengal in the Nineteenth and Twentieth Centuries*, ed. John R. McLane, 59–74. East Lansing: Asian Studies Center, Michigan State University, 1975.

——. "The Indian Women's Movement: A Struggle for Women's Rights or National Liberation?" *The Extended Family: Women and Political Participation in India and Pakistan*, ed. Gail Minault, 49–82. Delhi: Chanakya, 1981.

——. "Women's Movements in India: Traditional Symbols and New Roles." *Social Movements in India: Sectarian, Tribal and Women Movements*, ed. M. S. A. Rao, 149–65. New Delhi: Manohar, 1979.

Forster, E. M. *A Passage to India*. New York: Harcourt, 1952.

Foster, Robert. "Making National Cultures in the Global Ecumene." *Annual Review of Anthropology* 20 (1991): 235–60.

Foster, Thomas. *Homelessness at Home: The Transformation of Spatial Metaphors in Modern Women's Writing*. New York: New York University Press, forthcoming.

Foucault, Michel. "Nietzsche, Genealogy, History." *Language, Counter-Memory, Practice: Selected Essays and Interviews*, ed. Donald F. Bouchard and trans. Donald F. Bouchard and Sherry Simon, 139–64. Ithaca: Cornell University Press, 1977.

Freedgood, Elaine. "E. M. Forster's Queer Nation: Taking the Closet to the Colony in *A Passage to India*." *Bodies of Writing, Bodies in Performance*, ed. Thomas Foster, Carol Siegel, and Ellen E. Berry, 123–44. New York: New York University Press, 1996.

Furneaux, Rupert. *Massacre at Amritsar*. London: Allen, 1963.

Gardner, Judith Kegan, ed. *Provoking Agents: Gender and Agency in Theory and Practice*. Urbana: University of Illinois Press, 1995.

Gillis, John R., ed. *Commemorations: The Politics of National Identity*. Princeton: Princeton University Press, 1994.

Gilroy, Paul. "Police and Thieves." *The Empire Strikes Back*, by the Birmingham: Centre for Contemporary Cultural Studies, 143–82.

——. "You Can't Fool the Youths . . . Race and Class Formation in the 1980s." *Race and Class* 23 (autumn 1981–winter 1982): 207–22.

Gilroy, Paul, John Solomos, Bob Findlay, and Simon Jones. "The Organic Crisis of British Capitalism and Race: The Experience of the Seventies." *The Empire Strikes Back*, by the Birmingham: Centre for Contemporary Cultural Studies, 9–46.

Glynn, Sean, and Alan Booth. *Modern Britain: An Economic and Social History*. London: Routledge, 1996.

Gordon, Leonard. *Bengal: The Nationalist Movement, 1876–1940*. New York: Columbia University Press, 1974.

Gramsci, Antonio. *An Antonio Gramsci Reader: Selected Writings, 1916–1935*, ed. David Forgacs. New York: Schocken, 1988.

——. *Selections from the Prison Notebooks*, ed. and trans. Quintin Hoare and Geoffrey Nowell Smith. New York: International, 1971.

Greeley, Andrew. *Irish Gold*. New York: Doherty, 1994.

Grewal, Inderpal. *Home and Harem: Nation, Gender, Empire, and the Cultures of Travel*. Durham: Duke University Press, 1996.

Guha, Ranajit. "Dominance without Hegemony and Its Historiography." *Subaltern Studies VI*, ed. Ranajit Guha. Delhi: Oxford University Press, 1992.

——. "On Some Aspects of the Historiography of Colonial India." *Selected Subaltern Studies*, ed. Ranajit Guha and Gayatri Chakravorty Spivak, 37–43. New York: Oxford University Press, 1988.

——. "The Prose of Counter-Insurgency." *Subaltern Studies II*, ed. Ranajit Guha, 1–42. New Delhi: Oxford University Press, 1992.

Guha, Ranajit, and Gayatri Chakravorty Spivak, eds. *Selected Subaltern Studies*. New York and Oxford: Oxford University Press, 1988.

Hall, Stuart. *Critical Dialogues in Cultural Studies*, ed. David Morley and Kuan-Hsing Chen. London: Routledge, 1996.

——. "Encoding and Decoding in the Television Discourse." Stencilled Occasional Papers, no. 7. Birmingham: Centre for Contemporary Cultural Studies, 1973.

Handler, Richard. *Nationalism and the Politics of Culture in Quebec*. Madison: University of Wisconsin Press, 1988.

Harlow, Barbara. *Barred: Women, Writing, and Political Detention*. Hanover: University Press of New England, 1992.

——. "From the 'Civilizing Mission' to 'Humanitarian Interventionism': Postmodernism, Writing, and Human Rights." *Text and Nation: Cross-Disciplinary Essays on Cultural and National Identities*, ed. Laura García-Moreno and Peter C. Pfeiffer, 31–47. Columbia, S.C.: Camden, 1996.

——. *Resistance Literature*. New York: Methuen, 1987.

The H-Block Hunger Strike. Prod. Sinn Fein Prisoner of War Department, 1991. Video.

Hiltermann, Joost. *Behind the Intifada*. Princeton: Princeton University Press, 1991.

Hooks, Bell. *Yearning: Race, Gender, and Cultural Politics.* Boston: South End, 1990.

Hubel, Teresa. *Whose India? The Independence Struggle in British and Indian Fiction and History.* Durham: Duke University Press, 1996.

Inden, Ronald B., and Ralph Nicholas. *Kinship in Bengali Culture.* Chicago: University of Chicago Press, 1977.

Isaac, Jeffrey C. *Power and Marxist Theory.* Ithaca: Cornell University Press, 1987.

Islam, Shamsul. *Chronicles of the Raj: A Study of the Literary Reaction to the Imperial Idea towards the End of the Raj.* London: Macmillan, 1979.

JanMohamed, Abdul R. "The Economy of Manichean Allegory: The Function of Racial Difference in Colonialist Literature." *"Race," Writing, and Difference,* ed. Henry Louis Gates Jr., 78–106. Chicago: University of Chicago Press, 1986.

Jayawardena, Kumari. *Feminism and Nationalism in the Third World.* London: Zed Books, 1986.

Jeffery, Patricia, and Amrita Basu, eds. *Appropriating Gender: Women's Activism and Politicized Religion in South Asia.* New York: Routledge, 1998.

Jelinek, Estelle C., ed. "Introduction: Women's Autobiography and the Male Tradition." *Women's Autobiography: Essays in Criticism,* 1–20. Bloomington: Indiana University Press, 1980.

Jennings, Rachel. "The Fight against Union Carbide: Reclaiming the Strategy of Transnational Solidarity." Unpublished essay.

——. "The Union and Its Limits: Histories, Regions, and Empires in the Nineteenth Century British Novel." Diss., University of Texas, 1995.

Jhabvala, Ruth Prawer. *Heat and Dust.* London: Murray, 1975.

Joshi, Rama, and Joanna Liddle. *Daughters of Independence: Gender, Caste, and Class in India.* London: Zed Books, 1986.

Kandiyoti, Deniz. "Identity and Its Discontents: Women and the Nation." *Colonial Discourse and Post-Colonial Theory: A Reader,* ed. Laura Chrisman and Patrick Williams, 376–91. New York: Columbia University Press, 1994.

Kaur, Manmohan. *Role of Women in the Freedom Movement (1857–1947).* Delhi: Sterling, 1968.

Kaye, M. M. *The Far Pavilions.* New York: St. Martin's, 1978.

Kipling, Rudyard. *Plain Tales From the Hills.* Garden City, N.Y.: Doubleday, 1899.

——. *"Soldiers Three" and "In Black and White."* London: Penguin, 1993.

Kumar, Radha. *The History of Doing: An Illustrated Account of Movements for Women's Rights and Feminism in India, 1800–1990.* New Delhi: Kali for Women, 1993.

Kushnick, Louis. "Parameters of British and North American Racism." *Race and Class* 23 (autumn 1981–winter 1982): 187–206.

Laushey, D. M. *Bengal Terrorism and the Marxist Left.* Calcutta: Firma K.L. Mukhopadhyay, 1975.

Levenson, Leah, and Jerry H. Natterstad. *Hanna Sheehy-Skeffington: Irish Feminist.* Syracuse: Syracuse University Press, 1986.

Lind, Mary Ann. *The Compassionate Memsahibs: Welfare Activities of British Women in India, 1900–1947.* New York: Greenwood, 1988.

Llewellyn-Jones, Rosie, ed. *Souvenir Chowkidar.* London: Chameleon, 1986.

——. *Chowkidar* 5, no. 4 (autumn 1989).

Lloyd, David. "Discussion outside History: Irish New Histories and the 'Subalternity Effect.' " *Subaltern Studies IX*, ed. Shahid Amin and Dipesh Chakrabarty. Delhi: Oxford University Press, 1996.

——. "Nationalisms against the State: Towards a Critique of the Anti-Nationalist Prejudice." *Gender and Colonialism*, ed. Timothy P. Foley, Lionel Pilkington, Sean Ryder, and Elizabeth Tilley, 256–81. Galway: Galway University Press, 1995.

Loomba, Ania. *Colonialism/Postcolonialism*. London: Routledge, 1998.

Lyons, Laura E. " 'At the End of the Day': An Interview with Mairead Keane, National Head of Sinn Fein Women's Department." *boundary 2* 19, no. 2 (1992): 260–86.

——. "Feminist Articulations of the Nation: The 'Dirty' Women of Armagh and the Discourse of Mother Ireland." *Genders* 24 (summer 1996): 110–49.

——. "Writing in Trouble: Protest and the Cultural Politics of Irish Nationalism." Diss., University of Texas, 1993.

McClintock, Anne. "The Angel of Progress: Pitfalls of the Term 'Post-Colonialism.' " *Colonial Discourse and Post-Colonial Theory: A Reader*, ed. Patrick Williams and Laura Chrisman, 291–304. New York: Columbia University Press, 1994.

MacCurtain, Margaret. "Women, the Vote and Revolution." *Women in Irish Society: The Historical Dimension*, ed. Doncha O Corram and Margaret MacCurtain, 48–51. Dublin: Women's Press, 1978.

McKillen, Beth. "Irish Feminism and Nationalist Separatism, 1914–1923." *Eire Ireland* 17 (1982): 52–67.

McKinney, Robert B., Mark A. Rassas, and Geoffrey S. Corn. "Military and Civil Defense." *American Jurisprudence*. Vol. 53A. 2d ed. 1996.

MacMillan, Margaret. *Women of the Raj*. New York: Thames, 1988.

MacPherson, Crawford Brough. *The Political Theory of Possessive Individualism: Hobbes to Locke*. Oxford: Clarendon, 1962.

Mahajan, V. D. *The Nationalist Movement in India*. New Delhi: Sterling, 1975.

Majumdar, Niranjan, ed. *The Statesman: An Anthology*. Calcutta: Statesman, 1975.

Majumdar, Ramesh Chandra. *History of Modern Bengal, 1905–1947*. Calcutta: Bharadwaj, 1981.

——. *The Revolutionary Movement in Bengal and the Role of Surya Sen*. Calcutta: Calcutta University Press, 1978.

Malone, Linda A. "The Kahan Report, Ariel Sharon and the Sabra-Shatilla Massacres in Lebanon: Responsibility under International Law for Massacres of Civilian Populations." *Utah Law Review* 1985, 2:373–433.

Mani, Lata. "Contentious Traditions: The Debate on Sati in Colonial India." *Recasting Women in India: Essays in Colonial History*, ed. Kumkum Sangari and Sudesh Vaid, 88–126. New Delhi: Kali for Women, 1989.

Marcus, George E. "Ethnography in/of the World System: The Emergence of Multi-Sited Ethnography." *Annual Review of Anthropology* 24 (1995): 95–117.

——. "The Uses of Complicity in the Changing Mise-En-Scène of Anthropological Fieldwork." *Representations* 59 (summer 1997): 85–108.

Marmor, Andrei. *Interpretation and Legal Theory*. Oxford: Clarendon, 1992.

Marshall, Gordon, ed. *A Dictionary of Sociology*. Oxford: Oxford University Press, 1998.

Martin, Biddy, and Chandra Talpade Mohanty. "Feminist Politics: What's Home Got to Do With It?" *Feminist Studies, Critical Studies*, ed. Teresa de Lauretis. Bloomington: Indiana University Press, 1986.

Martin, Wallace. *Recent Theories of Narrative*. Ithaca: Cornell University Press, 1986.

Masani, Zareer. *Indian Tales of the Raj*. Berkeley: University of California Press, 1987.

Matas, David. "Prosecuting Crimes against Humanity: The Lessons of World War I." *Fordham International Law Journal* 13, no.1 (1989): 86–104.

Mayo, Katherine. *Mother India*. New York: Harcourt, 1927.

Mehta, Ved. *A Family Affair: India under Three Prime Ministers*. New Delhi: Sangam, 1982.

Mies, Maria. *Indian Women and Patriarchy: Conflicts and Dilemmas of Students and Working Women*. New Delhi: Concept, 1980.

Minault, Gail. "The Extended Family as Metaphor and the Expansion of Women's Realm." *The Extended Family: Women and Political Participation in India and Pakistan*, ed. Gail Minault, 3–18. Delhi: Chanakya, 1981.

——. "Purdah Politics: The Role of Muslim Women in Indian Nationalism, 1911–1924." *Separate Worlds: Studies of Purdah in South Asia*, ed. Gail Minault and Hanna Papanek, 245–61. Delhi: Chanakya, 1982.

Miyoshi, Masao. "A Borderless World? From Colonialism to Transnationalism and the Decline of the Nation-State." *Critical Inquiry* 19 (summer 1993): 721–51.

Mockaitis, Thomas. *British Counterinsurgency, 1919–1960*. New York: St. Martin's, 1990.

Modleski, Tania, ed. *Studies in Entertainment: Critical Approaches to Mass Culture*. Bloomington: Indiana University Press, 1986.

Mohanty, Chandra. *Third World Women and the Politics of Feminism*. Bloomington: Indiana University Press, 1991.

Moore-Gilbert, B. J. *Kipling and "Orientalism."* London: Helm, 1986.

Mother Ireland. Prod. Derry Film and Video Workship. 1988. Video.

Moya, Paula. "Postmodernism, 'Realism,' and the Politics of Identity: Cherríe Moraga and Chicana Feminism." *Feminist Genealogies, Colonial Legacies, Democratic Futures*, ed. Jacqui M. Alexander and Chandra Talpade Mohanty, 125–150. New York: Routledge, 1997.

Murphy, Cliona. "The Tune of the Stars and Stripes: The American Influence on the Irish Suffrage Movement." *Women Surviving*, ed. Maria Luddy and Cliona Murphy, 180–205. Dublin: Poolbeg, 1990.

——. *The Women's Suffrage Movement and Irish Society in the Early Twentieth Century*. Philadelphia: Temple University Press, 1989.

Naidoo, Indres. *Robben Island: Ten Years as a Political Prisoner in South Africa's Most Notorious Penitentiary*. New York: Vintage, 1983.

Nair, Supriya. " 'Of Hearts Tied in Sari Fringes': Women and Pariahs in Raja Rao's *Kanthapura*." Paper delivered at the annual convention of the Modern Language Association, Chicago, 28 Dec. 1990.

Najjar, Orayb Arej. *Portraits of Palestinian Women*. Salt Lake City: University of Utah Press, 1991.

Nandy, Ashis. *The Intimate Enemy: Loss and Recovery of Self under Colonialism.* New Delhi: Oxford University Press, 1983.

Narayan, R. K. *The Mahabharata.* New Delhi: Visions, 1978.

Narayan, Uma. *Dislocating Cultures.* New York: Routledge, 1997.

Nath, Shaileshwar. *Terrorism in India.* New Delhi: National Publishing, 1980.

Nehru, Jawaharlal. *An Autobiography.* London: Bodley Head, 1958.

New Americas Press. *A Dream Compels Us: Voices of Salvadoran Women.* Boston: South End, 1989.

Newsinger, John. "British Security Policy in Northern Ireland." *Race and Class* 37 (July–Sept. 1995): 83–94.

Ngugi, wa Thiong'o. *Detained: A Writer's Prison Diary.* London: Heinemann, 1981.

Norton, Charles Eliot. "Rudyard Kipling: A Biographical Sketch." *Plain Tales from the Hills,* by Rudyard Kipling. Garden City, N.Y.: Doubleday, 1899. xi–xix.

O'Dwyer, Michael. *India as I Knew It: 1885–1925.* London: Constable, 1925.

One Who Knows. *Mrs. Margaret Cousins and Her Work in India.* Madras: Women's Indian Association, 1956.

Owens, Rosemary, and A. D. Sheehy Skeffington. *Votes for Women: Irish Women's Struggle for the Vote.* Dublin: n.p., 1975.

Pandey, Gyan. "Peasant Revolt and Indian Nationalism: The Peasant Movement in Awadh, 1919–1922." *Selected Subaltern Studies,* ed. Ranajit Guha and Gayatri Chakravorty Spivak, 233–87. New York: Oxford University Press, 1988.

Panikkar, K. M. *Asia and Western Dominance.* London: Allen, 1959.

Papanek, Hanna. "Purdah: Separate Worlds and Symbolic Shelter." *Separate Worlds: Studies of Purdah in South Asia,* ed. Gail Minault and Hanna Pappanek, 3–53. Delhi: Chanakya, 1982.

Parry, Benita. "Resistance Theory/Theorizing Resistance, or Two Cheers for Nativism." *Contemporary Postcolonial Theory,* ed. Padmini Mongia, 84–109. London: Arnold, 1996.

Pheto, Molefe. *And Night Fell: Memoirs of a Political Prisoner in South Africa.* London and New York: Allison, 1983.

Philips, C. H., ed. *The Evolution of India and Pakistan, 1858 to 1947: Select Documents.* London: Oxford University Press, 1962.

Piatt, Hester. *Anne Devlin: An Outline of Her Story.* N.p., n.d.

Pratt, Mary Louise. "Fieldwork in Common Places." *Writing Culture: The Poetics and Politics of Ethnography,* ed. James Clifford and George F. Marcus, 27–50. Berkeley: University of California Press, 1986.

Rajan, Gita. "Subversive-Subaltern Identity: Indira Gandhi as the Speaking Subject." *De/Colonizing the Subject: The Politics of Gender in Women's Autobiography,* ed. Sidonie Smith and Julia Watson, 196–222. Minneapolis: University of Minnesota Press, 1992.

Ram, Raja. *The Jallianwala Bagh Massacre: A Premeditated Plan.* Chandigarh: Panjab, 1978.

Ramusack, Barbara N. "Catalysts or Helpers? British Feminists, Indian Women's

Rights, and Indian Independence." *The Extended Family: Women and Political Par-*
ticipation in India and Pakistan, ed. Gail Minault, 109–50. Delhi: Chanakya, 1981.

———. "Cultural Missionaries, Maternal Imperialists, Feminist Allies: British Women
Activists in India, 1865–1945." *Women's Studies International Forum* 13 (1990): 309–
21.

Ramusack, Barbara N., and Sharon Sievers. *Women in Asia: Restoring Women to History.*
Bloomington: Indiana University Press, 1999.

Randall, Margaret. *Sandino's Daughters: Testimonies of Nicaraguan Women in Struggle.* Van-
couver, B.C.: New Star, 1981.

Rolston, Bill. "The Training Ground: Ireland, Conquest and Decolonisation." *Race*
and Class 34 (April–June 1993): 13–24.

Roof, Judith, and Robyn Wiegman, eds. *Who Can Speak? Authority and Critical Identity.*
Urbana: University of Illinois Press, 1995.

Rooney, Ellen. "Commentary: What Is to Be Done." *Coming to Terms: Feminism, Theory,*
Politics, ed. Elizabeth Weed, 230–39. New York: Routledge, 1989.

Ross, Alan. *Blindfold Games.* London: Collins Harvill, 1986.

Roy, Santimoy. *The Revolutionary Nationalist Movement.* Calcutta: Antaranga Pra-
kashana, 1993.

Rubenstein, Richard E. *Alchemists of Revolution: Terrorism in the Modern World.* New York:
Basic Books, 1987.

Rushdie, Salman. *Imaginary Homelands: Essays and Criticism, 1981–1991.* London:
Granta, 1991.

———. *Midnight's Children.* New York: Avon, 1980.

Said, Edward. *Culture and Imperialism.* New York: Random, 1993.

———. Introduction to *Kim*, by Rudyard Kipling, 7–46. London: Penguin, 1989.

———. *Orientalism.* New York: Vintage, 1978.

———. *Representations of the Intellectual.* New York: Pantheon, 1994.

———. *The World, the Text and the Critic.* Cambridge: Harvard University Press, 1983.

Sangari, Kumkum, and Sudesh Vaid, eds. *Recasting Women: Essays in Colonial History.*
New Delhi: Kali for Women, 1989.

Sarkar, Hemanta K. *Revolutionaries of Bengal: Their Methods and Ideals.* Calcutta: Indian
Book Club, 1923.

Sarkar, Sumit. *A Critique of Colonial India.* Calcutta: Papyrus, 1985.

———. "Popular" Movements and "Middle Class" Leadership in Late Colonial India: Perspectives
and Problems of a "History from Below." Calcutta: Bagchi, 1983.

Sarkar, Tanika. *Bengal, 1928–1934: The Politics of Protest.* Delhi: Oxford University
Press, 1987.

Schaeffer, Robert. *Warpaths: The Politics of Partition.* New York: Hill, 1990.

Scott, David. "Colonial Governmentality." *Social Text* 43 (1995): 191–220.

Scott, Paul. *The Day of the Scorpion.* New York: Avon, 1979.

———. *A Division of the Spoils.* New York: Avon, 1979.

———. *The Jewel in the Crown.* New York: Avon, 1979.

———. *The Towers of Silence.* New York: Avon, 1979.

——. "What India Meant: *Plain Tales from the Raj.*" *London Times,* 24 Nov. 1975, 14.

Sharma, Radha Krishna. *Nationalism, Social Reform and Indian Women.* New Delhi: Janaki Prakashan, 1981.

Sharpe, Jennifer. *Allegories of Empire: The Figure of Woman in the Colonial Text.* Minneapolis: University of Minnesota Press, 1993.

——. "Scenes of an Encounter: A Double Discourse of Colonialism and Nationalism." Diss., University of Texas, 1987.

Simpson, A. W. B. "Round Up the Usual Suspects: The Legacy of British Colonialism and the European Convention of Human Rights." *Loyola Law Review* 41 (winter 1996): 629–710.

Singh, Baljit. "An Overview." *Terrorism: Interdisciplinary Perspectives,* ed. Yonah Alexander and Seymour Maxwell Finger, 5–17. New York: John Jay, 1977.

Sivanandan, A. "From Resistance to Rebellion: Asian and Afro-Caribbean Struggles in Britain." *Race and Class* 23 (autumn 1981–winter 1982): 111–52.

Smith, Sidonie, and Julia Watson, eds. *De/Colonizing the Subject: The Politics of Gender in Women's Autobiography.* Minneapolis: University of Minnesota Press, 1992.

Spivak, Gayatri Chakravorty. "Can the Subaltern Speak?" *Marxism and the Interpretation of Culture,* ed. Cary Nelson and Lawrence Grossberg, 271–313. Urbana: University of Illinois Press, 1988.

——. *In Other Worlds: Essays in Cultural Politics.* New York: Methuen, 1987.

——. "The Political Economy of Women as Seen by a Literary Critic." *Coming to Terms: Feminism, Theory, Politics,* ed. Elizabeth Weed, 218–29. New York: Routledge, 1989.

——. "Subaltern Studies: Deconstructing Historiography." *Selected Subaltern Studies,* ed. Ranajit Guha and Gayatri Chakravorty Spivak, 3–34. New York: Oxford University Press, 1988.

——. "Three Women's Texts and a Critique of Imperialism." *"Race," Writing, and Difference,* ed. Henry Louis Gates Jr., 262–280. Chicago: University of Chicago Press, 1985.

Stree Shakti Sanghatana. *"We Were Making History": Women and the Telanagana Uprising.* London: Zed Books, 1989.

Strum, Philippa. *The Women Are Marching: The Second Sex and the Palestinian Revolution.* New York: Hill, 1992.

Tarrow, Sidney. *Power in Movement: Social Movements and Contentious Politics.* Cambridge: Cambridge University Press, 1994.

Taylor, Charles. *Sources of the Self: The Making of the Modern Identity.* Cambridge: Harvard University Press, 1989.

Tennyson, Alfred. "The Charge of the Light Brigade." *The Norton Anthology of English Literature* . Vol. 2. 4th ed, ed. M. H. Abrams, E. Talbot Donaldson, Hallett Smith, Robert M. Adams, Samuel Holt Monk, Lawrence Lipking, George H. Ford, and David Daiches, 1175–76. New York: W. W. Norton, 1979.

Tomlinson, Mike. "Can Britain Leave Ireland? The Political Economy of War and Peace." *Race and Class* 37 (July–Sept. 1995): 1–22.

Torgovnick, Marianna. *Gone Primitive: Savage Intellects, Modern Lives*. Chicago: University of Chicago Press, 1990.

Townsend, Charles. *Britain's Civil Wars: Counterinsurgency in the Twentieth Century*. London: Faber, 1986.

Tripathy, Biswakesh. *Terrorism and Insurgency in India, 1900–1986*. New Delhi: Pacific, 1987.

Tula, Maria Teresa, and Lynn Stephen. *Hear My Testimony*. Boston: South End, 1994.

United Kingdom. *Parliamentary Debates* (Commons). 5th ser., vol. 131 (28 June–16 July 1920).

United Kingdom. Parliament. *Report of the Committee Appointed by the Government of India to Investigate the Disturbances in the Punjab, etc.* Cmd. 681. London: HMSO, 1920.

——. *Statements of Brig.-Gen. Reginald E. Dyer*. Cmd. 771. London: HMSO, 1920.

United Kingdom. War Office. *Manual of Military Law*. London: HMSO, 1914.

Varadharajan, Asha. *Exotic Parodies: Subjectivity in Adorno, Said, and Spivak*. Minneapolis: University of Minnesota Press, 1995.

Weed, Elizabeth, ed. *Coming to Terms: Feminism, Theory, Politics*. New York: Routledge, 1989.

Wichert, Sabine. *Northern Ireland since 1945*. London: Longman, 1991.

Wilkenson, Theon. *Two Monsoons*. London: Duckworth, 1976.

Williams, Raymond. *Keywords: A Vocabulary of Culture and Society*. New York: Oxford University Press, 1983.

——. *Marxism and Literature*. Oxford: Oxford University Press, 1977.

Wilson, James Q. *Political Organizations*. Princeton: Princeton University Press, 1995.

Wolpert, Stanley. *Massacre at Jallianwala Bagh*. New Delhi: Penguin, 1988.

——. *A New History of India*. New York: Oxford University Press, 1982.

Young, Robert J. C. *Colonial Desire: Hybridity in Theory, Culture and Race*. New York: Routledge, 1995.

Zuberi, Nabeel. "Paki Tunes." *SAMAR* 5 (summer 1995): 36–39.

culinity, 128–29; and India as
mother, 129; and Indian nationalism, 17, 129–23, 164–66; and Jugantar, 128, 131; and Kali, 16; and
narrative strategies, 139–45; and
subalterns, 18–20; and violent resistance, 128–29, 145–46. *See also*
Dutt, Kalpana
Hinduism: and All India Women's Conference, 78, 116–17, 122, 125; Baba
Firdaus, 206; and Bengali terrorist
movement, 151–54; and collective
agency, 24; and dominance, 38; and
feminist-nationalist individualism,
20; and gender, 119, 122; and heroic-
nationalist individualism, 16, 129;
and hunger strikes, 137; and Indian
nationalism, 119, 120–21, 126–27;
and Indian women's movement,
126–27; Kali, 16, 152–53; and narrative strategies, 143, 148–49; and purdah, 116, 121–23; sati, 151–52, 202;
and Women's Indian Association,
114
Hindu masculinity, 128–29
Hindu myth. *See* Hinduism
Hindus, 194
Historical research, 203–24
Holloway Prison (London), 101–3
Home and world, 114, 117, 118
Hunger strikes: and Bengali terrorist
movement, 137; and Hinduism, 137;
and Irish nationalism, 137; and Irish
political prisoners, 219; and Irish
Republican Army, 219; and Irish suffrage movement, 103–7, 137; and
Irish Women's Franchise League, 97;
and women, 137

Identity politics, 76–77
Immigrants, 215–16, 218
Immigration Act of 1971 (United King-
dom), 215
Immolation, 151–52, 205

Imperialism, 197
Imprisonment, 102–7
India: common law in, 56, 57–60; family structure, 157–59; funerary
customs in, 202; gender roles in,
117–18; immolation of women in,
204; Irish in, 220; martial law in,
55–57; martial races in, 148; as
mother, 129, 154–55; as necropolis,
182, 202, 207; police, 67–68; social
relations, 19; status of women in,
110, 111–12; survival in, 173; university system in, 199; violent resistance
in, 41–42
Indian culture, 185
Indian diarchy, 48–49
Indian family structure, 157–59
Indian nationalism: and All India
Women's Conference, 118–19; and
assassination, 189–91; and Bengali
terrorist movement, 139; and class,
13–14, 130–31, 192–93; and colonial
regimes of knowledge, 172; and
communism, 161–62; and Congress
Party, 190; C. Sehanabish on, 136–
37; and feminism, 223 n.3; and gender roles in India, 118–19, 120–21;
and heroic-colonial individualism,
188; and heroic-nationalist individualism, 17, 129–33, 164–66; and Hinduism, 119, 120–21, 126–27; and
Irish nationalism, 26–27, 32–33,
128, 136; and Irish Republican Army,
212; and Jugantar, 145, 167; and non-
Indian women's movement, 110; and
nonviolent noncooperation, 150,
190; and oral histories, 168; and
partnership with British, 49, 192;
and Quit India movement, 192, 193;
Ranajit Guha on, 13–14, 17–18, 130,
192; and resistance, 26–27, 160–61,
195; and violent resistance, 132–35,
147; and Women's Indian Association, 118–19; and women's move-

Purnima Bose is an associate professor of
English at Indiana University

Library of Congress Cataloging-in-Publication Data
Bose, Purnima.
Organizing empire : individualism, collective agency,
and India / Purnima Bose.
p. cm.   Includes bibliographical references and index.
ISBN 0-8223-2759-7 (cloth : alk. paper)
ISBN 0-8223-2768-6 (pbk. : alk. paper)
1. India—History—British occupation, 1765–1947.
2. Nationalism—India—History. 3. Feminism—India—
History. 4. Individualism—India—History. I. Title.
DS480.45.B586 2003   954.03—dc21   2003002263